# Pathways of Adult Learning

# Pathways of Adult Learning

PROFESSIONAL AND EDUCATION NARRATIVES

**JANET GROEN** and
**COLLEEN KAWALILAK**

Canadian Scholars' Press

Toronto

**Pathways of Adult Learning: Professional and Education Narratives**
by Janet Groen and Colleen Kawalilak

First published in 2014 by
**Canadian Scholars' Press Inc.**
425 Adelaide Street West, Suite 200
Toronto, Ontario
M5V 3C1

**www.cspi.org**

Canadian Scholars' Press Inc. gratefully acknowledges financial support for our publishing activities from the Government of Canada through the Canada Book Fund (CBF).

**Library and Archives Canada Cataloguing in Publication**

Groen, Janet, 1959–, author     Pathways of adult learning : professional and education narratives / Janet Groen and Colleen Kawalilak.

Includes bibliographical references and index. Issued in print and electronic formats. ISBN 978-1-55130-637-7 (pbk.).—ISBN 978-1-55130-638-4 (pdf).-—ISBN 978-1-55130-639-1 (epub)

   1. Adult learning.  I. Kawalilak, Colleen, 1952–, author  II. Title.
LC5225.L42G76 2014        374        C2014-904939-0        C2014-904940-4

Text and cover design by Susan MacGregor/Digital Zone
Cover image: iStock image 34869876

12   13   14   15   16           5   4   3   2   1

Printed and bound in Canada by Webcom

MIX
Paper from
responsible sources
FSC® C004071

# Table of Contents

# Preface

You have picked up this book for a reason! Perhaps this is required reading for a course you are taking or teaching in a post-secondary or continuing education context. Or you may be an instructor, learner, or leader (formal or informal) in another work and learning context—someone who facilitates the learning of adults—and you seek a deeper understanding as to how adults learn.

You may be a nurse, social worker, teacher, instructor at a community or vocational college, community worker, human resource consultant, training and development specialist, sports coach, career counsellor, or art teacher at a community recreation centre. Regardless of how we identify and where we are located, we assume, unless we are working in complete isolation, that our work and learning involves being with other adults and engaging in ongoing, formal professional development or informal learning activities. If any of these roles or contexts resonates with you, what you are interested in, or what you hope to do in the future, we invite you to participate in a conversation—a dialogue—as we reflect, make meaning of, and navigate our individual and collective pathways as lifelong adult learners.

On this journey, we will explore the exciting and often challenging diverse work and learning terrains that we navigate. It is also important to recognize that so much of our learning extends beyond the bricks and mortar of formal, traditional, educational, learning environments. In fact, the majority of our learning occurs beyond these walls. There is potential for learning whenever we pick up a book, watch a TV documentary, attend a continuing education class, collaborate with neighbours on a community initiative, or stop in the hallway at work to chat with a colleague about a project or to share an idea. These are only a few examples of the limitless invitations extended to us as adult learners. Most important is that we recognize that *we are all adult learners*. We will continue to repeat this throughout this text. Our hope is that we will gain a deepened and expanded awareness and appreciation of the potential for individual and collective learning by reflecting what we have learned *along the way*, through our experiences.

In order for this conversation to be meaningful and authentic, we, the authors, are committed to creating a space that invites personal reflection. This book, then, while informed by scholarly literature on adult education and adult learning, will have a personal and relational tone. We aim to achieve this by speaking directly to you in first-person narrative and as co-learners on this journey. We intentionally do this because we believe that scholarly, academic writing does not need to be removed, distant, or inaccessible from our day-to-day, lived, and applied experiences and understandings. Too often, as readers, we struggle to make an untenable leap from what we are reading in a textbook to relevance in our day-to-day lives. Simply put, we seek to make meaning of theories that inform adult learning by intertwining theories with stories, voices, and experiences.

These stories, voices, and experiences are animated in several ways throughout the book. First, we offer our own narratives of learning so that we may introduce ourselves as co-learners to you, the reader, and to emphasize the potential and possibilities for learning, individually and collectively, in a variety of personal, professional, and educational contexts. Second, we invited several graduate students, past and present, from the Adult Learning specialization program in the Werklund School of Education at the University of Calgary, to share their own narratives of learning. These featured student narratives were carefully selected to represent varied experiences, and multiple perspectives and contexts of adult learning. Finally, voices from the field offer succinct and timely commentaries on concepts and themes presented. These voices represent colleagues whose expertise we continue to draw from, individuals who have exhibited leadership in particular areas of adult education within Canadian higher education and post-secondary contexts. We would also like to acknowledge many voices that *have not* been individually highlighted in this text. We refer to adult educators and practitioners who continue to contribute significantly to our field of scholarship and practice. We all benefit from your ongoing commitment and contributions. In all honesty, it was simply not possible to highlight all of the good work that is currently going on in Canada. It is our hope, however, that the voices represented in the pages that follow provide a valuable lens through which to better understand and appreciate the rapidly growing and ever-changing landscape of adult education research and practice.

We hope that the personal and relational tone conveyed through student narratives of learning, our own personal stories, and voices from the field provides you, co-learners in this learning journey, the opportunity to see yourselves in some of these narratives and to make connections between the theoretical concepts presented and the various contexts and dimensions of adult learning.

We begin this text by focusing on *who we are as adult learners.* In addition to our diverse work and learning contexts, we all juggle many roles in our lives. Are we members of a sports team or singing group? What roles and responsibilities do we have in our social networks? Are we parents, grandparents, siblings, brothers, sisters, aunts, uncles, and so forth? Do we volunteer, mentor, or participate in any group or team activities? Perhaps we are members of a book club, gourmet gathering, quilting group, hiking group, or rock-climbing club. Within any of these roles and contexts, there is great potential for learning, co-creating knowledge, and knowledge sharing. Wherever we are located, it is important to acknowledge this potential and to remain open to possibility. We then spiral out to extend the conversation into areas that explore philosophies and history of adult education, theories of adult learning, and diverse paid and unpaid work and learning contexts. Throughout, we integrate a critical lens to explore how sociocultural and socioeconomic influences and experiences shape, inform, and influence our learning journeys.

We begin with a touching reflection written by Judith Duerk (1993). Judith invites us to spiral back to our early school experiences, a time when we were open and hungry to learn, a time when we were fascinated with learning and all of its possibilities:

How might your life have been different if, late one afternoon, near the end of the summer, as you thought of the opening of school ... and of trying, again, to learn to use our mind in traditional ways ... something wondrous had happened?

If [those] who were your teachers had invited their young ... students ... even the littlest girls [and boys] ... to come to sit in a circle ... and, of course, you went, too.

If you had sensed the excitement in the voices of the teachers as they spoke of a different way to use your fine, young minds. And you could feel the wonder of [your teachers] sitting in a circle, under the open sky, just outside the school ... gathered to share their wisdom with the younger [ones] in their care.

*How might your life be different?* (p. 67)

# About the Authors

We met 10 years ago, as newly minted assistant professors; we have been dialoguing ever since! In the early years, we shared experiences and perspectives and grappled with the many challenges we attempted to navigate along the way, as new academics. This was new terrain and we were comforted to know that our individual struggles were shared, appreciated, and understood by the other. Through dialogue, we came to know that experiences we had gained, prior to becoming assistant professors, had much to offer if we took the time to critically reflect on these experiences, explore for meaning, and discern past learning and linkages with this new work and learning environment that we now found ourselves in. Through dialogue, we also deepened our understanding of adult education and adult learning—of the history, philosophical beliefs, and underpinnings that informed our work—and of what it means to be a lifelong adult learner. These are some of the topics we take up in the chapters that follow and we invite you to join our ongoing exploration and conversation.

Our most recent endeavour involved developing a course, titled Professional Development and Lifelong Learning (PDLL), for learners enrolled in our pre-service teacher education (Bachelor of Education) program. Throughout this course-development process, we continued to ask ourselves, how can we convey to pre-service teachers that adult education and adult learning has relevance in a teacher education program? We then pondered other professional programs such as nursing, social work, business, and fine arts. The common ground that transcends silos that typically differentiate professional disciplines is that *we are all lifelong adult learners*, regardless of the career path we navigate.

As we explored the literature in support of the development of the PDLL course, we realized that much of the literature in adult education was directed toward those enrolled in graduate programs and that this literature focused heavily on the study of adult education. What was missing was a book that spanned and spoke to individuals participating in undergraduate, vocational, or continuing education programs and to learning that we acquire beyond traditional formal education contexts. This book has been written in response to this niche in the literature.

Do we dare admit that, collectively, we draw from 50-plus years of experience in our work with adult learners, in multiple contexts, and from the many different roles that we have assumed? We would like to stress that "50-plus years" speaks to our combined experience; we both launched our careers at a very young age! On a serious note, we have been social worker, staff development consultant, vocational teacher, college instructor, team leader, corporate trainer, spiritual director, ESL teacher, adult basic education instructor, family life educator, small group facilitator, artist, musician, community volunteer, activist, professional development coordinator, course developer, instructional designer, and leadership trainer. All of these roles have contributed, significantly, to our present work as associate professors in educational studies in adult learning, in the Werklund School of Education at the University of Calgary. Looking back, each experience we have gathered along the way has contributed richly to the tapestry of our learning journeys.

# Acknowledgements

This book provides a glimpse of some learning challenges, opportunities for growth, and significant learning moments shared by adult learners we have been privileged to meet and experience along the way. We refer to adult learners who span many disciplines and work and learning contexts that include adult learners currently enrolled in formal, more traditional education programs; graduates who now work in a variety of workplaces; and educators, leaders, and workplace trainers who teach and facilitate adult learning. What is most significant, however, is that, beyond our diverse work and learning contexts, what connects us all— our common ground—is that if we remain open to the challenge, we all are and will continue to be lifelong adult learners.

In the pages that follow, some of these voices speak to us directly about navigating the formal, informal, and incidental terrain of adult learning and of some insights gained as courageous sojourners on an often unpredictable, non-linear, frequently messy and circuitous, lifelong learning pathway. There are many other voices, however, not directly referred to by name in the chapters that follow, who have significantly guided the evolution and writing of this text. All of these individuals continue to enrich our own learning journeys and practice. We remain humbled by and grateful to all who continue to share their stories with us. We receive this as an invitation to delve more deeply into making meaning of our own learning narratives and into the exploration of adult education as a rich, diverse, and often challenging field of scholarship and practice. To all we have met thus far—those who have directly shaped, formed, and influenced our own learning narratives—and to those we have yet to meet, we extend our deepest appreciation. Without you, this book would not have been possible.

We would like to thank our families, friends, colleagues, and our own Werklund School of Education at the University of Calgary, for encouragement and the space you provided so that we could bring this text to fruition. Needless to say, we often "burned the midnight oil" and this meant that other commitments and responsibilities were put on the back-burner. Our heartfelt appreciation also goes to Canadian Scholars' Press for recognizing the need for and supporting the publication of this text. You were on board from the very beginning and your guidance, responsiveness, and wisdom provided us invaluable insight and guidance.

# PART I

## Pathways of Learning: Interpreting Our Story

Am I an adult learner? What does this mean? Is this different from how children learn? How do my past experiences inform who I am now and where I am located? How have all of these experiences shaped my lifelong learning narrative? How and what have I learned, informally and incidentally, beyond the bricks and mortar of formal education? Who has contributed to my learning? How and why?

How have gender, race, age, cultural background, religious beliefs and traditions, sexual orientation, economic standing, and other sociocultural influences impacted and shaped my learning journey?

In part 1, we explore our pathways of learning and how our lifelong learning narratives began long before we began writing this book.

# CHAPTER 1

# On Being
# an Adult Learner

## Introduction

We have had the pleasure and privilege of journeying with and learning from hundreds of adult learners over the past many years—learners who span a multitude of diverse contexts and cultures. Some were enrolled in certificate, diploma, and degree programs offered through traditional post-secondary and continuing education environments. Others drew from professional contexts—nurses, social workers, sports coaches, faculty members from colleges and universities, human resource personnel, and family life educators. We have also worked and learned with individuals employed in business and industry and with those working for pay or volunteering in community-based, non-profit contexts, such as retreat centres, social service agencies, self-help programs, youth centres, and Aboriginal communities. Most recently, some of our work has focused on personal and professional development and adult learning for individuals enrolled in a Bachelor of Education pre-service teacher education program. Regardless of context, however, we are reminded that *we are all adult learners, navigating the circuitous pathway of life and learning.*

Our learning environments have always been rich in diversity, even when, at first glance, participants appeared to have much in common. For example, the teacher education program was a very large class of more than 350 pre-service teachers. One would assume the presence of common ground in that all were embarking on a career that focused on teaching children and youth within the K–12 system. As the designated instructors for this course, we brought our knowledge and experiences that were deeply rooted in *adult* education and *adult* learning. We were not K–12 teachers. At the onset, it became clear that many who sat staring down at the podium where we were situated were puzzled and pondering, *Why is an adult education course a core course offering in my teacher preparation program? I am here to learn how to teach children, not adults.* Needless to say, we had our work cut out for us. As we gazed across the expansive science theatre during one of the large group lectures, we were mindful that, regardless of the commonality of career choice that united all those taking the course, there was little homogeneity represented here.

Over the months that followed, differences that were visible, and those less so, served as constant reminders that learning environments where adults gather to learn and to work are rich with opportunities and challenges. Diversity of age and life experience was particularly significant in that the pre-service teachers spanned 18 to 60 years of age. Who would have thought? There were gender differences, cultural differences, varied religious beliefs and traditions represented, and a diversity of sexual orientation, socioeconomic status, and ethnicity. Learning style preferences, interests, and abilities also became visible throughout the semester, as did differences in values, world views, perspectives, and beliefs. This richness of difference shaped our learning environment, our individual and collective learning experiences, and the dynamics in the class. We were once again reminded that *we are all adult learners* and that this was our common ground.

As we work our way through the many topics and themes presented throughout these chapters, we invite you to consider—regardless of profession, work context, age, gender, cultural beliefs, academic background, and all other life experiences that have contributed to who you are now and to where you are located in life—that the potential for learning is *lifelong* and that possibilities for learning greet us in the most unsuspecting and unexpected ways. To put it simply, some of the wisest and most educated people we have met along the way were individuals who lacked formal schooling or post-secondary education. Life was their teacher and they remained open to the power and possibility of making meaning from life experiences. It also goes without saying that being a highly credentialed individual is not a sole determinant of "smartness" or "wisdom." Learning is not confined, nor does it reside, within the boundaries of formal education environments. Indeed, although these can be tremendous sites of learning, lifelong experiences and the opportunities for learning from our experiences are often our greatest teachers. By aligning with this belief and philosophy, we embrace the adult learner within all of us—if we remain open, the learning potential and possibilities are endless.

## Pondering Our Life Histories

We believe that the best place to begin to deepen our understanding of what it means to be an adult learner is to reflect on some meaningful experiences that have shaped and influenced who we are and how we have arrived at this time and place. Some of you may reflect fondly on early formal schooling experiences, yearning to reclaim a time when life was less complicated. For others, exiting our childhood could not come soon enough, and perhaps we have made great efforts to leave our childhood behind. Regardless of where we are situated, most of us can recall a particular person who stands out in our memory—someone who influenced us greatly: a relative, friend, Elder, community worker, teacher, church leader, or mentor from some other context. Or perhaps it was a book that fed our fascination or imagination; a song that resonated at a particular time in our life when we were struggling with a dilemma; a first love; a coach; or a trip we took that transformed our perspective. Whichever morsel of memorabilia we find ourselves reflecting on, what did we learn? How did we learn it? Why was this significant?

In his seminal work on education biography, Dominicé (2000) takes up the significance of *learning from our lives* and invites us to reflect on the following:

- Out of my entire educational life history, what do I select as important to my learning process? Where do I begin? What stories do I tell?

- How does my particular location in life pertaining to gender, family of origin, experiences of learning (both inside and outside of school), socioeconomic status, and spirituality shape my response to these questions?

As we journey through the many themes and topics included in these chapters, we encourage you to hold these questions up as deserving and worthy of ongoing, critical reflection.

As authors of this text, we also respond to this invitation by pondering these same questions. We do this by sharing our own insights, experiences, and reflections and by drawing from the voices and experiences of other individuals who recognize and embrace the adult learner within. These good people represent teachers, nurses, social workers, adult learners challenged by physical impairments, community activists, college instructors, business and industry workers, volunteers, and others. In this way, we hope to create a safe and challenging space for dialogue—for knowledge sharing, and for the co-creation of new knowledge.

We begin by reflecting on some significant learning moments that brought us here, to this place and time, and to what we refer to as our lifework as adult educators and lifelong adult learners.

## JANET

 I did it! Standing outside the tea shop in Shenyang, China, one pound of tea was resting in my hand. Such a simple thing and yet it represented so much learning over these past two months. I had navigated the trip from the university to the shop by myself, on my bicycle, had walked into the shop, and with a tremor in my voice had asked for one pound of black tea in Chinese. Not only that, I understood the shopkeeper when he told me the price of tea and I was able give him the correct bills. I was euphoric. I knew I was going to be okay.

Who am I as an adult learner? What a complex and vague question! It involves so much—what does it mean to be an adult? What is learning? How do I learn? What is important to me? What am I drawn to and what leaves me disinterested? Why is that? When I think about these questions and my life, the only way I can respond is through stories. I go back to situations and experiences, almost like a video is playing in mind. Maybe that's the way it is with all of us. When we are asked questions like, how do you like to learn? What are your passions? I suspect that many of us respond by saying, well, let me give you an example. And then we tell a story of our experience. We move into story almost naturally because story allows us to paint a portrait—with brush strokes we include multiple aspects of our life to illuminate and contextualize our experience of learning and the knowledge we have gained. Perhaps we include storied bits from our family of origin, or a little about where we lived, or a kindergarten experience, or ... Partway through the story, we might say, "Oh, wait a moment, it is important that I tell you this!" And so, we interweave bits and pieces of ourselves that reflect the effects and influences of culture, family, gender, and socio-economic and cultural status to understand who we are as learners and how we arrived at this juncture in our lives.

For example, the little vignette I offered about my time in China is located within a broader life story. It is against the background of being a white, privileged female growing up in a middle-class Dutch immigrant family who valued formal education. I was "good in school." I listened, I did my homework, and I got good grades all through school—right from kindergarten through my doctoral work. My parents valued education and were interested in what I was doing and learning. My mom, in particular, was a wonderful model in that she returned to school at age 45 to complete her university degree, one course at a time. She graduated 20 years later!

I don't think I really took any deep risks as a learner throughout the stages of my development until I travelled with my husband, John, to China, when we were in our mid-twenties. We had completed our degrees, including our Bachelors of Education, and had taught in elementary and high schools for two years prior. We both knew that we wanted to step off the predicted pathway to experience something different. We went to Shenyang, China, to teach English as a Foreign Language. If I think about the potential that learning has for disrupting beliefs, values, and world views, I think this was my watershed moment. It was uncomfortable, stressful, euphoric, exhilarating, and humbling. It taught me that I hold particular assumptions, not only about learning, but also about how I am located in and respond to the world. I think it was at that point that I realized that I was an adult learner. This involved reflecting deeply: moving inward to really question, explore, and probe who I am, what I believe, and why I believe what I believe. Looping back to my earlier question—who is an adult learner?—I believe that when we are at a point in our lives where we are willing and able to look back, reflect, and make meaning of our experiences in order to continuously evolve and change, this is when we can claim to be adult learners.

Janet's experiences in China speak of the courage it takes to be open to the unfamiliar, to push beyond what is comfortable, and to respond to an invitation to make meaning of the world and our place in it, in new ways. Janet's life path, how she arrived at this place and time, aligned to a trajectory of milestone moments that resembled those of many of her peers: finish school, get a good post-secondary education, carve out a secure and rewarding career path, and find a loving and reliable partner to ensure a long and fruitful marriage. Colleen, on the other hand, in spite of having received similar messages growing up, assembled the pieces in her life path in an entirely different sequence.

## COLLEEN

 My parents had limited formal schooling. They were young adults at the onset of World War II. The economic and political realities at that time were not conducive to youth completing high school, let alone pursuing post-secondary studies. When the war ended, after having served in the army for several years, my father was employed as a civil servant with the federal government. His employee file read "Grade Eight Level Complete." My mother worked at home, raising five children.

Over Dad's 35-year career, he was regularly promoted under a clause that valued related work experience as the equivalent to a university degree. This did not sit well with some of his more highly educated and credentialed colleagues vying for promotion. By the time my father retired, in spite of his limited formal education, he was supervising several university-credentialed individuals. In many ways, he was a self-made man in that he acquired, informally and non-traditionally, the knowledge and skills needed to perform his work with excellence in the most circuitous ways and beyond the bricks and mortar of formal, traditional education. As I reflect on my father's learning journey, there are similarities that he and I share. To elaborate, I was midway through my grade 11 high school year when life informed me that it had other plans! A serious car accident turned my world upside down. My best friend was killed instantly and others sustained serious injury. After being pulled from the wreckage by the jaws of life—a hydraulic emergency rescue machine used to extricate crash victims—I managed to escape with minor abrasions and contusions. Although the trauma of this event left deep emotional scars, this was not visible to the naked eye. The survivor guilt I carried with me was immense, however; depression burrowed its way into the crevices when I wasn't paying attention, and took hold for several years to come.

I did not return to school that year. I was confused and disoriented. I constructed walls that others could not see. The world was no longer a safe place. The car accident had dissembled, overnight, any semblance of order to the world that I had once known. The following year, I was readmitted to high school under a "special circumstance" clause. This allowed me to undertake grade 11 and 12 coursework simultaneously. The agreement was that if I passed my grade 12–diploma exams, I would be awarded automatic credit for grade 11 coursework. Determined to graduate with my peers, I was focused on accomplishing this goal. I did pass all exams but remained four credits deficient to being awarded my high school diploma. I chose not to return to high school the following year. All of my friends had now graduated and many were university-bound. I walked the pavement looking for work, haunted by a voice in my head that said, over and over again, "No one will hire you; you don't have a high school diploma."

I did eventually find work as a telephone operator, then as a receptionist. I licked envelopes in the mailroom at a swanky law firm and fell in love with a court reporter that worked close by. I was very young but it felt like love at the time. I was also toying with how I might return to school in the evenings and still keep my job. Was there a chance that I could be admitted to the local college without a high school diploma? I made an appointment with a college counsellor to discuss my options. I recall sitting down across the desk from her. "Tell me a little about yourself, Colleen; what brings you here?" I burst into tears. "I don't have a high school diploma." She was thoughtful and compassionate; this calmed me down. The interview went well and I was admitted under probationary status in spite of not having completed high school. She referred to me as an "adult learner" whose volunteer and paid work over the past few years would be considered the equivalent to a high school diploma. I couldn't believe what I was hearing. I was now an adult learner? When did this happen? What does this mean? Although this terminology was foreign to me, I was not about to question or resist. Being labelled an adult learner was opening a door that I was eager to walk through.

The next several years brought many twists and turns. After successfully completing coursework in my first year of college, I was awarded full-time, regular student status. This delight was short-lived as I soon realized I was pregnant. Yet another layer of personal identity emerged. I was no longer simply a young adult learner, admitted to college without completing high school; I was also soon to be a single, unmarried mother who had been raised in a fairly traditional Catholic family. In the words of my girlfriend, this story had all the makings of a train wreck!

In spite of the challenges, I was clear that I would welcome this child into the world and that I had the ability to create a loving home and secure future for the two of us. In retrospect, I continue to ponder how and why this rootedness of conviction resonated so deeply in me. Regardless, I clung to this certainty. Once again, I put formal schooling on hold and set my sights on being a fully employed, single mom. As my baby's father chose to have no contact, I knew that I would be navigating this pathway alone. My decision invited criticism and scorn from him and others who accused me of being selfish. They thought I should have either aborted or given my child up for adoption. For me, neither was an option.

Now, almost 40 years later, I reflect on how my life story has unfolded along the way. Giving birth to my son and raising two other children, whose mother had died when they were both very young, were the best choices I ever made in my life. They have all grown to be amazing human beings.

I learned from so many experiences and, although I lacked a formal education and credentials, I managed to craft a strong career as a social worker, a family life educator, and then as a college instructor. I realized that what I was doing in my work must have held some credibility as I continued to be promoted within these various contexts. What gnawed at me, however, was the need for a clearer understanding of what it was I was doing. Were there theories that supported the approach I took to my work? My colleagues spoke of lifelong, incidental, formal, informal, and transformational learning. What were the differences? What didn't I know? And, if I did know it, how would this knowledge broaden, deepen, and change my work? These questions haunted me and contributed to a growing sense of discomfort and unease. I recognized that I had been raised with the message, "Finish high school, get married, have children, and if you ever have a major life problem, your priest or your doctor is your greatest resource." Well, I admit that I didn't follow the rules—I did do all of these things, but simply in a different sequence! I got pregnant, went on to pursue further education, and then got married. Needless to say, my priest and my doctor did not have the answers I was seeking.

I did find a way to complete an undergraduate degree; it only took 22 years! Shortly thereafter, I was ready to add the undertaking of graduate studies to the list. Why not! Regardless of the sequencing of my unfolding narrative, I was beginning to understand what it meant to be a "lifelong" adult learner; I was in it for the long haul. I discovered that others I met along the way also had stories, stories that were uniquely their own. Perhaps I was not so different after all!

At the time, Colleen was unaware that the traumatic experience of the car accident provided her significant tacit (or informal) knowledge. This life challenge propelled her into a world of unpredictability, chaos, and feeling out of control, and a life narrative that completely contradicted what she had been raised to expect if she had followed "the rules." Through this experience, she was propelled onto a pathway that brought unprecedented growth and transformation; all of this took root and germinated at a time when she felt that everything was coming apart. Her world view had been altered and assumptions that had guided her to this point in time were revisited and revised. Tacit knowledge acquired along the way included reaching deep down to discover self-reliance, determination, focus, and commitment. Over time, Colleen responded to an invitation to be more open, to trust others in new ways, and to revisit and reflect on the meaning of life, and on how difficult and painful experiences unexpectedly present moments of opportunity for growth and learning.

Although Janet and Colleen navigated different lifelong learning pathways brought about by life events and circumstances, they both needed to acquire a new language of sorts, a way of communicating, perceiving, and responding in and to the world. For Janet, this came by way of being immersed in a new and foreign culture. Colleen also experienced a profound cultural shift, but not one that necessitated her crossing any geographical boundaries. How we "know what we know" as adults comes to us in so many different ways. Adult learning creates a broad and deep space in recognition of this grand diversity of experience and perspective.

## Connecting Narratives

Sometimes, it is not until we engage in dialogue with another that we come to appreciate and realize new understandings or insights. This was the case when we shared snapshots of our life journeys with one another. In other words, our life narratives took on new meaning when we engaged in dialogue and put our stories into words. Words, or some other form of expression, help us to get our experiences out of our heads. In this way, we hold up our stories in the palm of our hand and, although we remain deeply connected to these stories on many different levels, we are provided the opportunity to *re*visit and to *re*view them—to reflect on these experiences in new ways. Dialogue provides this safe space within which to ponder, reflect, and make meaning of them. Dialogue also gifts us with the opportunity to explore our experiences through the interpretations and perspectives of others. These spaces for sharing need not rely only on the sharing of stories through words. Connecting our narratives may take the form of song, dance, poetry, film, photography, and other so many other art forms.

We view dialogue as being different from and deeper than conversation. The Greek roots of dialogue are *dia* (through) and *logos* (meaning). A great American physicist, David Bohm (1996), described dialogue as being "as old as civilization itself" (p. vii) and the dialogical process as a "never ending river ... a search for mutual, meaningful understanding rather than the attainment of consensus or truth" (Kawalilak, 2004). Where conversation often involves particular agendas being brought to the table and a desire to prompt or convince others to see and interpret something from our point of view, dialogue opens up a space that welcomes differences of perspective and understanding and focuses on inclusion and relationship formation through trust and being authentically present to one another.

Sharing our experiences through dialogue provides rich fodder and opportunity for exploration and learning. The most unsuspecting person may present to be a significant teacher, someone who offers a life lesson at a time of need, whether realized or not. Or, another might tell us that we have impacted him or her in ways that we would never have anticipated. An event that seems trivial may turn out to be laden with opportunities for self-discovery. We may find ourselves in situations where we feel a lack of connection with others, only to discover that we share more similarities than we do differences. In any and all of these ways, we come to realize that teacher and learner reside within each of us and that it is this ebb and flow of giving and receiving that feeds our passion and fascination with learning. In the search for vision, stories and narrative sharing are important. Through story sharing, life experiences and significant learning moments are reclaimed and revisited. In the oral tradition in Aboriginal cultures, stories "created a sense of landscape, community and place" (Attwood & Magowan, 2001, p. xii). Havecker (1991) reminded us that "knowledge ... [consistent with other Indigenous cultures and traditions] was derived from experience" (p. 17). This knowledge, embedded in experience, is passed on to others through story.

Dialogue is a form of narrative learning—its nature is to explore and to gain a deepened understanding of the perspective and lived experiences of self and others. David Bohm described dialogue as "a stream of meaning flowing among and through us and between us ... [to] make possible a flow of meaning ... out of which may emerge some new understanding" (1998, p. 6)—dialogue is *not* the same as discussion. Discussion often focuses on the back and forth of ideas, on breaking things apart, and on analysis. According to Bohm, discussion often resembles a Ping-Pong game in which points are earned depending on who speaks more loudly and convincingly. Power differentials based on gender, role, age, socioeconomic status, and race often play out in discussions with others. Dialogue, on the other hand, speaks to wholeness and is about emptying a space in support of co-creating new knowledge and understanding. In essence then, dialogue invites us to have the courage to let go of tightly held biases and assumptions, to leave these at the door, to make room to receive what we may not yet know or understand. It takes courage to loosen our grip on what is and has always been comfortable and familiar to free up this space.

In the words of the renowned Indian philosopher Jidhu Krishnamurti, "The cup has to be empty to hold something" (p. 312).[1]

Fritjof Capra, physicist, systems theorist, and international author, referred to the "web of life" (1996, p. 298) and to the interconnectedness of *all* members of the human community. We draw from the words of Capra to guide our own philosophy and practice as adult educators and lifelong adult learners and maintain that it is through our relationships with one another, in whatever context we work and learn, that we gain a deepened sense of understanding and place in the world and in our ability to grow, learn, and effect change in the world. According to Capra, "The success of the whole community depends on the success of its individual members, while the success of each member depends on the success of the community as a whole" (1996, p. 298). This is significant when we consider our own work and learning contexts. For example, as adult learners involved in formal education programs such as social work, teacher education, nursing or other health-related programs, business, continuing education, or vocational training, how do our learning journeys and experiences connect with other individuals in our program? What do we need from one another for the learning environment to be both safe and challenging? How might our experiences and perspectives benefit others? What do we need from others? What do we have to offer in support of their learning journey? Within professional and other work contexts, how do we learn together, formally and informally, to contribute to the vision, mission, and values of the organization? What professional development (PD) opportunities are available? How do we keep current with best practices beyond these formal PD opportunities?

## A Common Language

Throughout this text, the language and terms we use to describe and guide our reflections and dialogue may be familiar, or may be different from what you are accustomed to in your own work and learning context. Although these terms are elaborated on in depth in the chapters that follow, we felt it was important to promote a shared understanding and interpretation of terms and concepts. We do this by drawing from some definitions provided by many of our good colleagues in the field.

## Adult Learners

Most countries consider the age of majority (when we reach adulthood) to be 18. We align with Hansman and Mott (2010), however, who maintained that adulthood also includes "[taking] on the social, psychological, and/or economic roles typically expected of adults in their cultures and collective societies" (p. 14). Adult learners, then, referred to throughout this text, are individuals who are 18 years of age or older and who may be located at various points along this continuum of maturity and responsibility.

Beyond this broad definition, we resist any attempts to profile who and what an adult learner is. To elaborate, if you are an instructor, facilitator, or trainer within a post-secondary institution or in some other work or learning context, consider the range of adult learners along an "age and learner readiness" continuum. Consider that you have 30 participants enrolled in your course. During the first week, you focus primarily on getting to know participants. You are aware that the age range spans 18 to 50 years. It also becomes clear, at the onset, that some participants appear to lack focus and motivation. They come to the class or session unprepared and do not appear to be interested or engaged. Others are visibly ready to do the work that needs to be done, to learn, and to succeed. This scenario may leave you perplexed. As you reflect on those who appear unmotivated, you ask yourself why they are taking this course, as this is not how adult learners should behave. Indeed, this is a challenge for anyone in a teaching or training environment. Consider, however, that adult learning focuses on the learning process that occurs *within* individuals throughout a learning experience and that, rather than focusing too heavily on who they are when they enter the learning environment, the more important questions to reflect on are how and what might this person learn in this context, and who might they be when they leave this learning environment. What occurs inside the learner from the time they enter the session or program to the end of a particular learning experience? Adult learners represent diverse needs, interests, levels of readiness and motivation, learning challenges, learning-style preferences, life experiences, perspectives, and world views. Gender, cultural norms and traditions, religious beliefs, socioeconomic levels, family history, and so forth all contribute to the lifelong learning biographies of adult learners. We assert that a generalizable profile of a "traditional adult learner" does not exist, and perhaps it never did.

### Adult Learning

Learning in adulthood captures the entire range of formal, informal (and non-formal), and incidental learning taken up and experienced by the learner, whether this learning occurs within or beyond formal education contexts.[2]

*Formal* adult learning contexts are structured and defined. Formal adult learning environments include the program that you are currently enrolled in at a university or other post-secondary institution. This may also include a professional development event mandated by your organization or a workshop or training session you need to attend in order to retain a particular professional designation or certification. Typically, formal adult learning events involve specific learning objectives, structured activities, and measurable outcomes to guide and evaluate learning.

*Informal* learning, on the other hand, is not confined to the structures of formal adult learning environments. Consider Janet's and Colleen's narrative snapshots. Both referred to significant learning acquired that *did not* involve formal learning in traditional learning environments. What Janet and Colleen experienced was more aligned to the acquisition of *tacit knowledge*. Tacit knowledge is something that all human beings acquire through the day-to-day unfolding of life experiences that include observing others, associating with others, engaging in activities, trying new things, making meaning of our emotions, and paying attention to our intuition. Michael Polanyi, in his book titled *The Tacit Dimension* (1966), referred to tacit knowledge (or informal learning). Polanyi emphasized the significance of this more embodied, personal, and somewhat elusive knowledge that is acquired. Tacit knowledge or competence may also include inherited practices we gain that are difficult to account for in terms of how we have learned them. Tacit knowledge is also difficult to make explicit—to put into words (Polanyi, 1966). Examples of tacit knowing include learning how to ride a bike; being able to sense, read, or use emotions in order to impact or influence outcomes; being guided by our intuition in decision-making, even when it is difficult to explain the logic; reading another person's body language when communicating; or learning a language through immersion in a new and foreign culture. To add to the mix, the literature also makes reference to *non-formal learning*. This may include taking up a particular activity in order to learn something we are interested in or need to learn. Non-formal learning is typically non-structured and void of pre-determined time commitments.

*Incidental* learning refers to unexpected learning that comes along when we are involved in formal or non-formal learning activities (Werquin, 2010)—what we come to know accidentally or unexpectedly. We may be involved in some formal learning environment; for example, taking a course on how to make great Italian pasta. The unexpected happens when we realize that, six weeks into the course, we have acquired some knowledge of Italian expressions by listening to another participant who speaks to her friend in their language of origin. We may have never expected to acquire any understanding of Italian. Or consider how we come to acquire social skills in our early school years. Although the school day involves structured classes, this space provides an opportunity to learn how to communicate and relate to our peers. Who would have ever thought this type of "bonus learning" would be provided in math class!

There is tremendous potential for incidental learning if we remain open to opportunities and possibilities. Consider people who say that a career change occurred at the most unexpected time or that a friend met his significant other while sitting in the dentist's office. These are incidental moments—some are pleasant and unexpected, while others are not always welcomed. We say "not always welcomed" because sometimes we hope to remain true to a particular learning pathway and then, out of nowhere, something hits us on the side of the head and causes us to change direction. If we are more comfortable with structure and predictability, incidental learning may sometimes feel like an inconvenience. The choice as to how we respond to these moments, however, is ours to make.

## *Adult and Community Learning*

Adult and community learning refers to a wide range of settings and is aimed at adults who may not normally participate in education and training—often involving a collaboration between local authorities, community-based organizations, and traditional providers. This covers structured adult education classes taught by professionally qualified teachers, unstructured activity that leads to learning, informal courses delivered in the private sector, independent study online, and self-organized groups.[3] Examples of community learning may include literacy classes or drop-in technology workshops offered by a community organization, health and wellness programs offered by the YWCA, parenting classes located in a rural public-health centre, seniors' stay-fit programs, theft-prevention information nights sponsored by a local business, one-on-one tutoring, or general interest programs offered in basic home repair or photography. Community learning initiatives may span from one to several hours and may be single offerings to one or more individuals or may involve multiple offerings.

## *Adult Education*

Adult education refers to

> the entire body of organized educational processes, whatever the content, level and method, whether formal or otherwise, whether

they prolong or replace initial education in schools, colleges and universities as well as in apprenticeship, whereby persons regarded as adult by the society to which they belong develop their abilities, enrich their knowledge, improve their technical or professional qualifications or turn them in a new direction and bring about changes in their attitudes or behaviour in the twofold perspective of full personal development and participation in balanced and independent social, economic and cultural development. (UNESCO, 1980, p. 3)

Merriam and Brockett (1997) defined adult education as "activities intentionally designed for the purpose of bringing about learning among those whose age, social roles, or self-perception define them as adults" (p. 7). Malcolm Knowles (1980), in *The Modern Practice of Adult Education: From Pedagogy to Andragogy*, made an important distinction between adult education and adult learning:

One problem contributing to the confusion is that the term 'adult education' is used with at least three different meanings. In its broadest sense, the term describes a process—the process of adults learning.... In its more technical meaning, 'adult education' describes a set of organized activities carried on by a wide variety of institutions for the accomplishment of specific educational objectives.... A third meaning combines all of these processes and activities into the idea of a movement or field of social practice. In this sense, 'adult education' brings together into a discrete social system all the individuals, institutions, and associations concerned with the education of adults and perceives them as working toward common goals of improving the methods and materials of adult learning, extending the opportunities for adults to learn, and advancing the general level of our culture. (p. 25)

We are guided by all of these scholarly voices in locating adult education as formal structures, activities, and initiatives designed to support adult learning. We regard adult learning as that which occurs by and within the learner when participating within or beyond the formal structures of adult education. This distinction is important as it emphasizes that learning can occur at any time, in any space, and at any pace.

## Communities of Practice

Communities of Practice (CoPs) have received a lot of attention in the literature and in business and professional contexts. A community of practice refers to a group of people who gather together (through any variety of mediums) and through their unity of common concern, interest, or passion for something that they do, interact regularly to focus on how to do something better. CoPs are designed to enhance, develop, and strengthen individuals' knowledge, skills, and/or abilities pertaining to an identified focus (Wenger, 1998). A professional learning community is also understood to be a CoP and is not limited to a particular discipline or work context. Within an education context, a professional learning community (or CoP) is present "when teachers come together to collaboratively search for and resolve the problems of practice in their schools" (Roberts & Pruitt, 2003, p. xi). We further extend Talbert and McLaughlin's (1994) definition to include other discipline and work contexts where members, united by a collective identity, knowledge base, and common commitment, focus on strengthening and improving a service or practice to better meet the needs of individuals and communities they serve.

Individuals who come together informally to explore or resolve a particular problem may be referred to as a community of practice. As discussed by Wenger (n.d.), a community of practice need not always reside within formal structures and organizations. For example,

> Communities of practice have been around for as long as human beings have learned together. At home, at work, at school, in our hobbies, we all belong to communities of practice, a number of

them usually. In some we are core members. In many we are merely peripheral. And we travel through numerous communities over the course of our lives.

In fact, communities of practice are everywhere. They are a familiar experience, so familiar, perhaps, that it often escapes our attention. Yet when it is given a name and brought into focus, it becomes a perspective that can help us understand our world better. In particular, it allows us to see past more obvious formal structures such as organizations, classrooms, or nations, and perceive the structures defined by engagement in practice and the informal learning that comes with it. (p. 3)

As we, the authors, reflect back over the years, we realize that we formed our own community of practice and that this has provided us with tremendous opportunities to grow individually and together as colleagues, to explore new and emerging theories and practices in adult education and adult learning, and to prompt, probe, and nudge one another to face some of our learning challenges and tensions, both personally and professionally. We recognize the latter as being the greatest gift of our own experience of incidental learning, in that, out of this, engaging in authentic and meaningful dialogue has been our constant go-to and companion. Not unlike other communities, large or small, that evolve, develop, sustain, and thrive, our community of practice relationship has emerged out of a purposeful and intentional focus on developing and nurturing trust, care, compassion, and mutual respect. Without these elements that have all contributed to "safe space," we would not have had the courage to risk and to be vulnerable with one another.

## *Diversity*

Diversity refers to a very broad and deep range and layering of differences, varieties, and points of unlikeness. For this reason, it is simply not possible, in any single text, to address the depth and breadth of different groupings, elements, contexts, places in the world, and ways of knowing and being. Within the context of conversations focused on in the chapters that follow, we refer, when speaking about diversity, to the "protected areas and grounds" identified in the Alberta Human Rights Act (Alberta Human Rights Commission, 2014). These protected grounds of difference relate to race, religious beliefs, skin colour, gender, physical disability, mental disability, ancestry, age, place of origin, marital status, source of income, family status, and sexual orientation. We also acknowledge that each one of these protected grounds deserves significantly more attention, exploration, and analysis than is possible to undertake in these chapters. We recognize that we are only scratching the surface here and that it would require volumes of publications on *each* of these differences to do justice in addressing and capturing the complexities, intricacies, and interplay within and across differences.

Our commitment to the need and significance of *engaging with differences* is transparent in how diversity is represented and made visible through the integration of voices, perspectives, and experiences of adult learners, adult educators, scholars, and practitioners in the chapters that follow.

## Lifelong Learning

Individuals and societies, and more specifically, educators, governments, and employers, interpret lifelong learning through multifaceted lenses. Field (2006) identified the 1990s as a time when lifelong learning became highly fashionable as "the new educational reality" (p. 9). Discourses around knowledge marketability, the learning age, global competitiveness, human capital, and a knowledge economy cited lifelong learning as a means to an end and, subsequently, the promotion of lifelong learning emerged as "convenient political shorthand for the modernizing of education and training systems" (p. 12). This new reality was linked to the repeated warnings by policymakers that a lack of knowledge would threaten a competitive, future advantage. This narrow, vocationally focused interpretation as to all that lifelong learning entailed and offered lacked acknowledgement that continual learning throughout one's lifetime had the potential to significantly support individual growth, personal health and well-being, more active and engaged civic participation, and community involvement that informed social change.

In this text, we apply a wide-angle lens to appreciate and understand lifelong learning as including different types, ways, contexts, and mediums of learning. This is significant in that

> the concept of lifelong learning stresses that learning and education are related to life as a whole—not just to work—and that learning throughout life is a continuum that should run from cradle to grave. This learning does not need to be linked to the attainment of formal qualifications. (The European Older People's Platform, 2007, p. 2)

Lifelong learning then refers to making meaning, making sense of life experiences, and "using these meanings in thinking, solving problems, and making choices and decisions; and acting in ways that are congruent with these choices and decisions as a means of obtaining feedback to confirm or disconfirm meanings" (MacKeracher, 2004, p. 8). Lifelong learning encompasses diverse learning pursued and experienced throughout a lifetime. This is flexible learning, accessible and available at times and in places that align to the needs and interests of who we are as learners. Crossing numerous sectors, lifelong learning recognizes, supports, and promotes learning *in* and *beyond* traditional schooling to include post-compulsory education and the four pillars identified by Delors (1996): 1. Learning to know, 2. Learning to do, 3. Learning to live together and with others, and 3. Learning to be.[4] Christine Wihak, a voice from the field whose research and practice are deeply steeped in advancing support for and recognition of prior learning acquired throughout adult life, speaks to the importance of learning acquired beyond the walls of traditional schooling.

Prior learning assessment and recognition (PLAR) is one of adult education's greatest success stories. PLAR, the recognition of learning acquired outside the formal education system for academic credit and/or professional certification, is a practice grounded in adult learning theory. Research evidence shows that adult learners who have access to PLAR as part of formal programs of study complete credentials more quickly, at less cost, and gain increased confidence as well. Some form of PLAR is now incorporated into lifelong learning policies around the world—most recently in the European Council, where all member states are now expected to provide this service to their citizens by 2018.

At present, however, the vast potential of PLAR to benefit adult learners has not been reached, primarily because of the indifference of many post-secondary institutions to their needs. What can you, as an adult educator, do to make PLAR more widely known and accepted?

—Dr. Christine Wihak,
Director of PLAR, Thompson Rivers University

## Guiding Assumptions

It is a great privilege to journey with adult learners who work and learn within and across professions, organizations, and community and education contexts. We continue to be inspired by their passion for learning and deep commitment to explore and make meaning of challenges and opportunities experienced "along the way." We remain humbled by all that we continue to learn from adult learners, many of whom have become our greatest teachers.

It is also our privilege to collaborate with and learn from colleagues, leaders in the field, who "walk the talk" by embracing their inner adult learner, while simultaneously sharing expertise and providing ongoing support for adult learners who are navigating their own pathways. Tim Loblaw, a graduate student currently working on his doctoral degree in the United Kingdom and a leader in adult education at a local college, speaks of his passion for learning and to his deep commitment to share his passion with others.

 The terrain of Western Canada is symbolic of my journey through the terrain of adult learning. Over the years, I have traversed the mountain vistas of undergraduate and post-graduate education, discovered hidden coulees of vocational educa-tion and training, and settled into a rich parkland that I have come to call "my professional identity." Upon reflection, my journey through the terrain reveals a phenomenological approach so beautifully captured in the conversations between activists Myles Horton and Paulo Freire in *We Make the Road by Walking*.

My "walk" started as a hike up the mountainous terrain of formal adult education; namely, an undergraduate degree from an established university. As a young man seeking an identity, I believed this was the summit one was expected to climb—a self-evident rite of passage into adulthood. I initially chose a path that led toward the physical sciences. Two years into my degree, however, I encountered my first crossroads as a traveller along the path of adult learning. In essence, I became disillusioned with the realities of working in the "real world" of the physical sciences. Leaving university seemed impractical, so, haphazardly, I chose another path. Partially driven by a need to find a degree I could apply to the "real world" and partially driven by a desire to create an identity, I chose the social sciences. Here, I discovered the fields of ethnography, sociology, and anthropology. They appeared as rolling foothills that seemed worthy of exploration yet less sharply defined by the harsh cliffs and ledges of the physical sciences. It was a terrain where I felt I could find myself.

To some extent, I have been playing in the field of social sciences ever since. Upon graduation from university I immediately applied my social science degree toward a semi-professional job. However, I was still a young man and felt an undercurrent pulling at my iden-tity. My road still needed walking. Eventually, I struck out toward per-sonally unexplored territory in adult learning: the realm of vocational education and training. Driven by yet another desire to create an identity, I returned to post-secondary education, this time at a technical institute. I decided it was time to start "plying a trade"; time to travel another road. Skills-for-work and training-for-growth: this new landscape of career-focused education seemed so foreign to me. I successfully trained for and entered the field of media advertising, but interestingly enough, I realized my emerging professional identity was actually a product of my entire prior adult learning experiences. I had become an advertiser who looked at the world through a lens of social science. I thought I had finally achieved the career I was supposed to have as an adult. But this road was not the end. There was still more to make by walking.

My professional career in radio advertising eventually brought me back into post-secondary education. An opportunity presented itself to teach media advertising at the same technical institute where I had graduated years earlier. From here, a new identity emerged out of this fertile terrain within adult learning. I embraced the role of adult educator such that I allowed my career to evolve. I shifted into educational development within the post-secondary setting. In order to support this transition, I leveraged my undergrad social science degree back into formal education, first as a graduate student in education and then as post-graduate researcher in lifelong education.

Looking back on these experiences, I have come to appreciate a central theme in my journey as an adult learner. I am an explorer at heart. Curiosity and a sense of adventure for the unknown have certainly driven me to explore and learn. However, the road I am making as I walk involves exploring my own identity.

—Tim Loblaw, Graduate Student

Our own learning journeys as adult learners and adult educators have contributed to some assumptions that continue to guide our teaching and practice. Some of these assumptions include the following:

- Learning is lifelong
- Learning can be fun
- Learning is relational
- Learning is circuitous
- Learning can be emotional
- Learning is deeply personal
- Learning is a natural process
- Learning is multi-dimensional
- Learning is influenced by context
- Learning is impacted by culture
- Learning is affected by emotions
- Learning can be transformational
- Learning involves meaning-making
- Learning involves internal processes
- Learning is body-, brain-, and mind-related

These underlying assumptions are foundational in navigating, understanding, and supporting pathways of adult learning. Indeed, lifelong learning extends *far beyond* the knowledge, skills, and abilities acquired through formal education gained from traditional learning contexts.

## Concluding Comments

We have learned that an *educated heart* is a meritorious credential in its own right—book learning does not tell the whole story. An educated heart shows wisdom in knowing and extending care, compassion, and authentic presence to others. An educated heart also appreciates the potential for learning by *leaning into opportunities*, often unfamiliar, sometimes uncomfortable, to openly engage in dialogue with others of difference in search of a deepened understanding and desire to know the world through the eyes and life events of others.

As we dig deep to explore the themes and topics in this text, we draw from the perspectives of many we have learned with and from over the past many years. These voices enrich and deepen the dialogue we invite you to engage with in the chapters that follow.

## Endnotes

1  Jidhu Krishnamurti (n.d.) cited in L. Nichol (Ed.), *The essential David Bohm* (2005), New York, NY: Routledge.
2  An adaptation of *adult learning* as defined in the report for the *Study on European Terminology in Adult Learning for a common language and common understanding and monitoring of the sector* (July, 2010), p. 6.
3  An adaptation of *adult and community learning* as defined in the report for the *Study on European Terminology in Adult Learning for a common language and common understanding and monitoring of the sector* (July, 2010), p. 6.
4  Delors's (1996) "Four pillars" of education for the future, cited in *Learning: The treasure within: Report to UNESCO of the international commission on education for the twenty-first century.*

# CHAPTER 2

# Adult Development

## COLLEEN

 When did I become an adult? At one time I was led to believe that I would wake up to be an adult on my eighteenth birthday. I recall looking in the mirror for some sign, a new look, a deeper understanding of what being an adult referred to. I recently had a similar experience when I turned 60. Would the mirror be as kind? Likely not! Some said that 60 years marked entry into the seniors' domain. What did this mean, anyway? Didn't I have until I was 65? Yet, others stated that I had been a senior since age 55. Now, the government is saying that, to collect seniors' benefits in the future, I may need to be older yet. So, now I am too young to be a senior. Who decides? The fulcrum kept shifting.

As I pondered, the answers to my questions were not so clear or simple. So much depended upon whose lens I was looking through. Through a legal lens, I was an adult when I turned 18. I could legally purchase alcohol, get married without parental consent if I chose to, and vote. Through the lens of my parents, I was years from being ready to marry, was too young to drink, and still required a curfew for as long as I lived at home. From a financial (student loan) perspective, I was old enough to sign on the dotted line to apply for funding to attend college. If I defaulted on the loan, I would be responsible, not my parents. Through the eyes of the bank, I was an adult assuming financial obligation and responsibility.

I admit that I was thrust "out of childhood" after the car accident at age 16. This rocked my world. Nothing was the same. I no longer believed that my parents could protect me from harm's way, nor did I believe that falling asleep would take away the bad and the ugly with only the good being there in the morning. Prior to that night on December 15, 1968, I had lived my life in the moment. I believed I would live forever. I saw no reason to think otherwise. Something changed for me back then, however. Being hit by a drunk driver, losing my best friend, and leaving school propelled me to a place where I spent most of my time alone and reflecting. What does life mean? Who am I? Am I significant? Why didn't I die? And what is it that I am learning from these experiences that seem to come out of left field? I recall writing in my journal, "I have no idea how all of this will impact who I am in future but I suspect it will be monumental."

I was a young, white, typical girl, the middle child in a family of five children. Although I don't recall my father ever working fewer than three jobs, I used to think that I didn't have much to fear. On the surface, we presented as a middle-class family and, at some level, I knew that this was a privilege. I was deeply impacted and influenced watching my father who worked almost every day of the week and continued to upgrade his skills in all ways available to him, and by a mother who had survived the war and come to Canada as a war bride. Indeed, she bore the scars of the choices she had made back then, but she was never able to completely embrace the freedoms she wanted for her daughters. She did, however, break some of the chains to provide us with a pathway of freedoms and opportunities that she had never had.

After the accident I no longer felt like a child. The innocence was gone. The world became more complicated. In many ways, and in retrospect, it was all quite transformational. Within a few years, I had entered the world of work and I became a single mother. My life was no longer just about me. I did not have complete control, nor could I anticipate all that was to come my way. I took a deep breath and held on for dear life!

## JANET

 Do I follow the classic trajectory as an adult? Have I moved through the stages of development neatly and system-atically? If development theory tells us when key events and milestones are to occur, I guess I modelled the classic stages of development in Western society. I could be a textbook case. I completed my undergraduate education without interruption by the time I was 23. I got married and engaged in a career path that reflected my love of teaching in my mid-twenties. Then, I was a mother of three children—all by 33 years of age. Through all of this, we were busy with the external demands of life—being parents, crafting our careers, purchasing a home. The only pushback I remember was from my in-laws—there was the expectation that I stay home with the children. I chose not to conform. I embarked on a Master's degree in Adult Education and continued to work part-time. They began to realize that I could fulfill my duties as a parent, while still working and studying.

During this time there wasn't much time for introspection or self-development; nor did I feel a hunger for this. We were just too busy. Development theorists tell me that this is fairly normal; that we often do not turn inward and become self-reflective until many of these external demands have been completed. Then there is space—space to pause, to look around, to think about things a little differently, space to journey inward.

If I was going to point to a time in my life when this really happened and pointed me on the career path and research direction that I am exploring in the now, it would have to be my time at the Ignatian Centre for Spirituality when I was a staff development consultant. I was in my mid-thirties. Up until this point, my faith had been shaped by external influences in that I was deeply connected, throughout my upbringing, to the Dutch-based Christian Reformed Church. However, during my times of retreat at the Centre, it became about so much more—my story and my experiences were experienced as central to my spiritual journey. This was such a revelation to me! When I delve into Fowler's work around faith development, I now realize that I was undergoing a profound shift and progression in my spiritual journey. In his work, Fowler talks about a gradual shift in our stages of faith, from being externally driven and involving child-like acceptance to experiencing rebellion, questioning, and even denial of our heritage. Ultimately, if we continue our journey, we move into a reclamation and growth of our faith journey, but we can only do so by moving inward to probe our assumptions and to claim what we believe. I am still on this journey, pushing myself to live an undivided, more cohesive and coherent life, where my outward actions and inward thoughts and beliefs are congruent with each other. Easier said than done!

## Introduction

As noted in chapter 1, many of us love telling stories. When we get together with friends we share stories about our families, our high school teachers and classmates, special vacations, and critical life events. Often, we revisit and retell the story of an experience in our lives multiple times, altering and nuancing the story based on shifting life experiences and perspectives—same event, different story. For example, Janet's mother once told her that she did not understand, for the longest time, how hard it was on her family to say goodbye as she left the Netherlands in the early 1950s with her husband and three young children. While Janet's parents were nervous, they were excited about their new adventure in Canada; they were looking forward with anticipation. They really did not or could not look backward to the loved ones they were leaving behind. It was 30 years later, when Janet's sister moved away to Hong Kong, that her mother's story of leaving the Netherlands changed. She then spoke about how hard it must have been on her mother to wave to the ever-receding figures on the ship that took them out to sea and away from Rotterdam. Now she understood, as she was the parent who was being left behind as her daughter flew off to new adventures in Hong Kong. Her perspective on that experience widened and was reflected in her more recent versions of stories she told of leaving the Netherlands.

When we tell stories of our experiences, it is important to consider *how we are changing or developing through these experiences*. We take a step back, reflect, consider, and reconsider if and how we are being shaped, developed, and ultimately changed through our experiences. Furthermore, if we consider Janet's mother's shifting story of leaving the Netherlands, we also realize that the process of change and development is ongoing; we can return to an event over and over again and still learn something new. As our circumstances change, we are offered a new lens through which to see and make meaning of our experience.

In this chapter, we explore the field of adult development in order to enrich our understanding of the storied and changing experiences of adult learners. Theories of adult development are particularly helpful because the phases of life we undergo and the transitions we experience provide insight into the rich possibility of adult learning that emerges throughout our life journey. Looking specifically at the word *development*, the idea of development has typically been associated with change over time and/or change with age, whether we consider adults or children (Merriam & Clark, 2006). Our lives offer a much more complex, ever-shifting, and multi-faceted picture of change and development than does this neat and tidy definition. This was evidenced by Janet's story of her mother. At the beginning of this chapter, we spoke about life changes and development as teenagers transitioning into early adulthood. And yet, our pathways were quite different from one another. For Colleen, change came suddenly with the event of a car accident; she speaks of being catapulted into adulthood. For Janet, change was gradual; she transitioned into adulthood in a more traditional way that resembled many of her friends' paths. Whatever pathway we take, there are life transitions and events that impact how and what we navigate as we journey to adulthood. This is the focus of this chapter.

Before we investigate various aspects of adult development and learning, we want to point out that much of the scholarship in this area holds an underlying assumption regarding change and development as being a movement toward "higher, more mature, more integrated levels of functioning ... [and] the potential for growth, for life-changing interventions bettering both individuals and society" (Merriam & Clark, 2006, p. 29). This positive growth perspective is located within a humanistic orientation to adult education. A humanistic orientation is rooted in the inherent human potential for goodness and the idea that our underlying quest is to become self-actualized in order to create a better world and to strive for the highest good (Lange, 2006). Stepping back and pausing for a moment, you realize that this is quite an assumption. What do you think? Does this value statement align with your position on development, learning, and change?

While you might agree with this positive growth–oriented perspective, we are sure that you can likely point to times in your life when change or a learning event had the opposite effect. This might have felt like a step backward in your learning journey. Jarvis (2006) spoke of this as *non-learning*. While he suggested that non-learning could occur when we are too busy and/or refuse to undertake the effort to undergo change, he also indicated that non-learning for adults might occur due to negative, early experiences. As a result, the unsettling emotions of anger and anxiety associated with the process of learning may cause us to retreat, to disengage from learning, and to barrier ourselves from potential positive change and development.

It is also important to acknowledge how cultural and gender-bound qualities are associated with growth and change. Tennant (2006) reminded us that an emphasis on separateness, independence, and self-generation, typically associated with healthy adult development, is derived from a predominantly Western, male perspective. For example, Gilligan (1982), who has conducted extensive research on women and identity, stated that mature womanhood is rarely associated with the notion of autonomy; rather, the qualities of engagement and interdependence are valued.

So, while we still align ourselves with the belief that change and development is generally growth-oriented and positive, we also acknowledge that notions of growth are culturally laden. Additionally, we recognize that our life experiences can result in perspectives that are inhibiting, restrictive, and less developed. As we enter into the various approaches to development and change, we ask you to consider your own story of development and learning and to reflect on how you have changed and why. How has your perspective on your experiences and stories shifted through your life journey? Has your journey always been growth-oriented? Have there been times when your life experiences and events set you back a step or two, making your more cautious and hesitant? In addition, in our role as educators, do we take the time to learn and understand the stories of our learners? Do we consider how their stories inform our practice? We offer you Marlene Atleo's reflection as an important parable for the stance we need to take, in seeking to deeply understand our learners' lives, their ongoing development, and the impact these dimensions have on their learning journey.

 It was a foggy Clayoquot Sound day. Lineage womenfolk were gathered around a plywood table processing dog (chum) salmon for the smoke house. The smell of smoke was acrid on the October air. The men brought up more salmon that the women beheaded, gutted, cut, and prepared for smoking. I loved the opportunity to do fish with my husband's female relatives. The stories around the table were inviting, entertaining, and instructive. There was much to see and learn. Standing across the table, I diligently copied Nan Margaret's every move. Gutting male and female salmon differently so that they could be cut uniquely because they had distinctive levels of fat and lean, which was important for drying for the winter stores. I used my chitulth (fish knife) with increasing expertise. It looked like I had done well securing the fish for hanging ... until we hung them in the smoke house. Mine were notably all backwards to the others. I had mimicked Nan's work and cut mirror images rather than been relational as if I were by her side learning to cut them from her perspective. It was a graphic lesson for me about teaching and learning. She did not adapt her perspective to mine; I had to adapt my perspective to hers. While I can't but figuratively be in the shoes of my students, I can be beside them to scaffold their learning.

—Dr. Marlene Atleo, Associate Professor,
University of Manitoba, Ahousaht First Nation

Now let's review various aspects of adult development and their impact on learning: biological development, cognitive development, psychological development and life transitions, and identity development.

## Biological Development

We are all getting older; we cannot push back the hands of time even though we might have a yoga practice, eat right, use the right creams, or take vitamins. Biological development highlights the inevitable march of time and refers to physical changes experienced over a lifetime. When we think about biological development and adult learning, we are interested in how our physical well-being, sensory acuity, and physiological and physical responses impact our ability to engage in learning and associated activities. From a strictly biological perspective, we enter adulthood by our early twenties and, typically, until our late forties we experience few physical changes that impact our ability to learn, other than those as a result of childbirth, accident, stress, degenerative illness or disease, and lifestyle. Our overall lifespan has increased dramatically in Canada, from 59 years for males and 61 years for females born in 1920s to 79 years and 83 years, respectively, for males and females born this past decade (Statistics Canada, 2012). However, we need to be cautious when reading these statistics, as there are variances beyond gender, based on our location, socioeconomic status, and racial and ethnic background.

Although we undergo changes in our bodies and to our physical wellness over our lifetime, the impact of most of these changes on our ability to learn is largely unknown (Merriam, Caffarella, & Baumgartner, 2007).

However, even though we do not yet have a strong research base regarding changes to our bodies and the connection to learning, we intuitively know how important our physical well-being is to everything we do. Jarvis (2006) reminded us that, when we learn, we are not only learning with our mind, but with our senses. While we may take this for granted in our day-to-day living, and may not consciously incorporate the majority of these senses into our learning experiences, the gradual diminishment of their acuity will cause us to pay attention to their importance.

Turning to vision and hearing, the acuity of these sensory receptors slowly declines, particularly from our forties onward. Age-related vision changes are associated with a loss of close vision, a mild reduction in the ability to distinguish between some colour combinations, and an increase in time needed to adjust to changes in light intensity. Turning to hearing, its loss is progressive, typically starting in our late thirties. However, adults usually do not notice any significant change until their late fifties or sixties, when sounds—particularly those in the high-frequency range—become more difficult to hear, making normal speech muffled and hard to understand. However, vision and hearing changes can typically be attended to, making it possible for individuals to carry on learning, relatively unimpeded (MacKeracher, 2004; Merriam, Caffarella, & Baumgartner, 2007).

Another physical change we experience as we age relates to changes in our nervous system, the primary biological basis for learning, which consists of the brain and the spinal cord. In ongoing research that focuses on the aging brain, researchers refer to aging as a "complex phenomenon characterized by reorganization, optimization, and enduring functional plasticity that can enable the maintenance of a productive—and happy—life" (Reuter-Lorenz & Lustig, 2005, p. 249). For example, we now understand that, despite a reduction of brain cells as we get older, remaining neurons increase their connections with each other. Plasticity allows the brain to maintain much of its function throughout our lifespan. In addition, recent research focusing on the role of the frontal lobes of the brain in adulthood, and their pivotal role in governing reflective thought and the connection between reason and emotions in processing and acquiring knowledge, holds potential in helping us understand how to maintain cognitive nimbleness as we age.

One change associated with an older adult's changing nervous system is our declining reaction time, typically resulting in increased time to complete certain psychomotor tasks such as putting together furniture or reacting quickly on the tennis court. Regretfully, these two examples relate to both of us. So, while we cannot categorically say that all older people are significantly physically slower or need more time to process information than young people, "on the average, people over the age of 65 react less rapidly" (Lefrancois, 1996, p. 506). However, the need for an increased amount of time to learn something as we get older is not really a problem, the only possible exceptions being in times of emergency or when a learning situation is particularly unique, requiring a multi-faceted response, or when your child is on the other side of the tennis net. In summary, while the physical changes of sensory acuity, reduction of brain cells, and decreased speed of response are inevitable as we get older, there is typically no corresponding decline in our ability to develop, to change, and to learn. We do, however, need to incorporate adaptive strategies and adjustments in order to continue on our pathway of learning.

## Cognitive Development

Cognitive development involves "changes in thinking patterns that occur in conjunction with learning" (Merriam & Clark, 2006, p. 32). Underlying this description is the gradual maturation of our cognitive development so we, as adult learners, have the ability to think *reflectively* about our experiences "to question the status quo, ask why, and examine assumptions underling practice. Adults *learn* to do this as they encounter life experiences and find that their usual coping mechanisms no longer work" (Merriam & Clark, 2006, p. 32). Therefore, while we may be able to assimilate new ideas and knowledge as the concepts and ideas easily fit into our own understanding of the world, there will be other times when such ideas and concepts are so new and/or contradictory to our understanding and experiences of life that we can no longer just assimilate this knowledge. This is when we are called upon to move into accommodation and adaption that requires dramatic shifts in our thinking and ways of being. Let's return to Colleen's story to illuminate the profound shift she had to undergo as a young adult. After her car crash, Colleen's way of being in the world was dramatically different; so changed was she that she was no longer able to just live in the moment and assimilate experiences from the perspective of a protected young adult. Colleen's identity fundamentally changed and she needed go back to the drawing board to determine who she was and how she would engage in and with the world. *"Being hit by a drunk driver, losing my best friend, and leaving school propelled me to a place where I spent most of my time reflecting. What does life mean? Who am I? Am I significant? Why didn't I die? And what is it that I am learning from these experiences that come out of left field?"* As you will see later in this book when we explore several adult learning theories that include experiential learning and transformative learning, *reflective thinking*—the ability to think abstractly and to reason hypothetically—is absolutely fundamental when we engage with knowledge that pushes us beyond our usual way of being in the world. This is the central platform for much of adult learning and mature adult development.

However, prior to abstract thought and reflective thinking associated with adult learning, Piaget, a pioneer in cognitive development research, indicated that we move through four phases of cognitive maturation: sensory motor thought, preoperational, concrete operational, and finally, formal operational thought (1973). This final stage, considered by Piaget to be the pinnacle of mature adult thought, is typically arrived at during adolescence. This stage allows us to problem-solve and engage in abstract reasoning. Other theorists, however, believing that Piaget's model relied too heavily on a biological model, focused more on how social contexts affect the development of our cognitive processes (Goldberger, Tarule, Clinchy, & Belenky, 1996).

In addition, several researchers believe in a fifth stage of cognitive development, beyond Piaget's final stage. This fifth stage is called *post-formal thought* (Sinnott, 1994). Key dimensions of post-formal thought include the ability to "think relativistically, sustain contradiction and paradox, integrate, and reconcile alternatives in moving towards dialectical thinking" (Boucouvalas, 2005). An example of dialectical thinking or multiple ways of thinking about everyday life where contradictions or complexities abound could be illustrated in this way: a friend might take a principled stand on the importance of reducing our impact on the environment and yet choose not to recycle.

Kegan, a researcher who intertwined both the psychological and sociocultural variables into dialectical thinking, believed that our thinking as adults needs to evolve and change to higher levels of thinking in order to deal with the challenges and complexities of the twenty-first century (1994). We all have multiple roles within and across our professional and personal lives and the ensuing demands pull us in all directions. Kegan's model of cognitive development proposed that we have two powerful desires that are at odds with each other:

> the desire to be connected to others and the desire to be independent of others. These two forces are very difficult to keep in balance; in fact, we move back and forth in a spiral-like movement between an emphasis on one or the other. (Merriam, 2005, p. 33)

As we navigate the tension between these two forces, we move through different levels of thinking—from concrete views of the world, to more abstract inferences, to abstract systems, and ultimately, to dialectical thinking. The demands of our sociocultural context push us to develop further in order to navigate and function within contradictions and ideological differences. When you think about it, this is what adult learning is all about.

# Psychological Development and Life Transitions

As children, we were often told that we were not old enough to do something. This assumed societal rules that enforced an age-appropriate perception of when we are able to do something. Examples would be when we were old enough to drive, when we could vote, how old we should be before getting married, when to start university and develop a career, and when to have a family. Psychological development, typically viewed as an internal and almost automatic process, is the foundation for stage and age theories. These theories are built upon the assumption that our ongoing development relies upon a patterned and orderly progression of life transitions that are based upon chronological time associated with specific ages and/or life stages. The most well-known models linked to age are Levinson's (1978) and Levinson and Levinson's (1996) studies of male and female development, Gould's (1990) psychoanalytical theory of development, and Loevinger's (1976) stages of ego development. Again, age theories have been problematized as being culturally and gender specific, and increasingly out of step with life in the twenty-first century. For example, Levinson's theory of life stages indicated that adolescence ends at age 17 and that early adulthood begins as one prepares to move out into the world of school, work, and independence. However, such a clear-cut transition does not acknowledge the rapidly changing economic and social conditions in today's world; a place where young people are entering an unstable and temporary world of work and, in turn, are delaying departure from the family home. The challenge lies in the earlier generations' expectations that the current millennial generation move through the same life stages at the same time and in the same way as their own generation.

In stage theories, there is a subtle difference in that, while there is still an upward movement of growth and development, it is not automatically associated with chronological age. Fowler's (1981) stages of faith development provide a good example of this. While there is some connection with one's age, Fowler's stages of faith development argued that one can arrive at a mature level of faith in one's twenties, or perhaps one might never arrive at the final few stages of faith development even later in life.

Underlying the theories of age and stage development is the belief that the structure of our lives revolves around times of stability interspersed with times of transition or periods of change, raising the spectre of learning through such transitions. *Anticipated transitions* are life events that are typically expected to occur in most adult lives, such as having a child, securing our first job, getting married, buying a house, and eventually retiring. While there are normative expectations around when these might happen and in what order, our current reality challenges these expectations at every turn. People are no longer retiring at age 65; adults return to formal education several times throughout their lives; and the typical age to get married has dramatically shifted over the past decades from the early twenties to the late twenties or early thirties. However, Merriam (2005) indicated that the potential for learning from such a transition greatly increases when friends and peers are going through similar experiences. For example, Janet, like several of her friends, is experiencing empty-nest syndrome and is finding it very helpful to compare notes with friends as their children also gradually become more and more independent.

*Unanticipated transitions*—or "what to do when life happens"—can occur unexpectedly. You are fired or downsized from your job; you are diagnosed with a life-altering illness; you are offered a huge opportunity through a friend or at work; or you, like Colleen, are the victim of a tragic accident. Whatever the likely extremely stressful event, the potential for significant learning is often greater than the learning resulting from typical and expected life transitions.

Schlossberg, Waters, and Goodman (1995) also highlighted *non-event transitions* in our lives; in essence, something that we expect to happen does not happen. For example, you might not get married, or have a child, or get into your first program of choice at university. Or you may not get the job promotion you had been working toward for years, potentially resulting in some significant reflection on your life goals and your future career pathway. While some powerful learning opportunities can emerge out of these nonevent transitions, adult educators have rarely delved into this learning potential (Merriam, 2005).

Finally, Schlossberg (1989) described the *sleeper transition* as something that occurs so gradually over time that we might not even notice that it is occurring. The erosion of communication between a couple that ultimately results in the ending of a marriage, or the diligent practice of a novice guitarist that elevates her or him, over a long period of time, to a level of guitar playing that is envied by many. These are but two examples.

In summary, psychological development that we undergo and transition that we experience, throughout our lives, provide opportunities to learn. However, it is only through self-awareness, acknowledging the tensions associated within the transition, and engaging in reflective thinking—an ongoing theme throughout this text—that the possibility of learning is realized. The process of learning through these times of transition will be explored further when we delve into transformational learning.

## Negotiating Identity

Underlying our discussion on biological development, cognitive development, psychological development, and life transitions is the quest to understand how all of these contribute to our understanding of who we are. When we tell a story about ourselves or describe our lives, we are highlighting certain qualities that provide clues to how we perceive ourselves at that moment; as a mother, as a teacher, as a middle-aged man, as someone who has immigrated from a different culture, as a young woman who has grown up on a farm in Saskatchewan, and so on. Merriam and Clark (2006) indicated that "the self, as a concept, is socially and historically constituted; there is no fixed understanding of the notion across time or across cultures" (p. 33).

Merriam's statement about the self is an important one to unpack, as it challenges the dominant way we, in the Western world, have viewed the notion of *self* since the time of Enlightenment. Specifically, the prevailing view—also categorized as a modernist notion of self—argued that there is a fixed and unitary concept of self and that, as individuals, we have the power or agency to find our true, authentic, and core self. Indeed, much of the humanistic orientation to adult development has been built on this quest. Rogers (1961) stated that the goal of life is "to be that self which one truly is" (p. 166). And Maslow (1970) argued that within the individual is the ability and power to work toward self-actualization.

Like Clark and Dirkx (2000) in their chapter titled Models of the Self: A Reflective Dialogue, we believe that we need to reconsider the notion of a unitary self, where all of the power or agency to change oneself resides within the individual. We turn to a voice from the field, Shahrzad Mojab, professor and director of the Women and Gender Studies Institute at the University of Toronto, to offer an alternative perspective, one that illuminates how culture, context, and gender become intertwined to create a shifting and relational sense of self. Much of Shahrzad's research explores adult learning and women within the context of war.

 Learning theories are highly contested. So, in my research on women, war, and learning I have muddied this already cluttered field by dislocating its pedagogical, theoretical, and policy frames to sites of war, violence, and occupation. I have tried to understand the processes of learning, the content that is being taught and learned, and the consequences of what is being learned or unlearned in places where displaced and disposed women turn up, such as refugee camps, adult language classes, or skills training programs. In my research, I have observed the emergence of "life in transition" as a universal mode of being and learning. By this phrase, I mean women's mode of living, which is unsettled, precarious, tempo-rary, unsafe, or unstable. These are the women whose experience and knowledge of the actualities of violence fall outside the boundaries of learning policy, practice, and theorization. But learning is happening regardless of this neglect, omission, and exclusion. Therefore, learning theories must begin to identify learning modalities in women's experience within the condition of war and violence that have been outside of their purview, such as survival learning and resistance learning. We should also note that learning theories and practices often are formulated on the experience and knowledge of atomized individuals rather than on persons in relations. Women's experience and knowledge of violence, trauma, and displacement unfolds itself through social relations of race, class, sexuality, and other socially differentiating forces. The current learning modalities are either less than optimal for, or can indeed fail, women learners who have experienced war and violence first hand. We should recognize that survivors of violence and conflict have their own good knowledge of their lives and experiences, that their survival has more often than not been based upon their intelligence, and that they have the ability to adapt, improvise, and innovate.

—Dr. Shahrzad Mojab, Professor, Director,
Women and Gender Studies Institute, University of Toronto

Shahrzad's story is a compelling example of a self that is not unitary; these adult learners demonstrate a non-unitary and relational notion of self, located in a post-modern world. They live in the socially constructed reality of war that dictates tenuous living conditions and creates a culture of violence and fear. In addition, they epitomize a multiplicity of selves in their relationships with others, responding to and engaging with events outside of their control while also living out prescribed cultural and gender roles, as opposed to pursuing the perception of a core, authentic, and true self that never changes. They are a multiplicity of selves: women, mothers, wives, and daughters. They are also providers, protectors, victims of trauma, and survivors.

## Concluding Comments

As we close this chapter, we return to the beginning: we love to tell stories about our lives, and we tell these stories in order to make meaning of our experiences. The meaning we derive from these stories is ever shifting; adjustments are being made as we journey through our lives. We experience multiple transitions and we engage in numerous roles that cause our perspective and interpretation of these experiences to undergo ongoing revisions. The telling and retelling of our stories reflect a *narrating notion of identity*, in which the self is understood as an ever-unfolding and changing story. We take one experience within our life and change our narrative about that experience. For example, in Shahrzad's exploration of women, learning, and war, there are multiple narratives for each woman occurring simultaneously. There are narratives of victimization, trauma, and loss for each of these women. There are also narratives of survival, learning, and hope. These multiple narratives probably jostle for dominance in each woman's narrative identity. The ongoing choices these women, and each of us, make about the narrative we tell—how we make sense of an experience—will then determine how we respond and move forward from that experience. And so, as we take up a narrative orientation to consider biological development, cognitive development, and age and stage development, we understand ourselves and the life changes we experience as a story unfolding. To extend this notion, the shaping of our narrative is not just a personal process; we live in a story-shaped world (Sarbin, 1993).

CHAPTER 3

# Sociocultural Influences

## JANET

As a child, when I thought of the Netherlands, my parents' home until their early thirties, it was always associated with Christmastime and the big box of goodies we received from Oma and Opa. With anticipation, we unwrapped what we always knew would be inside, a chocolate letter for each of us. I had an S, even though my name is Janet, because I was named after an aunt whose name started with an S. There was also salted licorice, underwear, and perfume for my mom. I was an immigrant child, the youngest of seven—three of my siblings were born in the Netherlands and we final four were born in Canada.

My parents spoke of coming to Canada as a relief, a space that offered them freedom from World War II and the daily reminders of their wartime experiences. I don't think I realized how profoundly this background marked me until two events in my recent history. The first event had to do with my visit to Pier 21 in Halifax—the immigration entry point for my family when they arrived by ship from the Netherlands. For the first time, I was able to see the names of my parents and my three oldest siblings in the passenger registry of the ship that arrived in Canada in March of 1953. Seeing those names made the stories come alive; there they were—the names of my parents and siblings! From Halifax, they immediately took the train to Edmonton—four days in duration. As they gazed out of the train, the vast, white expanses of land were foreign to them and created feelings of anxiety. Upon arrival in

Edmonton, they connected with other Dutch immigrants and gradually created a life. Having Dutch friends contributed to a sense of "home." There were many differences, however; the abundance of open land, the houses, the frontier feeling of the town had little resemblance to their past surroundings.

Once my parents settled into daily life, pictures were sent back to Holland. In these photographs, my parents and my older brother and sisters were carefully positioned in the corner of the room where there was furniture; the rest of the room was empty. This gave the illusion of prosperity. However, despite these challenges and in hindsight, I now know we were fortunate as my father had a great job as a draftsman with the government of Alberta waiting for him. Our family rapidly expanded and our transition was fairly smooth and easy. We were from Europe—we looked like many others that arrived at the same time in the 1950s and the 1960s. My parents were high school graduates; they had some English skills and my father was a trained professional. Life in Edmonton offered my family the possibility of a fresh start. Fifty years later, that wisp of hope translated into the reality of full lives, rich in experiences. Memories were created here in Canada and grandchildren and great-grandchildren scattered across this land.

I didn't realize that the immigrant experience marked me in other ways until I visited relatives in Holland as a teenager. When spending time with my Dutch cousins, I realized that their understanding and experience of family was so different than mine. They told me stories of visiting their Oma every Sunday and being forced to kiss her cheek, not their favourite thing. They shared birthdays, Christmases, and family vacations with other cousins and with aunts and uncles. That wasn't my experience growing up—aunts and uncles came from afar for short visits, we visited Niagara Falls and then they left. We were a family unit of nine and the notion of extended family pretty much existed in the Christmas box. We were raised to be independent, to make our way in the world, and to travel. However, I also realized that our independence came at a cost. I felt a sense of loss as I heard my cousins' stories of growing up. I did not know my extended family well and, in particular,

I never really knew who my grandparents were. Now, while I cannot change the past, I have the privilege of trying to capture lost time by travelling to the Netherlands, more than once, to visit the places where my parents grew up and, more importantly, to build connections with cousins recently discovered, before it is too late.

Why do I tell this story? Cole and Knowles (2001), in their work on life history methodology, remind us that our identities and our stories are contextualized. In other words, gender, socioeconomic standing, culture, and race inform and shape our lives and experiences. These factors also contribute to the very foundation of our story. Because I am white, middle-class, and a woman of European descent, my story is shaped in certain ways. Doors open for me because of this and doors also close for me for the very same reason. I venture down certain pathways because of my context. Other pathways are not revealed or are not chosen, also because of societal influences and context.

## COLLEEN

 I was raised in a middle-class neighbourhood in the province of Alberta, Canada. My father, Stanley Michael Kawalilak, was the "breadwinner," working six days a week to put food on the table. My mother, Mary Agnes Logan, like all other mothers in our neighbourhood, worked at home raising five children. She hated the name Agnes and would get visibly irritated when others did not respect her preference to be called Mary. Being a dutiful Catholic wife, birth control was not an option; so, she remained pregnant for many of her younger years. We went to church every Sunday, ate fish on Fridays and said the rosary afterwards, and visited relatives on the farm in the summer months. We always had a dog as a family pet.

From all outward appearances, most would have described us as a typical, middle-class family. From the inside, however, looking back, we lived month to month and were only a few steps ahead of other families labelled low income. I found out in later years that my dad would often juggle bills needing to be paid at the end of every month. He learned that skipping one payment would not create too much of a problem, as long as he was sure to pay that particular bill the following month. The mortgage payment was always paid, however, to ensure that we retained the security of a roof over our heads. Mortgage and groceries always came first. These were always the first bills to be paid.

I became aware, at a very young age, that money was always an issue. Consequently, money was the root of most arguments between my parents. I don't think they thought that my siblings and I knew as much as we did about our financial struggles as a family. Regardless, there were many summer holiday excursions that involved travelling to a lake a few short miles away. Although we seldom drove beyond the provincial border, I recall a particular trip taken when I was in my early teens. We drove west into British Columbia. The terrain was beautiful. We drove through mountain passes and forests. Further along, we found beaches, lakes, fruit trees, and vineyards. I had never experienced any of this before. Even though we had only travelled to the adjoining province within my own country of Canada, I felt that I was now a seasoned "international traveller"!

My school experiences were both typical and somewhat limited. To elaborate, I lived in a middle-class neighbourhood, and all of my classmates were white and from families that shared similar socioeconomic advantages and challenges. No one seemed very rich or terribly poor. We were a working-class family and, on the surface, we all looked quite similar. I remember when "Victor" came to our school in grade four. He walked in wearing leather shorts and suspenders. His knee socks covered his trembling legs and his thick, black ankle boots looked too big for his feet. He was from Germany and when he mustered up the courage to actually speak, a few weeks later, he struggled with broken English. Shortly thereafter, another student joined our class. He was a very tall boy with ebony skin. He was from Kenya and also struggled with English. Other than spending time with one of my girlfriends whose older sister had cerebral palsy, these few experiences defined the extent of diversity in my world. I did have a pen pal who lived in Ukraine, however. Pen pals for girls my age were quite typical. I never told any of my friends that she was from the Ukraine, however, as they might ask me why would I be corresponding with someone from the Ukraine. Why not India, or Africa, or Brazil? I was trying to avoid admitting that my father's heritage drew from Ukrainian/Polish as jokes about the old country ran rampant and were hurtful. Acknowledging my own heritage would have opened up a window for ridicule. I wanted to keep this secret.

Being the middle child in a family of four girls and one boy, with siblings on either side of me being several years apart, I think that I spent a fair bit of time on my own. Being the middle child also afforded me the opportunity to go unnoticed when this served to my advantage. I would spend hours thumbing through travel magazines and dreaming of travelling to faraway places.

Growing up, I was constantly reminded of how lucky I was to have food on the table. When I wanted to leave some on the plate I would be scolded and told, "Think of all the starving children in Africa." I must admit that there were times when I resented those children who I didn't even know. Wasn't it their fault that I had to eat those horrible Brussels sprouts! This didn't stop me, however, from romanticizing about what it would be like to live in India, China, Holland, and the Philippines.

At some level, and in spite of the financial tensions in the family, I was always aware that I lived a privileged life. Indeed, I was reminded of this regularly and especially at Sunday mass. My awareness, however, went much deeper than this. I always felt a yearning, a deep desire to connect with those who seemed different from me. I wanted to know what they knew, what they experienced in the "other" world, how they celebrated Christmas—or did they—and if accents were all the same when singing or laughing? In other words, I was more interested in what we had in common and in what we shared, beyond our differences—our common ground.

It wasn't until I was in my late thirties that I had the opportunity to travel abroad. I travelled to Scotland with my mother to visit her birthplace and to connect with relatives that I had never met before. I met aunts, uncles, and cousins that I had only known in photographs. How was it that we were so much alike and, here we were, only meeting each other for the first time?

Although mom had many stories to tell about immigrating to Canada as a war bride, post–World War II, it wasn't until we travelled together that I began to see and understand her through other lenses. Why had I never realized that her narrative began long before she was my mother? She was once a young girl with so many unrealized dreams and aspirations. She was a daughter, a sister, and an aspiring singer. She was a young woman who ran to the underground shelter when bombs were falling on Glasgow. She was the loyal, loving daughter who stayed to care for her father after her mother died of a brain aneurism. Although she was to travel to Canada by ship to join my father, she would not leave her dad until her two brothers had returned from the war. Why had she shared so few of these memories with me before?

Many of the places we visited harboured deep emotion for my mother. Some were happy memories and others … well … not so much. I realized that, in sharing her stories with me, she was actually revisiting them herself for the very first time. Although coming to Canada to join my father held great hope and promise, she had hidden the pain, all of these years, of having left her beloved homeland. I felt profound gratitude when she gifted me with her stories. We cried together as she unveiled some of her memories and struggle. At other times, and in my mother's words, "we laughed so hard that we almost peed our pants." Seven weeks of travelling; seven weeks of sharing; seven weeks to relive some of my mother Mary's history, much of which had remained hidden, even to her, all of these years. Pieces of the puzzle began to take shape as she slowly peeled back the layers to uncover the storied memories within. My understanding deepened as to why my mother reacted to certain situations in ways that she did when I was growing up. Her unwavering faith and commitment to the Catholic Church was deeply rooted in her own childhood upbringing. Her words, "get a good education, Colleen, as this will give you the freedom to never be dependent on a man" were rooted in her own reality of being fearful that, one day, my father might leave and, if this happened, she would be stranded and alone, with no way to support herself.

## Introduction

As we spiral down to make sense and deeper meaning of experiences and factors that have shaped and impacted our life stories, we reflect on how social, societal, and cultural factors and experiences—our habits, traditions, beliefs, have influenced our own development. On Pier 21 in Halifax, Janet pondered the plight of her parents, immigrants who welcomed a new beginning and freedom from the hardships and events brought about by World War II. She realized that the unfolding narratives of her parents—all of their experiences abound with emotions, adjustments, transitions, opportunities, and challenges when immigrating to Canada—constituted an emerging prelude to her own life narrative. Although Janet's parents adopted Canada as their new home before she was even born, features and influences that would contribute to her life story were already being recorded.

Colleen's appreciation of the prelude that preceded her birth surfaced when she travelled with her mother back to her mother's homeland. Along the way, after a bit of prodding, her mother responded to the invitation to uncover, reconnect, and relive some of the pain and sadness experienced, having left her beloved homeland at a young age to follow Colleen's father to Canada as his new bride. He was a handsome Canadian soldier and it all seemed very romantic to her at the time. As time wore on, however, the struggles of immigrating and living in a foreign country took shape. She was referred to as "the wife" and as someone who spoke with a curious Scottish accent. Becoming aware of many hurts that had been buried deep within the crevices of her mother's story, but never forgotten, Colleen began to connect her own life journey to that of her mother's. She now understood the emotion that fuelled her mother's messages to secure a good education, to have dreams, and to always have enough put away in a savings account to "get home in a day," if need be. These messages were not just about hopes that Colleen's mother harboured for her children; they also provided a window into some regrets that her mother had kept secret and guarded for so many years.

These are only snippets of what we have learned about our parents, their stories, and some of their challenges, tensions, and opportunities. We also know that there are still so many untold stories, stories of our parents, grandparents, and great grandparents, stories that continue to influence and impact our own lives and learning journeys. As we seek to render meaning to our learning, we cannot discount the influences and greater narratives of our immediate and extended families of origin. Our family histories, however, although significant, are only part of the story.

## How We See Ourselves

Drawing from French sociologist, anthropologist, and philosopher Pierre Bourdieu and his theorizing of *habitus,* our sense of place and how we interact in the world takes shape and form from earlier experiences growing up, from where and how our families were and are positioned and valued within particular social and societal contexts, and from the power relations that play out within and across these social and societal structures. Bourdieu focused on the acquisition of practical knowledge— tacit and embodied knowing—and on unconsciously following the social rules and norms prescribed within social, cultural, and physical environments that we grew up in. He described the habitus as

> something *non natural,* a set of *acquired* characteristics which are the product of social conditions and which, for that reason, may be totally or partially common to people who have been the product of similar social conditions.... habitus is not something natural, inborn; being a product of history, that is of social experience and education, it may be *changed by history,* that is by new experiences, education or training ... dispositions are long-lasting; they tend to perpetuate, to reproduce themselves, but they are not eternal. They may be changed by historical action oriented by intention and consciousness and using pedagogic devices. One has an example in the correction of an accent in pronunciation. (2005, p. 45)

Bourdieu (2005) insisted that "the habitus is not a fate, not a destiny" (p. 45). Rather, it is generative and open to creative configuration when we engage with and encounter new contexts and environments. Although we may reproduce, knowingly or unknowingly, existing structures that have guided our development, these same structures may also serve as impetus for new ways of interpreting and responding in the world.

Bourdieu's work has been the focus of much critique in scholarly literature (Hillier & Rooksby, 2005). Whether or not we believe that the dispositions we acquire growing up are determinants or precursors of our ultimate dispositions, reflecting on dimensions of identity formation that influence how we see ourselves and other people in the world warrants our consideration.

Indeed, our own life narratives are intertwined and influenced by the narratives of our parents, the families we grew up in, the communities where we lived, and our childhood friends. It is also critical to consider our positionality; that is, *where* and *how* we are located in our respective communities, cultures, and contexts. To extend this notion, we are reminded by Tisdell (1995) that positionality provides valuable insights with respect to power and agency, relative to the existence of "multiple systems of privilege and oppression" (p. 61). One might refer to this as our standpoint and the ruling relations (Smith, 2005; Smith & Sparkes, 2008) at work that organize class, gender, race, religion, ableness, sexual orientation, education, and so forth. All of these factors significantly shape our life narratives and represent some of the many sociocultural influences that impact how we interpret our experiences, how we see ourselves, and how we respond to and engage with others.

Religious affiliation, whether we are located within an organized church community as part of our childhood upbringing or, align to a particular spiritual practice as adults, is also a revealing sociocultural influence. Afroza, a woman of Muslim faith, speaks to this significance.

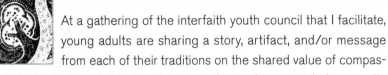At a gathering of the interfaith youth council that I facilitate, young adults are sharing a story, artifact, and/or message from each of their traditions on the shared value of compassion. A Sikh participant explains how the gurdwara regularly opens its doors to feed the poor and less fortunate. A Christian member shares a quote from the Bible, describing how she personally puts the verse into action. A Jewish colleague tells a story of his family's experience with shiva, a ritual of mourning that demonstrates compassion for the bereaved and the community. As I hear and reflect on what is shared, I think of my own Muslim tradition and the personal voice I have given to the value of compassion. After sharing our stories, art, and symbols, the group plans, implements, and evaluates a service project to put the value of compassion into action.

My experience with this interfaith initiative has taught me a great deal about program planning, transfer of learning, and evaluation. What has been most profound, however, is learning about how diverse faith traditions are lived, experienced, and made meaningful and relevant in daily life. As we engage in dialogue around the values of compassion, hospitality, and caring for our elders, the group realizes we are united in our shared values and diverse in their expression.

At the end of our cycle, I ask the group to reflect on their learning journey. A Baha'i participant shares the sense of wonder and relief she has felt. As she heard from other participants, she wondered more and more about their backgrounds. She felt immense relief at having found a space where she could openly and comfortably reveal her Baha'i-Canadian identity.

What has this experience revealed to me about interfaith adult learning? I have learned we need to have open and meaningful conversations about religion beyond the private spaces of our homes and places of worship. For many, religious belief or lack thereof is an important part of one's world view and integral to whom they consider themselves to be. Being able to share this and to see the diverse cultural expressions within each faith tradition is a magnificent learning journey.

I have also realized that we gravitate toward safe, comfortable conversations about our diverse traditions and heritages. Perhaps we are reconciling our diversity, on one hand, with concerns for cohesion and shared values, on the other. However, in trying to protect ourselves from uncomfortable conversations, we don't genuinely come to know those that are different from ourselves. We don't gain insight on the impetus and personal convictions of fellow citizens and members of their community. If we allow for conversations that may cause some discomfort to reveal themselves, we are authentically encountering diverse others and increasing our understanding of the complex and dynamic nature of religious beliefs and expressions.

Very importantly, I have learned that interfaith learning does not dilute our religious identity, but rather strengthens it. Through inquiring about a story, piece of art, or message from our religious tradition and sharing it with others, we become more confident and articulate in "who we are." By hearing from and being more present to others, we are coming to know them and, as we come to know the other, we further come to know ourselves.

Now, whenever I hear or read about the gurdwara, the Bible, and shiva, I understand with greater depth how meaningful they are for others. I am grateful for being part of a program that creates space for conversations about religion. Next time, I aim to deepen the learning by considering that which may cause me to question and clarify. For it is this that will encourage further self-examination, critical analysis, and reflection on the origins and consequences of my attitudes and behaviours.

—Afroza Nanji, Graduate Student

Afroza's ongoing examination of her beliefs, attitudes, and behaviours contributes to a deepened awareness and appreciation of differences from and connections with those who follow other faith traditions. Religious affiliations and engagements provide us with a sense of identity and purpose, a definition of sorts that can potentially guide our behaviour and practice. The same holds true for those who push back and stand up against certain dogma and traditions espoused by any given religion, as an oppositional stance also conveys differences, and connectivity to others.

Cultural diversity also exists, not only across but also within religions and faith community contexts. This becomes apparent when we consider, for example, different sects, schools, or denominations that emerge within each of the Christian, Muslim, Jewish, and Buddhist traditions. Although often united by foundational beliefs, each sect, school, or denomination, within any given context, may take up a unique interpretation on the teachings and on how these teachings should manifest and be practised in the day-to-day. Afroza speaks of the comfort and learning potential when engaging in safe space with others to explore and examine differences *and* a sense of "oneness" and common ground. Safe space supports an authentic expression of openness to share, to explore, and to examine differences. The paradox made clear in Afroza's reflection is that our diversity as human beings actually serves to unite us as "human community," more so than do our differences.

Mark reflects on the significance of human community, on the importance of a fully supportive social learning environment, and on how this support influences learning for adult learners with physical disabilities.

 My reflections on learning are based on my background as a 62-year-old man who has an inherited, slowly deteriorating eye condition. There are two parallel and consistent learning necessities for a person who has a disability. The first is to attain one's ultimate learning objective and the second is how to accommodate one's disability in and of itself while venturing down the learning pathway. The best contexts and circumstances where I have learned effectively have related to learning at my own rate, with my slow and reflective style of learning, both by observing others and through my own personal interactions and experimentations, and where I can understand how what I am learning may be applied.

It has been my experience that there are three dimensions of learn-ing that constitute a favourable learning circumstance for a person with a visual disability: 1) being immersed in a learning framework that nurtures varied perspectives and provides for a flexible learning setting; 2) having access to current technologies that are appropri-ate for the individual with a specific visual disability; and 3) being accepted into a fully supportive social environment that provides for the sustained learning and growth of the learner with the disability.

A learning framework that provides for a nurturing learning setting can exist in both formal and informal environments. A classroom learn-ing setting, where a student with a visual disability can be involved with peer learning discussions and strategies—with the intention of future integration into regular classroom settings—has been an ideal framework for my formal education. Even boarding schools specializ-ing in learning about one's disability, along with appropriate academics, may be advantageous for some individuals who are more reliant upon such specialized supports.

Technologies should not be viewed as panaceas. It is a fallacy to assume that a learner is fully competent and competitive in any learn-ing environment once they have access and the knowledge to apply a specific adaptive technology. Technologies only function as one of many vehicles and supports needed to adequately and successfully access and navigate the learning environment. Paradoxically, however, I do admit that technology has played an increasingly important role in my education, progressing from high-contrast miner's chalk on a blackboard and a low-tech, basic magnifier to a closed-circuit camera–large-print reading system that actually listens to a printed text through synthesized speech.

I assert that a fully supportive social learning environment is per-haps the most vital of the three dimensions of learning for those with a visual disability. Without the feedback, bantering, sharing varied perspectives, coming to understand common ground around disability issues, consistent interactions, and ensuing dialogues with peers and instructors, any technological adaptations in any learning frameworks become absolutely meaningless and ineffectual. Even though a perfect learning framework in an ideal setting for a particular learner may be provided alongside a learner having the ideal adaptive technology in place, these are mere accommodations. Learning frameworks and adaptive technologies do not ensure actual inclusion in the social setting constructed to provide an overall learning experience.

One of the major advantages of having a disability and becoming a learner in any instructional situation is how we automatically and implicitly also assume the role of "educator." By this, I mean people with disabilities will assume the major responsibility in sensitizing others about our learning requirements (and daily life issues, for that matter). We have no choice but to do our best to teach others about our individual, professional, and learning requirements. I admit that this instruction is not always successful or applied in the most appropriate manner. The point is, we, as learners with disabilities, often have a genuine understanding of the teacher's needs and perspectives and, in this way, we learn simultaneously.

—Mark Iantkow, Graduate Student

Mark's narrative emphasizes the importance of inclusion, belonging, and being valued and attended to in the learning environment and an essential social/relational connection between learner experience and the learning process. Having a physical disability or impairment does not have to equate to being disabled socially. Mark frequently assumes a "teacher" role to help guide others' understanding of his learning needs. In discussions beyond those that have been captured in Mark's narrative, he distinguished "having an impairment" from "being disabled." Making reference to physical impairments that included visual, hearing, or ambulatory challenges, he shared experiences of "not being disabled" in particular environments that were sensitive and responsive to his visual challenges. He then referred to "being disabled" when attempting to navigate an environment that was neither constructed nor sensitive to his visual impairment. Mark's perspective provided valuable insight in that the same person with a particular impairment may be disabled in one environment but not in another. Digging deeper, the same analysis can be applied to how we experience relationships in learning environments. Relationships contribute significantly to our sense of self and to the formation of our identity. When, as learners, we feel empowered through caring, compassionate, and supportive relationships with others, we develop certain beliefs about ourselves and about how we are perceived and valued by others. This then impacts our sense of place and experience in the world, our habitus.

We applaud Mark and other voices heard throughout this text for pushing back against structures that serve to barrier some learners, and in the ongoing work that they do to reconfigure some of these ways of organizing, in support of creating more socially responsive adult learning environments. These voices are testimony to the potential and possibility when we draw from *our power within* and from *our power as community* to upset structures that barrier and to push against dominant discourses that thwart personal and collective potential and well-being.

## Power

In chapter 1, "On Being an Adult Learner," dialogue was introduced as a pathway to ponder, to reflect on, and to make meaning of experiences through authentic, caring, and compassionate engagement with others. Within this dialogue space, we feel a sense of safety born out of being respected *by* others and extending respect *to* others. Jane Vella (2002), in her book *Learning To Listen—Learning To Teach: The Power of Dialogue in Educating Adults*, connected dialogue with "sound relationships for learning [that] involve respect, safety, open communication, listening, and humility" (p. 10). Vella referred to power relationships between students and teachers in formal education settings and maintained that "our efforts through dialogue education to build a world of equity and mutual responsibility cannot be designed without attention to the power of sound relationships" (p. 11). Afroza's and Mark's narratives speak to the gift of reciprocal learning experienced when learners and educators come together to learn simultaneously within a space of sound relationship.

As adult learners, it is critical to acknowledge that any sense of safety and sound relationship calls for a much broader and deepened understanding of sociocultural influences and for a desire and openness to engage in authentic dialogue about the meaning and significance of differences. Any discourse about power in the lives, relationships, and work and learning experiences of adult learners would be sorely lacking without addressing how culture, race, ethnicity, norms and traditions, gender, socioeconomic background, literacy level, sexual orientation, age, physical and mental abilities (ableness), and religious affiliations influence our development and how we ultimately see and understand ourselves as lifelong adult learners. With this said, it is simply not possible to explore diversity in any deep or meaningful way in one single book, let alone one book chapter. Many of our colleagues across Canada and beyond publish extensively on diversity within adult learning, in formal and informal contexts; we continue to be guided by their expertise, vision, informed practice, and wisdom. For this reason, we have attempted to integrate some of the many layers of influence, challenge, tension, potential, and opportunity that diversity brings to individuals, communities, and societies, *throughout* the chapters in this text. In other words, limiting any focus on challenges and opportunities related to diversity to one single chapter might reinforce and contribute to a more fragmented and non-inclusive understanding and discourse as to how our differences actually have potential to connect and to unite us as humankind.

Carl James (2010), in his text *Seeing Ourselves: Exploring Race, Ethnicity and Culture*, referred to how factors of difference "are interrelated; hence, it is difficult to disentangle them and point to a particular factor operating independently in any given situation or at any one time" (p. 3). James also cautioned against essentialism. Essentialism involves applying broad brushstrokes and assumptions that promote beliefs that, as humankind, we have fixed characteristics predetermined by our biology or culture. We align with James's assertion that, "While there are many common experiences to be found among people of the same ethno-racial groups, the experiences of group members are mediated by a myriad of other identities and constructs including, but not limited to" (p. 3) diversities that include culture, race, ethnicity, norms and traditions, gender, socioeconomic background, literacy level, sexual orientation, age, physical and mental abilities, and religious affiliations.

While keeping with our intention to support a more integrated experience for readers who engage with the topics in this text, we have chosen to highlight some voices from the field to enrich our understanding and appreciation of difference. We locate these voices and perspectives against the backdrop of individual and collective power. We have chosen this approach as we believe that power relations and differentials within and across individual relationships, organizations, and societies are what tip the balance in determining who wins, who loses, what counts as legitimate knowledge, and what and whom are discounted.

Discourses about power in work, learning, and societal contexts are plentiful and date far back in the literature. As one example, back in 1926 Eduard Lindeman wrote in his original *The Meaning of Adult Education*, that

> "Great Society" has come to be a vast network of power-groups, each vying with the other for supremacy. Nationalism and imperialism are merely outward manifestations of this "pseudo-power" which degrades us all; beneath these more glamorous units lies the pervading economic structure of our civilization based upon a doubtful competitive ethic and avowedly designed to benefit the crafty, the strong and the truculent. (1961, p. 26)

Making reference to industrial organization, industrial control, and labour movements, Lindeman advocated for a more "cooperative enterprise, before 'power *over*' [could be] transposed into 'power *with*' in industry" (1961, p. 27). Then, almost 20 years later in a paper published in 1945, titled The Sociology of Adult Education, Lindeman posed the question, "*Why don't American sociologists do something about adult education?"* (p. 4). One reason that Lindeman cited for this lack of doing on the part of American sociologists was that "they are themselves enmeshed in the academic system, most of whose administrators still hold their noses at the mention of adult education" (p. 4). Inglis (1997) added his critical voice and perspective to the discourse and cited the attractiveness of "the notion that enabling people to take control of their own lives and [freeing] themselves from the structures that dominate and constrain them" (p. 3). Inglis argued that being empowered required so much more than personal transformation. He maintained that autonomy, individual agency, and empowerment are elaborated on and emphasized in the literature to a greater extent than is "a critical analysis of discourse and power structures and the way they operate in the lives of people" (p. 8).

Budd Hall, co-chair of community-based research and social responsibility in higher education for the United Nations Educational, Scientific and Cultural Organization (UNESCO), and professor of community development at the University of Victoria School of Public Administration, speaks passionately of power within the context of social movement learning.

 How many of you remember the Idle No More movement for the recognition of Indigenous rights in Canada? Do you remember the democracy movements in Egypt and elsewhere in the Middle East? Perhaps you have heard of various environmental movements in Canada or your own part of the world? All of these are examples of social movements. Usually when we think of social movements, we think of them as political movements or perhaps movements about identity or protest movements. What we often overlook is that social movements are remarkable and rich spaces of adult education. Learning that is part of or influenced by social movements we call social movement learning.

Social movements are particularly rich spaces for learning. They are some of the most powerful incubators of new learning and new thinking that exist. How or where does learning take place in social movements? Well, first of all we need to say that it happens both inside and outside of the movements themselves. Inside the movements, we will often find that there are formal opportunities to learn more about the issues of the movement or the campaign itself. There may be educational sessions for activists within the movement to learn more about, for example, the implications of legislation related to land use of Aboriginal peoples in the case of the Idle No More movement or formal learning opportunities about global issues in the peace movement. There are also structured opportunities to learn about campaigning skills or strategies within the movement, such as how to use social media to reach out, how to contact and deal with the media, how to contact politicians, and more. But perhaps the largest part of the learning for those inside the movements is the informal learning that happens when people talk about the movement to their friends and families or in other ways try to explain the issues on the table.

I have often said that social movements have a magical power to create learning because through the actions, the demos, the theatre, and the social media, thousands of people outside the movements have an opportunity to learn about the issues at the heart of the movements themselves. This form of social movement praxis actually allows people to explore and sometimes transform their thinking as they develop new understandings of power, knowledge, and issues of difference or exclusion or denomination. What are some of the social movements that you are aware of? Can you think of what kinds of adult learning have happened either within or without those movements?

If you want to read more about social movement learning take a look at *Learning and Education for a Better World: The Role of Social Movements* (Hall, Clover, Crowther, & Scandrett, 2012).

—Dr. Budd Hall, Professor, Director,
Office of Community Based Research, University of Victoria

Linking informal learning to the power of collective learning and social action continues to play a significant role in the important work of Indigenous peoples and communities. Many non-Indigenous scholars, educators, and activists, like Budd, also work tirelessly as allies in addressing the many injustices inflicted by a colonial government on the First Peoples of Canada. A stark example of cultural genocide here in Canada is found in the residential school system where First Nations, Métis, and Inuit peoples endured many horrors under the mantle of education.

André Grace, a leading researcher and adult educator in queer studies and adult learning, expands and deepens the sociocultural lens and discourse. André advocates for ethical practices, policymaking, and inclusivity pertaining to the needs and rights of queer or sexual and gender minority individuals.

 In my work regarding learner access and accommodation, I include a core focus on queer or sexual and gender minority (SGM) individuals—including lesbian, gay, bisexual, and transgender persons—and our issues in relation to inclusion, equity, and social justice in education, health care, other institutional contexts, and culture. Here I emphasize SGM-inclusive policymaking and its implementation in ethical practices in education and other caring professions. Indeed there has been a move to focus on sexual and gender minorities in North American academic adult education since the early 1990s. The contemporary effort to include queer theorizing and queer studies in academic adult education contests its usual omission and ensuing silence, making it a profoundly political endeavour. Queer theory exposes heterosexism and homo/bi/transphobia as it examines how ignorance and fear of SGM people often lead to violence against us. Queer studies places queer theory in a dynamic, interactive relationship with queer research and practice. Queer studies works best when it links knowledge building to advocating for sexual and gender minorities in life, learning, and work contexts. Here advocacy is about recognition, respect, and accommodation that affirm queer integrity.

—Dr. André P. Grace, Professor, Director of Research, Institute for Sexual Minority Studies and Services, University of Alberta

André's advocacy work, teaching, and scholarship focus on the exploration of self, others, and cultures by examining the positionalities and needs of learners and teachers across sexual and gender minority differences. As sexual and gender minority individuals are represented in all areas and walks of life, André's message is one that invites all caring individuals to actively support and advocate for inclusion, safe space, and ethical practice.

## Concluding Comments

*Pathways of adult learning* is an appropriate metaphor that encompasses the road we have travelled, the road we are on, and the road that we have yet to experience and explore. We offer this metaphor to capture the diversity of landscape that we navigate as adult learners, the diversity of experiences and activities that guide and inform our journey, the diversity of humankind that we experience along the way, and all other factors, elements, and influences that impact our learning journeys and narratives. In the words of Lindeman (1961), "The whole of life is learning, therefore education can have no endings" (p. 5).

The adult learners and voices from the field who spoke to us in this chapter are a powerful reminder of our human need for care, compassion, inclusion, ethical practice, and community. Power *in* and power *with*, versus power *over* others supports pathways for healing, learning with and from others, individual and collective transformation, and social change. A genuine desire to *engage with difference* takes courage and a loosening of our grip on tightly held assumptions, beliefs, agendas, and practices. We emphasize courage because, by stepping out beyond our own comfortable and familiar, we risk having our world view altered and even transformed. Margaret Wheatley, in *Turning to One Another: Simple Conversations to Restore Hope to the Future* (2009), speaks to this courage as

> a gesture of love ... [a] conversation [that] can only take place among equals.... Those who act superior can't help but treat others

as objects to accomplish their causes and plans. ... When we are courageous enough to honor ourselves, we offer everyone else their humanity. (pp. 140–141)

# PART II

## Philosophy and History: Navigating the Landscape

What are some of the philosophical underpinnings that inform theories of adult learning? What is important and valuable in education and how has my own educational biography shaped my beliefs and values?

How does my conception of reality, truth, knowledge, values, and logic affect my ideas about education and my philosophy of teaching and learning?

What do I know about the history of adult education as a field of scholarship and practice? Has this history impacted me without my knowing? How does this field inform my work and learning in my particular context?

In part 2, we explore the philosophy and history of adult education and become aware that we have been part of this rich heritage all along.

# CHAPTER 4

# Philosophical
# Orientations in Adult
# Education

## RAND

 I came into the role of Dean, School of Information and Communications Technologies, at SAIT Polytechnic, straight out of a 29-year career in the business world, a career that spanned several industries. Although I was originally trained as a civil engineer, at both the undergrad and graduate levels, and also trained in business, I had spent most of my work life managing the development and operations of information technology. In truth, I had very little idea of what the dean's role entailed, although I suspected it had a lot to do with managing a large number (120) of technical and administrative staff. I also knew I had a lifelong attraction to educational environments, although I never quite understood why. I was particularly attracted to the nature of the institution I joined, which prides itself in preparing "job ready" graduates who design, construct, and operate a vast variety of technologies used to support almost every corner of the economy.

The first year on the job was quite disorienting. The institution was business-like, and therefore familiar in its operation, but very unlike the business world I had experienced in its philosophy and values around core purposes. The yearly activity cycles were far more process- and measurement-based than I expected. We seemed to have measures for everything imaginable—learner satisfaction, instructor classroom performance, employee satisfaction, graduate employment rates, employer satisfaction, and many others. For the first couple of years it seemed a new and mysterious measure would arrive almost weekly.

Eventually, I learned the rhythm of the place, the very pronounced cycles, but more significantly, I learned what was at the heart of the way we worked. During my early days, in particular, I was constantly questioning and reflecting to myself about those things that seemed to be important in my role—it was a perplexing world. At one point well into my tenure, in a state of irritation, I set up a special meeting with our vice-president (my boss) simply to ask him directly what he thought was truly important in my role. I was desperately trying to put together the pieces I'd been seeing.

In time I came to believe very strongly in the importance of our students and their learning experiences at the institution. If customers were important in the business world, then our students were our customers, but even more significantly, our raison d'être. Our faculty, as well as our administrative and technical support people, were the key to creating the type of learning experience I increasingly saw as essential. I'd believed in the importance of customer service in my previous business-based roles, but I found the conviction was much more profound in the highly interpersonal world of post-secondary technical education. I went into the classroom myself to understand the life our instructors lived and the challenges they faced. If our instructors and staff focused on the students, I realized it was very much my role to focus on the people who delivered our services, their growth and progression as professionals, and—to the degree appropriate—their fulfillment as people.

I did truly learn my role as dean on the job, although I will admit much of my previous management experience was invaluable. The institution also provided numerous professional development opportunities, which certainly helped in my journey. However, I would say, in summary, that much of what I learned about my role came from interacting with the people around me; it came from reflecting and putting the pieces together. Many people helped, but I suppose only time will tell if I got it right.

—Rand Ayres, Dean, School of Information
and Communications Technologies, SAIT Polytechnic

## Introduction

Throughout this book, we have emphasized the importance of reflection as part of the learning process. By reflecting, we have the opportunity to deliberately and carefully probe our values and beliefs versus simply taking our assumptions and our surroundings for granted. Lange (2006) argued if learners take the freedom to think and make their own decisions for granted, they may "hold ideas that are indiscriminately eclectic and inconsistent in values ... [or] merely reproduce how they were taught or how they learn best" (p. 93). For example, we see in Rand's narrative that when he first arrived on the job as the dean of a large polytechnical institution, he spent a great deal of time trying to determine the values and beliefs held by the administration and instructors. He could sense the philosophy of this institution was different than the world he had previously occupied—the corporate setting—but he had difficulty uncovering it. At one point Rand's frustration is evident when he indicates that, without an understanding of what was important at SAIT, it would be hard to determine what was really important in his role. However, over time Rand, through persistent and deep reflection, developed his philosophy of education. Like Rand, we believe it is important, as learners and educators, to hold a philosophy of education and learning; it provides us with an anchor: "A conceptual framework, essentially a philosophy of education, can provide teachers with a sense of personal integration and professional coherence that places ongoing elements and episodes in teaching and learning in relation to and in perspective with each other" (Gutek, 2014, p. 3).

At this point, we would like you to take some time to develop your own statement of philosophy on education. As you reflect on what education means to you, what do you consider to be important and valuable in education? And how have your own educational experiences shaped your beliefs and values? We turn to a voice from the field, Elizabeth Lange, to help us understand both the importance of developing a philosophy of education and reflective ways we can use to create our own statement of philosophy.

The word philosophy often conjures images of draped ancient Greeks or bespectacled scholars behind ivy-draped brick university walls, conjuring up feelings of philosophobia. Yet, every educator daily enacts their philosophy. Every statement a teacher or facilitator makes in a classroom or learning context is value-laden, demonstrating their philosophy-in-action. One's working philosophy is connected to ideas about the purpose of human nature, the purpose of life, and the shape of a "good" society. More specifically, educators convey their views about education, learners, and the process of learning. Therefore, it is vital that educators take the time to name, reflect on, and more fully understand the values and philosophical assumptions that impact their educational practice.

The most important role of developing a statement of philosophy is to articulate what you most fundamentally believe about education. This will prompt you to consider the belief systems you were socialized into as a child—in your family, school, and societal era—and consider whether these are still relevant. You may recognize that your life experiences have caused you to change aspects of your belief systems. Creating a reflective space to undertake this analysis of your beliefs is important to ensure that you are not habitually recreating your past educational experiences or conveying contradictory messages when your practices are not in alignment with your beliefs. It also provides a set of principles by which you can judge the ever-changing innovations in education and the changing demands in your workplace. Often, conflicts in the workplace can be traced back to philosophical differences. The word philosophy means "love of wisdom." Therefore, a clear and conscious philosophical statement can provide a guide for action in a complex, fluid world, fostering ongoing reflection on practice—all processes of wisdom.

—Dr. Elizabeth Lange, Associate Professor,
St. Francis Xavier University

As we engage with several philosophical orientations that ground research and practice in adult education, we encourage you to determine where you are located. Do some of these philosophies reflect your own experience? Also consider, as we present various philosophical orientations, your values and beliefs about what is good, true, and important in education. When you have finished this chapter, we hope that you will have your own statement of philosophy on education, providing you with a conceptual framework for your learning and teaching pathway.

As we indicate later in chapter 6, our fascination with how we learn and teach can be traced back to the teachings of Socrates and Plato in ancient Greece. Plato, in particular, established the foundations of philosophy, especially idealism. "Idealists have emphasized that the teacher should embody the finest and highest qualities of the cultures. The teacher, as a model, knows and values these finest qualities so students can come into contact with them" (Gutek, 2014, p. 21). Of course a long line of thinkers has followed Plato over these past 2,500 years, many of them addressing the purpose and meaning of education. Augustine, Aquinas, Kant, Spencer, Montessori, Addams, and Dewey are but a few. Classical and modern philosophies of education have evolved into six schools of thought: idealism, realism, pragmatism, existentialism, and post-modernism. Contemporary theories of educational thought include progressivism, perennialism, essentialism, reconstructionism, behaviourism, anarchism, and constructivism. Finally, as noted by Lange (2006), the analytic movement in philosophy emerged as a reaction against underpinnings in these dominant philosophical discourses, arguing that the core issues to be understood are not about reality, truth, and values, but about language and meaning. Proponents of analytics argue that our language around such terms as *andragogy, autonomy,* and *transformation* is confusing and we lack clarity around the means of learning and the end of learning (i.e., transformative learning).

Turning to adult education, we are in the beginning stages of developing our philosophical orientations. In our emerging orientations, we have relied on the schools of philosophical thought just described, our own influential adult educators, and practices out in the field. In this chapter we first explore the dominant philosophical orientations in adult education—including liberal, progressive, behaviourist, humanist, and radical/critical orientations—identified more than 30 years ago in a highly influential text written by Elias and Merriam (1980). Secondly, we turn to recent philosophical orientations that are having a significant impact on our current vision of adult learning and education.

## Traditional Philosophical Orientations to Adult Education

### Liberal Orientation

In liberal adult education, the oldest philosophy of education originating with Plato's Academy, "the emphasis ... is upon liberal learning, organized knowledge, and the development of the intellectual powers of the mind" (Elias & Merriam, 2005, p. 34). The dominant approach to learning in this philosophical orientation is the critical reading and discussion of classical writings: "With experienced leadership, the reading of these books brings one to intellectual understanding and enables a person to relate the great ideas to present experience and problems" (Elias & Merriam, 2005, p. 34). This educational philosophy is thought to be the predominant orientation in the Western world and is likely one that many of us experienced as learners. Knowledge is presented in an organized, discrete, content-specific manner with the goal to develop organized, rational, and literate citizens. As we considered this particular philosophical approach, we were both reminded of our own learning experiences in high school. Subjects were organized in a discrete fashion and we moved from one class to another: We went to History. The bell rang and we went to English. The bell rang and we went to Mathematics. Rarely did we experience an interdisciplinary approach to learning; teachers had their own curriculum focus and agenda.

Critiques challenge this orientation's assumption that the ultimate questions and truths of existence are universal across culture and history and can be adequately represented by texts "of White, Western, upper-class men" (Lange, 2006, p. 96), and for its relatively isolationist approach to content.

## Progressive Orientation

Progressivism, located in the philosophical school of pragmatism, has had a tremendous influence on the field of adult education over this past century, with its emphasis on learning from our experience (Walter, 2009). In particular, Dewey, the father of the Progressive era, advocated for a pragmatic approach to learning; that learning should be accessible to all and that experience is central to learning, mirroring many of the tenets of experiential learning. Lindeman, a seminal adult educator who also took up a progressive orientation to learning, firmly believed in a lifelong and holistic learning approach that captures all aspects of our life from childhood to adulthood and includes learning in all contexts; from formal institutions of learning to the workplace, community, and broader society. In the following quotation from Lindeman, we see that he turned the liberal approach to education on its head, advocating that the subject is not the driving force in education; rather it is the learner that is at the centre:

> The approach to adult education will be via the route of *situations*, not subjects. Our academic system has grown in reverse order: subjects and teachers constitute the starting, students are secondary ... in adult education, the curriculum is built around the student's needs and interests ... subject-matter is brought into the situation, it is put to work, when needed. Texts and teachers play a new and secondary role in this type of education; they must give way to the primary important of the learner. (Lindeman, 1961, p. 6)

It is interesting to note that, in addition to the emphasis on learning from experience, this orientation holds a larger agenda to unleash the talents of everyone in society in order to contribute to a strong democracy of "thoughtful responsible citizens" (Lange, 2006, p. 97).

With the learner taking centre stage in this particular orientation, the role of the teacher shifts from the "sage" to the "guide" and the relationship between teacher and learner is collaborative. The teacher is "organizing, guiding and evaluating learning experiences while engaged in such experiences him or herself" (Price, 1999, p. 4).

However, despite its tremendous influence on the field of adult education, critiques focus on the lack of clarity around the teacher's role in this orientation to education. As well, there is a worry that an education so heavily reliant on activity-centred approaches and the experiences of students could simply be self-perpetuating and indulgent, not leading to new and important ideas. Finally, notions of what constitutes progress and development, particularly assumptions based on a Western model, have also been challenged. Advocating for social change without questioning the underlying political and economic systems and considering who benefits from the push for progress and development is seen as naïve and simplistic.

## Behaviourist Orientation

Looking ahead, we will explore behaviourism in greater detail in our presentation of various traditional educational theories in chapter 6. Briefly, however, this orientation comes out of a psychological theory of education, emphasizing the importance of the external environment in shaping our learning: "education is a matter of environmental stimuli in such a way that learners respond emotionally and cognitively with specific desired behaviors" (Walter, 2009, p. 14). In this orientation the educator is responsible for controlling the learning environment in order to work toward specific desired behaviours. Positive behaviours in the learner are rewarded, by receiving something of value, and negative behaviours are extinguished through punishment or by removing something of significance. Typical contexts where this approach is still used include vocational and technical training, particularly skills training where we want observable and measurable results.

Humanists have critiqued this approach as being manipulative; power and the end goal typically reside outside of a learner's control. For example, employers promoting learning within a workplace might be accused of only being focused on developing specific behaviour-change outcomes in their staff in order to increase productivity, efficiency, and profit.

At this point, we ask you to consider critiques levelled against a behaviourist orientation to learning. Are they all warranted? Are there examples from your educational biography, as a learner and/or educator, where you felt this was an appropriate philosophy of learning to hold? We push the pause button here because this orientation is probably one of the most contested orientations in adult education as it typically positions the learner in a negative or deficit position and it reduces learning to processes strictly associated with the brain.

## *Humanist Orientation*

Much like the progressive orientation, the humanist orientation has had tremendous influence on adult education. This particular philosophy or orientation to education, drawing from humanism, "holds sacred the dignity and autonomy of human beings" (Elias & Merriam, 2005, p. 111). Therefore the emphasis on learning is not externally driven, as is the case in a behaviourist orientation, but is centred on the needs of the learner and their pursuit of personal growth and self-actualization through the learning process. In particular, andragogical and self-directed learning approaches to adult learning are anchored within this orientation, as is the focus on *personal* transformation under the umbrella of transformative learning theory. Drawing on the work of humanist psychologists Maslow and Rogers, educators using this approach strive to develop a strong relationship with each of their learners so each one can work toward their own personal growth and self-actualization. Rather than being directive in their approach, educators take on a facilitative role; holding the underlying assumption that their learners are internally motivated and, with support, will rise to their potential. For example, considering Janet's experiences within her yoga class, the instructor typically begins each class by thanking each person for coming to class. She reminds the students that this is not a competitive space; rather, all students have their own purpose for coming to this yoga class and she trusts they will work toward their own goals in their yoga practice. Her role is to guide the yoga practice, moving around the room to offer suggestions and modifications in order to support each person's practice.

While the humanist approach to instruction is congruent to the educational context of a yoga class, we remind you of critiques levelled against this orientation in chapter 2: too much emphasis is placed on the individual and their own individual goals, and the problematic notion that whatever each person visualizes will certainly happen. However, we are all located within a particular context and we hold a particular set of experiences and identities that we have developed over time. As a result, we need to acknowledge that there can be multiple external and internal barriers to our learning. External barriers, such as power relations and economic limitations, and internal barriers, such as resistance to growth or change and/or negative experiences associated with learning, remind us we are not autonomous learners on our individual paths toward self-actualization. Finally, from the educator's perspective, the drive to meet the individual needs of all learners within a particular learning context, especially if there are a large number of learners, can be daunting.

### Radical/Critical Orientation

While the humanist orientation focuses on the individual, a radical/critical philosophy turns its gaze outward to focus on collective conscientization, praxis, and action for social change (Elias & Merriam, 2005). Returning to the heart of the discussion in chapter 3, where we explored sociocultural contexts of learning, unless we understand how we are situated within our society (our gender, class, race, religion, sexual orientation) and our socioeconomic structures, we will not be able to reach the goals aspired to within a humanistic orientation. The possibility for self-actualization of *all* learners can only occur through an analysis and a critique of society and the inherent inequalities that are built into our existing structures. As learners engage in this critique of society, there is the possibility for agency to create both personal and social change. Probably the educator most strongly identified with the radical/critical orientation is Paulo Freire and his book *Pedagogy of the Oppressed* (1970). Freire was particularly critical of the dominant approach to formal education in Brazil, calling it a banking style of learning. "Teachers 'deposit' their knowledge into the 'empty' students, who withdraw the deposits on exams" (Lange, 2006, p. 101). Freire aspired that learners become actively engaged in their lives by participating in a problem-posing educational approach that would have them deeply understand, question, and challenge the societal structures of oppression—poverty, discrimination, sexism and/or racism—in order to liberate themselves. His approach to education "embodies political struggle in liberation movements of all forms" (Walter, 2009, p. 18).

Brookfield (2005b) argued that Freire's approach actually intertwined radical/humanist orientations to learning. While adult education's role is to "raise people's consciousness so that they realize their oppression and act to liberate themselves ... [it] also draws strongly on the humanistic emphasis on love as a powerful force of change. The oppressors are viewed as deserving of love" (p. 476). The oppressors themselves are caught in the same overarching system in which they have no control. They were born into their position in society and they also need to be liberated, as much as those who are more obviously oppressed. We return to a deeper exploration of Freire and his views on education as we delve into the historical underpinnings of adult education in the next chapter.

Turning to another pivotal figure from the 1970s also located within a radical/critical orientation to adult education, Ivan Illich advocated for the total elimination of schools, arguing that their very existence perpetuated our "over-industrialized and over-consumerized society" (Elias & Merriam, 2005, p. 166). Building somewhat upon a progressive orientation to learning, Illich argued that most of our valuable learning occurs through engagement in our daily experiences and that we do not need institutions of education for formal learning; rather this type of learning can be gained along the way through books, experts, and peers. While his notion that there should be access to education for all people through the development of learning networks seems rather simplistic, his criticisms of our current educational institutions as being too bureaucratic and self-serving (Collins, 1998) are important.

Ohliger, an adult education professor from the United States, took up Illich's ideas during the 1990s to present his concern with the direction of adult education institutions: "In numerous articles and talks, Ohliger alleged that more and more adult education institutions define people as inadequate, insufficient, lacking and incomplete" (Elias & Merriam, 2005). Ohliger advocated for the loosening of bureaucratic demands on adult educators and programs, the development of programs outside the institutional structures that focus on political and economic awareness, and finally a focus on grassroots learning and living by individuals, small groups, and new communities that suggest alternative pathways for a future society (Elias & Merriam, 2005).

Most recently, some of Ohliger's ideals for adult learning have become visible through the growth of social movements. We turn to Carol Roy who describes the history and emergence of social movements.

 Social movements have been intimately linked with informal and non-formal learning. However, we often take for granted gains by people before us who were concerned by injustices, and cared enough to learn about particular situations and take action. As a result, we have the eight-hour workday, paid vacations, sick days, and access to higher education for women. In the 1930s, the Antigonish movement used study circles and created credit unions, producer and consumer cooperatives, and housing cooperatives. In the 1960s, the women's movement demanded equal pay for equal work, laws against sexual harassment and assault, and laws against violence against women. In the 1960s and 1970s, the American civil rights and the anti–Vietnam War movements were prominent in the United States. In the 1980s, the peace movement led to the end of the Cold War and to the dramatic fall of the Berlin Wall. In the 1990s, pro-democracy movements resulted in the demise of the Soviet Union. Recently, social movements successfully ousted dictators in Tunisia and Egypt; and the Occupy movement highlighted the gap between the rich and the poor with "We are the 99 percent." In Canada, Idle No More is a movement demanding Indigenous rights and environmental protection. Throughout the world, local movements successfully challenged unfair and polluting practices of forestry/mining/water corporations, yet their successes do not make the six o'clock news. Social movements have their origin in learning about social and political issues, and result in further learning from the actions they generate.

—Dr. Carol Roy, Associate Professor, St. Francis Xavier University

Turning to critiques associated with a radical/critical philosophical orientation to learning, Lange (2006) cautioned this approach might be too optimistic, relying heavily on the inherent goodness of people who will place the interests of the community over and above their own self-interests. Also, educators themselves may become too presumptuous in assuming that they have the right and the ability to transform and empower others—particularly problematic if there is a significant disparity in power between the educator and learners.

Up until this point we have engaged in almost a historical excavation of the traditional philosophical orientations that informed the early growth of the field of adult education. While these orientations have played an important role in framing our practice as adult educators, Brookfield (2005b) argued that we should reformulate the typical classifications of liberal, progressive, behaviourist, humanist, and radical/critical orientations. "New forms of practice such as online and accelerated learning programs, feminist pedagogy, or racially-based forms of provision, are hard to link directly" (p. 476) to these philosophical categories.

# Emerging Philosophical Orientations to Adult Education

Drawing from Brookfield's overview of five philosophical movements currently influencing the research and practice of adult education, we now turn to critical theory, in particular neo-Marxism and the work of Habermas from the Frankfurt school of critical theory, post-modernism, post-structuralism—including an exploration of feminist theories—and other philosophies of learning outside a Western paradigm.

## *Critical Theory*

A critical orientation to adult education, holding many of the similar values as the radical/critical orientation to education, is grounded in Marxism and later interpreters of Marxism such as Gramsci (1971) and Althusser (1971), otherwise known as neo-Marxists. Neo-Marxism applies Marx's analysis of the inherent contradictions in capitalism, the alienation of the workforce, and the need for revolution, and determines how these concepts can be applied to conditions in the twentieth and twenty-first centuries. Indeed, many scholars in the field of adult education would argue that rapid globalization, mixed in with neo-liberal values and a corporate agenda of learning, make neo-Marxist principles even more relevant today. Similar to the agenda of adult educators within the radical orientation to learning, the task for neo-Marxist "adult educators [is to] work as organic intellectuals, a term coined by Gramsci, to develop critical consciousness among the people in order to combat ruling class hegemony and to replace this with proletarian hegemony" (Brookfield, 2005b, p. 477). Note, in this quotation, critical theory is not only about critical thinking; it is undergirded by the assumption that critical consciousness will translate into social action, as noted in our previous example regarding social movements. For Freire (1970) in particular, critical reflection and social action came together in a term he coined, *praxis*.

We now turn to the work of Habermas, a German social philosopher from the Frankfurt School of Critical Theory. While his work

Philosophical Orientations in Adult Education    87

has had a significant impact on the larger arena of the social sciences, we look more specifically at his contribution to adult education, particularly his influence on Mezirow's work on transformative learning theory. Habermas (1971) contended there are three types of learning: instrumental learning, communicative learning, and finally—the one most commonly associated with transformative learning—emancipatory learning. Instrumental learning, generally associated with the sciences, concentrates predominantly on behaviourist or external-goal oriented learning. It is task-, information acquisition-, and skills-oriented learning and it does not involve critical questioning. Communicative learning is built on the assumption that people have a need to communicate with each other and understand their world. "Communicative learning involves developing an understanding of social norms and expectations, socially acceptable behaviours and actions, and how actions are perceived by others. Education systems, legal systems and social systems are all founded on communicative learning" (Cranton, 2013, p. 99). Similar to instrumental learning, the questioning or challenging of systems is not associated with this level of learning. Finally, emancipatory learning is based on radical/humanist assumptions that humans have an innate need to grow and develop, to become self-aware, and to become free from oppression, which can also include being released from the oppression of not knowing, or of not being able experience or have access to experience (Cranton, 2013). We turn to Karen Magro and her analysis of learning occurring within an adult literacy context, to help us understand there are many situations in which all three levels of learning—instrumental, communicative, and emancipatory—occur simultaneously.

 I believe that literacy and learning are interconnected. Learning is discovery and personal development; it is the development of new knowledge about oneself and the world. A strong foundation of literacy is a key to unlocking different dimensions of learning. I view literacy as lifelong and multi-dimensional; linguistic, mathematical, artistic, scientific, environmental, and technological literacies develop within unique cultural contexts. As adult educators, we need to encourage more emotional and social literacy. Resilience, practical problem solving, and intercultural intelligence are critical skills to possess in our world today. As our adult literacy classrooms in Canada today are becoming more multi-ethnic and multicultural, the roles and responsibilities of adult educators have also transformed. We are co-learners, advocates, cultural guides, facilitators, and reflective practitioners. Paulo Freire emphasized that it is not enough to teach "words;" rather, adult learners need to be able to explore their worlds in critical and expansive ways that engage, inform, and enlighten. In over 30 years of teaching, I continue to encourage my students to respond personally and critically to cultural, social, and political issues that impact them; through this process, we explore alternative ways of thinking, feeling, and acting.

Before becoming a professor and completing my doctoral studies, I worked as an adult literacy practitioner in the inner city of Winnipeg for over 20 years; my insights into "effective" teaching practices with culturally diverse adult learners has shaped the perspectives I present in this chapter. Experiential and authentic learning experiences are crucial when working with adult literacy learners. Adults need an opportunity to reflect on the way a particular text connects with their own lives. They also need to be able to apply the skills they are learning to practical activities such as making a speech, writing letters and reviews, and preparing portfolios.

–Dr. Karen Magro, Associate Professor, University of Winnipeg

In Karen's example, we realize instrumental learning is occurring through the gradual acquisition of reading skills; communicative learning is happening as learners apply their literacy skills to life situations, such as making a speech and writing letters; and emancipatory learning is sustained as students apply their literacy skills to critically self-reflect on their story and their understanding of social and political systems. Ultimately, Karen has provided us with a powerful example of how these three levels of learning, occurring simultaneously, contribute to the possibility of transformative learning for these adult literacy students.

## Post-modernism

Post-modernism, at its heart, is about challenging the truth of the grand narratives associated with the modern world. It questions all of the sureties and assumptions we hold about our world, particularly the beliefs and values of the modern world that have developed and solidified since the time of the Enlightenment's "assurance that scientific progress would be the cure for all that ails us. It also disrupts the many binaries created by the modern structural need to classify and divide: examples include mind/body, theory/practice, private/public, individual/group, literate/non-literate, and motivated/unmotivated" (English, 2006, p. 105). Lange (2006) explained that post-modern thought emerged when the security and certainty the grand narratives offered to us no longer seemed to fit our world. Science was no longer our "go-to place" to explain the universe and our reality, and previous philosophical orientations such as Liberalism, Marxism, and Progressivism could not explain the diverse range of experiences across cultures, genders, classes, nations, and classes. Turning to the implications for adult education, Usher, Bryant, and Johnston (1997) and English (2006) indicated that a post-modern perspective calls into question many of the practices, values, and beliefs we have held near and dear as important narratives for our field: "self, motivation, rationality, and community, individual autonomy, self-directed—all used as if they applied to all people regardless of difference signifiers such as race, gender, class and sexual orientation" (English, 2006, p. 58).

Evidence of a post-modern perspective can be seen in an emerging interest in spirituality in Canada (Bibby, 2004; English & Gillen, 2000), which has not necessarily translated into parallel growth in religion. Indeed, in several graduate courses within our faculty that intertwine spirituality and education, we see that a post-modern approach is required in our teaching, in which we are respectful of the multiple pathways our students use to understand spirituality and how it is lived out in their lives. While this does not apply to all, we need to be sensitive to the fact that many of our students have become increasingly disenchanted with traditional religious approaches, associating these formal institutions with patriarchy and exclusionary doctrines. However, they still want to engage spiritually by exploring questions about meaning and purpose in their professional and personal lives and they want to feel a deep connection to each other and our world.

Critiques of post-modernism suggest this approach is too fragmented to guide our actions and it is too relativistic. Because there is no firm foundational basis for knowledge-making, post-modernism—preferring to hold a stance of despair regarding our existing structures—will resist any attempts to work toward new possibilities or structures for our society that could cultivate inclusion and diversity.

## Post-structuralism

Post-structuralism, like post-modernism, offers a critique of the structures of society and the influences they have on individuals within our society. The additional layer in this orientation is the following argument: it is we, as individuals, who proactively reproduce and reinforce broader structures such as economic, political, linguistic, and, of course, educational structures. As English and Mayo (2012) indicated, adult education theorists and practitioners are especially interested in the work of Michel Foucault (1926–1984) because his ideas on power, governmentality, discipline, and control can be related to learning contexts. Foucault argued the structures of modern society created a new type of power—a disciplinary power—that is exercised by individuals, rather than being reinforced by larger systems. "Disciplinary power stresses self-surveillance and is seen most explicitly in the functioning of prisons, but its mechanisms are also at play in schools, factories, social service agencies, and adult education" (Brookfield, 2005b, p. 479). For example, we can all identify a time when we had to write an exam, and we engaged in self-surveillance to make it an individual experience relying solely on our own knowledge and understanding of the content to answer the questions. Turning to another example, in many learning contexts there is a set amount of time to teach and to learn a certain amount of content. At the end of the allocated time, we as educators may move onto the next part of the curriculum regardless of whether we feel that we have fully engaged in this aspect of the curriculum and or have the assurance that our learners understand this particular portion of the curriculum. From the learners' perspective, in this particular instance, we might berate ourselves as being too slow and as being deficient learners. We self-discipline ourselves, berating ourselves for falling short and seeing ourselves as transgressing the norms of society for not moving at an acceptable pace. Of course, there may be some resistance to this self-imposed power from educators who will not comply with external timelines of curriculum completion.

In their analysis of Foucault's notions of disciplinary power, English and Mayo (2012) offered several valuable connections to our practice as adult educators, particularly the importance of questioning the truths, core concepts, and values we hold in such high esteem, known as *regimes of truth*. In particular, English and Mayo (2012) highlighted the ambiguities associated with andragogy, the first adult learning theory we will explore in chapter 7. While andragogy suggests that all adults want to learn and that they are self-directed, the reality is much more ambiguous; both learners and adult educators may be resistant to this particular regime of truth. Our various theories of adult learning are not the whole truth; they serve merely as guidelines. "It is tracing the lines of power, the acts of resistance, the circumstance of learning, which entails that one observes closely what is happening in each educational situation, that one can challenge, in a grounded manner and through ethnographic data, such regimes of truth" (English & Mayo, 2012, p. 62). We need to understand what compliance means, what resistance means, and why and when learners are self-disciplining themselves to cooperate fully within a learning situation. In turn, learners can and may resist many approaches that are valued by adult educators. For example, they may resist the often utilized reflexive practice of journal writing, arguing that it is too personal; or they can resist dialogic practices by remaining silent. Ultimately, we need to critically examine forms of learning that we judge to be affirming, democratic, and honouring of learners, which in turn can be seen as forms of surveillance by learners.

## Feminism

Feminism, like post-modernism and post-structuralism, challenges how knowledge has been constructed; specifically, men have been the primary creators of formal knowledge. In turn, feminism seeks to construct knowledge in a way that validates women's experiences at the same time that it critiques existing social, economic, and political structures. According to Taber and Gouthro (2006), there have been three overlapping waves in feminist theory over the past 50 years: the first wave focused on attaining basic equality and recognition as citizens; the second wave advocated for social change, based on an increasing awareness of the powerfully limiting influences of the existing social, cultural, economic, and power structures on women; and the third wave, emerging in the 1990s, was broader and more fragmented, addressing a variety of concerns from a diverse range of perspectives.

Taber and Gouthro (2006) also highlighted several schools of feminist thought reflecting many of the more recent philosophical orientations we have just described: liberal feminism, Marxist feminism, post-modern feminism, post-structural feminism, and most recently, ecofeminism. Ecofeminism argues that all oppression is interconnected; therefore in order to remove women's oppression, we must address oppression at all levels.

As we consider feminism and the implications for adult education, we call on the work of Patricia Gouthro (2005), an adult education professor from Mount Saint Vincent University who has used a critical feminist approach, drawing on Habermas, to "examine the structural factors that have marginalized the concerns of women learners by broadening the debates on lifelong learning to take the home-place into consideration" (Taber & Gouthro, 2006, p. 64). Below, in her contribution from the field, Patricia elaborates on the impact these limitations have had on women and the diminished value placed on learning within the homeplace. Through her commentary, we realize we need to unearth and challenge societal tenets that place higher value on public spaces of learning and negate work and learning occurring within the private space of home, typically associated with women.

 As many feminists note, the perceptual divide between "public" and "private" rarely benefits women. While personal privacy should be protected, it is equally important to recognize that inequalities in gender divisions of labour, caregiving expectations, and domestic violence are not just "personal problems" to be negotiated by individual women within the home. It is only by realizing that these are social issues as well as personal problems—developing what C. Wright Mills characterizes as "the sociological imagination"—that women (and men) can work toward change.

How do learning and the homeplace connect? When women defer or choose not to continue their education, it is often linked to caregiving responsibilities in the homeplace. When female academics or executives decide it is impossible to have children and a successful career, their "choice" is one that men do not have to make. When women enter university or the workforce after years of raising children, rarely is there recognition that they may have learned something from that experience (even by advocates of Prior Learning Assessment). The homeplace is invisible in most educational discourses—but it is always present, and quite often a factor, in determining women's learning pathways.

—Dr. Patricia Gouthro, Professor, Mount Saint Vincent University

Turning to public spaces of learning, Hayes and Flannery (2000) argued women are also disadvantaged in this arena because of their socioeconomic class and the associated tasks more often than not assigned to women. Using the notion of Hochschild's (1989) "second shift" or Patricia's description of homeplace or invisible work to describe the domestic, family, and community work that women come home to when they finish their time at the office, education often becomes the "third shift" for many women.

When considering the implications for our practice as learners and as adult educators, we need to be cautious about the type of conclusions we make. While it is critical to understand underlying structures that impede the learning journeys of women, we can often default to believing that we are addressing women's concerns by designing a particular type of learning experience, instead of looking at the underlying societal barriers. We can become too simplistic in believing that all women like to learn through connection, collaboration, and sharing, falling into the trap of essentialism—a concept introduced in chapter 3—or the belief that women are all alike. It is important to recognize that there is a diverse range of learning approaches within this group and labelling women, as a particular *group,* is a problem as there is incredible diversity within this particular identifier. Hayes and Flannery's (2000) work on women as learners reinforced the significance of paying attention to gender, but also of being aware of the effects of race, class, and sexual identity on learning.

## *Locating Ourselves*

As we conclude our exploration of philosophical orientations and how they have informed the evolution of adult education, we are reminded that this story has unfolded within a particular intellectual orientation, as we typically trace our beginnings and our academic approaches back to the Greeks. This means "essentially the ways and thoughts of Pythagoras, Archimedes, Homer, Aeschylus, Euripides, Socrates, Plato, Aristotle, Herodotus, Thucydides, and a host of lesser lights still shine brightly for us and are the official beginning of the traditions to which we still hold" (Winchester, 2013, p. 67). Even in our exploration of critical theory, post-modernism, post-structuralism, and feminism, which all share a motivation to critique our social, cultural, economic, and political structures, the backdrop for this critique is a Western world view and context. Having said this, we do acknowledge by disrupting what constitutes valid knowledge; many academics and educators are also encouraging communities who have been marginalized to demand that their voices, perspectives, and sources of knowledge be heard.

Indeed, Winchester stated, "the Chinese and the peoples of India can lay claim to having longer-standing intellectual traditions and ways than our own. The Inuit can claim to have survived for millennia in what is perhaps the most inhospitable conditions for human life" (Winchester, 2013, p. 67). We remind you that multiple stories, traditions, world views, and approaches to learning have been a constant thread throughout this book. As we have already touched upon in the previous chapter in our exploration of other ways of being and learning, we believe—as all knowledge exists in relation to specific times and places—that recognizing the centrality of *Indigenous knowledges* is critical. As a reminder, "Indigenous knowledges speak to questions about location, politics, identity, and culture, and about the history of peoples and their lands (Sefa Dei, Hall, & Goldin Rosenberg, 2000, p. 3). In addition, for many Indigenous peoples, the process of teaching and learning about their cultures and histories is an act of resistance to Western world view, linked to colonization and imposed ways of knowing.

Returning to the fundamental philosophical questions we asked you to consider at the beginning of this chapter—What is important and valuable in education and how have your own educational experiences shaped your beliefs and values?—we turn again to Sefa Dei, Hall, and Goldin Rosenberg (2000) to illuminate some of tenets of Indigenous cultures' world view:

> For millennia, many indigenous cultures were guided by a world view based on the following: seeing the individual as part of nature; respecting and revising the wisdom of elders; giving consideration

to the living, the dead, and future generations; sharing responsibility, wealth and resources within the community; and embracing
spiritual values, traditions, and practices reflecting connections to
a higher order ... this form of knowledge, accrued over time, is a
critical aspect of any culture. It is accumulated by the social group
through both historical and current experience. Through the process of learning the old, new knowledge is discovered; this is what
makes indigenous knowledges dynamic rather than static. (p. 6)

When we consider the implications of recognizing the situatedness of
our own knowledge, the dominance of the Western world view, and
seeking more inclusive philosophical orientations for our practice as
adult learners and educators, it is not enough to simply add some readings or learning activities to our existing programs of study or practice.
This requires us to draw on principles and processes of transformative
learning; we must fundamentally transform our way of understanding
knowledge and learning and teaching, a journey not undertaken thus far.

To reinforce the notion of the road not yet travelled, Marlene Atleo
(2013), in her outline of two ontological and epistemological traditions of
knowing and being (Aboriginal/First Nations/Métis/Inuit and Canadian
Euroheritage), mapped out how these two traditions have interacted over
time and in policy phases, reinforcing how the dominant Western world
view has been perpetuated and expanded within Canadian society. "The
first phase is based in assimilationist policies, the second phase in accom-
modationist responses by Aboriginal people, and currently, a phase in
which there is a critique and convergent discourse via dialogue" (Atleo,
2013, p. 41). It is in this current phase, where there is an interaction
between the life worlds—manifested through political, ideological, and
economic systems—that the possibility for a genuine discourse, transformative learning, and the reshaping of "adaptive institutions and educational systems" (Atleo, 2013, p. 42) might be realized.

## Concluding Comments

At the outset of this chapter, we conveyed that a philosophy of learning and education is important for all of us. As learners and educators we should be able to articulate why we do what we do, and how we have come to hold our beliefs and values. We encourage you to take some time to write out your own statement of philosophy on education, drawing on the various orientations presented to you in this chapter. What orientations were you drawn to? What orientations had little, if any, resonance for you? Were there certain themes across orientations that drew you in? Why was that? How do various orientations connect with your experiences of learning? In the upcoming chapter, we take a look at the history of adult education, presenting events that have informed the trajectory of our scholarship and practice. As we engage in this exploration, we will be drawing from several of the philosophical orientations presented in this chapter. Like you, these important historical adult education figures within our history hold certain values and beliefs about what is important in learning and education and this has informed their practice.

# CHAPTER 5

# Historical
# Underpinnings

## PAULO FREIRE AND MYLES HORTON

### –A CONVERSATION IN DECEMBER, 1987[1]

Paulo: Myles, I think we could start our conversation by saying something to each other about our very existence in the world.... You could speak a little bit about your life and work, and I will say something about my life.... (p. 5)

Myles: Well, I know exactly where I was born because a few years ago an FBI agent came by and said in kind of an embarrassed way, "If you ever have any need to prove that you were born in the United States, why the FBI has a record. I was sent down to find out whether or not you were an American citizen, and I found the cabin in which you were born, so you were born here." I thanked him because I had told him I was always under the impression that I was born there.

[When I was born] in 1905, my father and mother, who had been through grammar school, were schoolteachers. Of course, at that time there were so few people with advanced education that when they started trying to get teachers for the primary schools they had to employ people who had had just a little bit more education. Something like popular education in Nicaragua; they had a little bit more education than the people they were teaching. That's important because I think that's probably the basis of my interest in education, having parents who were teachers to start with. Before I was school age, they were no longer teachers because the requirements had increased to where you had to have one year high-school education before you could

99

teach. They couldn't afford to go back to school and get that educa-tion; therefore they had to stop teaching. But that interest stayed on.

My father was out of work for a while and took all kinds of odd jobs, manual labor jobs. Then he got into local politics and became a county official, a circuit court clerk. The reason he got elected to that office was that he was one of the few people in the county who could write legibly—which I never learned to do! The county kept all the records in longhand, and his qualification was that he could write. Later on when more people learned to write, he lost his job, and then he was a day laborer for a while. Worked as a salesman. Learned to fix sewing machines and tried to figure out all kinds of ways to make a living. My first real memories of what I now know as poverty—at that time I didn't know it was poverty, I just thought that was the way people lived—was when we were trying to raise cotton as sharecroppers out in the western part of Tennessee, where there was a lot of flat land. The nearest school was at the town of Brazil. (pp. 12–14)

Paulo: My father died very young. He was 52 years old when he died.... He was a military man but a democratic one, a very democratic one.

.... I was 13 years old.... We did not have at that time in Recife (it's my city) public schools at the level of secondary school. My mother had to try to find a secondary school where I could start without paying. She tried a lot. Every day she left the house to search for a school. I was waiting for her, full of hope … but one day she arrived. I went to receive her on the train, and she was smiling. She said, "Today I got a school for you." Until today I have a strong feeling of gratitude to the couple … who gave me the possibility of being here today.

.... When I started studying at school, I felt so challenged by some of the teachers that in three years I could teach Portuguese language and syntax.... I discovered that reading has to be a loving event.... I had such an almost physical connection with the text. It was this experience that began to teach me how reading is also an act of beauty because it has to do with the reader rewriting the text. It's an aesthetical event. (pp. 25–27)

Myles: I can remember, when I was in high school, how sad I was that my classmates didn't like to read poems, stories, literature. I enjoyed it so much and they hated it. I thought it was the teachers that did that to them, and I resented that.... to them it was something that you had to learn, memorize, and you hated it because you had to do it. (p. 27)

## Introduction

How do we do justice, in one brief chapter, to a history of adult education that has been shaped and informed, over so many years by events, initiatives, individuals, and communities that continue to inspire? We refer to stories of perseverance, intentionality, generosity, care, compassion, and to stories of great courage and commitment, all contributing to the colourful tapestry, texture, and historical underpinnings of the adult education movement. This tapestry has been contributed to and constructed by a rich and long history spanning English, European, Australian, and North and South American contexts, movements, initiatives, and pioneer adult educators, each illuminating and contributing layers and linkages to the evolution of adult education history and practice. Although all have contributed, in unique ways, to the ongoing narrative of adult education, there is an interconnectedness that unites these contributions with respect to the purposes of adult education. These purposes continue to receive much attention in the literature and span a range of foci, a diversity of perspectives, and a progression of thinking over time on the following:

- the cultivation of intellect, self-actualization of the individual, and organizational effectiveness (Darkenwald & Merriam, 1982);
- facilitating change in a dynamic society, supporting and maintaining a good social order, promoting productivity, and enhancing personal growth (Beder, 1990);
- vocational, social, recreational, and self-developmental needs of adult learners (Selman, Cooke, Selman, & Dampier, 1998); and

- adult education for economy, adult education for social change, and adult education for diversity (Spencer, 2006).

After much deliberation, we decided to open this chapter with excerpts of an extended dialogue between Paulo Freire and Myles Horton from December, 1987. Although we could have illuminated any number of individuals or initiatives, we felt that this seminal dialogue provided a glimpse into *some* of the history that guides the work of adult educators in the present day. This exchange between Freire and Horton also illuminates the power of dialogue, a central theme throughout this text, when space is created in search of a deepened understanding informed by the exploration of experiences, meanings derived from experiences, and perspectives. Documented in *We Make the Road by Walking* (Bell, Gaventa, & Peters, 1990), two adult education pioneers sat down to "speak a book," something that Freire had dreamed of doing for quite some time. They shared great respect for one another—as teachers, as educators, and as advocates for the poor and marginalized. Tim Loblaw referred to this same text in his narrative in chapter 1, referring to the phenomenological essence that informed Freire and Horton's conversation.

Myles Horton was born in in 1905 in Savannah, Georgia, to a poor family. He was an educator, socialist, and co-founder of the Highlander Folk School (1932). Highlander played a significant role in the civil rights movement in the American South by "teaching blacks and whites to challenge entrenched social, economic, and political structures of a segregated society. Because of his stand on social justice, Horton came under attack by the rich and power[ful]" (Davis, n.d., para. 2). Horton's grandfather was a mountain man; he was illiterate. Although his own parents knew how to read and write, their formal education was limited. Horton found a way to secure his own formal education, however, and earned a degree from Cumberland College and attended Union Theological Seminary. It was during his time at Union that Horton "developed an idea for a school that would teach the crafts and wisdom of the Appalachian People while empowering them to stand against the greed and tyranny of the corporate establishment that was taking advantage of the people" (Davis, n.d., para. 5). Acclaimed for human rights and social change advocacy, Horton and Highlander received a nomination for the Nobel Peace Prize. The work of Myles Horton lives on through the Highlander Research and Education Center. He died in 1990.

Paulo Freire was born in 1921, in the northeast of Brazil. Although born to a middle-class family, Freire came to know poverty during the Great Depression in the 1930s. He often attributed the focus of his work as an adult to early childhood experiences, having played and attended school with children who lived in poverty. In later years, Freire connected his own difficulties with learning to the fact that he had lived in poverty and, subsequently, to his experience with hunger:

> I wanted very much to study, but I couldn't, as our economic condition didn't allow me to. I tried to read or pay attention in the classroom, but I didn't understand anything because of my hunger. I wasn't dumb. It wasn't lack of interest. My social condition didn't allow me to have an education. Experience showed me once again the relationship between social class and knowledge. So, because of my problems, my older brother began to work and to help us, and I began to eat more. At that time, I was in the second or third year of high school, and I always had problems. When I began to eat better, I began understanding better what I was reading." (Gadotti, 1994, p. 5)

Freire championed liberation of the oppressed in society and anti-colonialist thinking. As discussed in the previous chapter, he advocated for a critical pedagogy in which the oppressed are supported to upset unjust, power-over conditions by becoming active participants in their own liberation. By disrupting colonialist attitudes, practices, and political agendas, Freire maintained that

> no pedagogy which is truly liberating can remain distant from the oppressed by treating them as unfortunates and by presenting for

their emulation models from among the oppressors. The oppressed must be their own example in the struggle for their redemption.

The pedagogy of the oppressed, animated by authentic humanist (not humanitarian) generosity, presents itself as a pedagogy of humankind. (2006, p. 54)

Although Freire was educated and eligible to practise law, he chose to teach and to work with the illiterate poor—those with no voice. His work focused on enhancing community and advocating for a more just society where "developing consciousness … is understood to have the power to transform reality" (Taylor, 1993, p. 52). Freire's work in the literacy movement and education, and his active political engagement in upsetting social injustices against those in society marginalized by gender, race, class, and caste also focused on empowering individuals to "break free from their historically contingent and entrenched vocabularies to face up to their fallibility and strength as agents of possibility" (Gadotti, 1994, p. xiii). Freire died in Brazil in 1997.

## Looking Back

While we continue to pay tribute to a multitude of individuals and initiatives that guide the work of adult education in Canada, it is simply not possible to mention them all. We have, however, selected a few stories and initiatives to provide a deepened understanding and appreciation of how philosophies of learning, education, and collective action continue to guide individual development, co-creating community, and social change.

### Adult Education and Literacy

Both Myles Horton and Paulo Freire developed a love of reading in their formative years. As their conversation continued,[2] they elaborated on how reading provided both a lens and increased confidence to probe, to challenge, and to question, as they sought to make sense of the world.

Myles: There's two things in my life that were very important in terms of where I spent my time, one was school and the other was church. In that little town, many of us were interested in education or religion. That's where people were. That's where the social life was. Part of my life was in a church community, part was in the school community, the other part was in a work community. (Bell, Gaventa & Peters, 1990, p. 28)

.... As a high school kid, I was active in the church. I was head of the youth group at the church at the time and an active church worker, but I was beginning to get very critical. I was willing to speak up because I felt comfortable there. I felt at home and I thought I could do that. Of course I found out after I did that, I wasn't supposed to ask questions or even think about anything like that. (p. 29)

.... It was at that stage that reading took on a completely different meaning to me because I was beginning to deal with real problems in life. When I'd read, I was informed that by reading, I'd get ideas from the reading. I'd get emboldened by it, especially poetry, and it took a new meaning. I was no longer reading to pass the time away. (p. 30)

Paulo: What fascinates me in reading good books is to find the moment in which the book makes it possible for me or helps me to better my understanding of reality, of concreteness. In other words, for me the reading of books is important to the extent that the books give me a certain theoretical instrument with which I can make the reality more clear vis-à-vis myself, you see. This is the relationship that I try to establish between reading words and reading the world. I always was interested in understanding, as you were, the reality, which I mean reading reality. But the process of reading reality in which we are enveloped demands, undoubtedly, a certain theoretical understanding of what is happening in reality. Reading of books makes sense for me to the extent that books have to do with this reading of reality. (p. 31)

For Myles and Paulo, learning to read opened up a new world, stimulated thinking critically, deepened their understanding and perspective, and provided a lens through which to experience and make meaning of the reality that surrounded them.

Deeply rooted in the development and delivery of community-based literacy programs, adult educators have been supporting children, youth, and adults in learning how to read for the past 100-plus years. The Reading Camp Association, founded in 1899 by Alfred Fitzpatrick, is regarded as the oldest adult education institution in Canada. The Reading Camp provided non-formal education (formally organized and delivered, but not credentialed) to individuals who had little or no access to formal education. The Reading Camp Association was renamed to become Frontier College in 1919. Fifty years later, Frontier College expanded its focus to address the needs of many marginalized populations in society—persons incarcerated in prisons, the homeless, children and youth (including children and youth in over 60 Aboriginal communities in Ontario, Manitoba, Quebec, and Saskatchewan), and many others with specific needs and challenges. In an attempt to address these needs, this national literacy organization works with literacy volunteers and learners across Canada with a focus on reading circles, youth programs, one-on-one tutoring, workplace literacy (essential skills), computer skills training, writing and math skills, GED (General Educational Development/high school equivalency diploma) preparation, and migrant workers and new immigrants.

The Canadian Literacy and Learning Network (2013) reported that

the latest literacy study by Statistics Canada shows that millions of Canadians do not have the literacy skills they need to keep pace with the escalating demands of our society and economy. This loss of potential impacts on the social and economic well-being of individuals, families, communities and our country.

and that

42% of Canadian adults between the ages of 16 and 65 have low literacy skills.

55% of working age adults in Canada are estimated to have less than adequate health literacy skills. Shockingly, 88% of adults over the age of 65 appear to be in this situation.

Impoverished adults often do not have the literacy skills required to get into job training programs. They may need literacy skills upgrading before they can succeed in training programs but only about 5–10% of eligible adults enroll in programs.

Less than 20% of people with the lowest literacy skills are employed.

Adult educators continue to lobby and advocate for impoverished individuals and communities where literacy challenges contribute to profound social, economic, and political injustices. The voices of Paulo Freire, Myles Horton, and other pioneers of the past continue to be the foundation of this work.

## Adult Education, Community Development, and Social Action

The Antigonish movement that emerged in the late 1920s is another prime example of liberatory adult education. Based out of the Extension Department at St. Francis Xavier University in Antigonish, Nova Scotia, Father Jimmy Tompkins, Father Moses Coady, and other educators led farmers, fishermen, and miners in cooperative action to improve the impoverished economic and social circumstances of Maritimers who worked off the land and sea. This call to purposeful and local action was fueled by the belief that informed collective action focused on upsetting the socioeconomic reality would contribute to a deepened understanding of one's situation, empowerment of individuals and communities, and sustained social and economic change, so that all people of society could live a "good life." Ultimately, the focus of Antigonish was to a build critical consciousness and support the skill development of the people, with an aim to empower communities to cooperatively own economic institutions.

The dominant message was that people should not fear, be ignorant of, nor be subservient to matters of finance and business that directly impacted their own livelihood. Mass meetings, study clubs, and leadership schools were designed to support people in the region in achieving this goal.

Colleen recalls the passion and commitment of her good friend and colleague, Dr. Anne Alexander, who dedicated the last several years of her life, while battling cancer, to writing the story of Antigonish in *The Antigonish Movement: Moses Coady and Adult Education Today* (1997). Anne believed that by "'immersing' in the flames of the past we can develop a consciousness that impels us to pose critical questions about current trends" (p. 16) and referred to

> a contextual understanding [and appreciation] that a tradition exists within Canadian adult education in which people shared a vision of a more human community and of how it could be achieved. Steeped in this knowledge, we can reflect anew upon our contemporary situation. We can take "the fire" of the past and challenge ourselves in thought and action. (p. 16)

Moses Coady grew up in a Roman Catholic community of hard-working farmers and fishermen. He was known to attribute his fighting spirit to his Irish ancestors. His parents home-schooled him until he was 15 years old. Coady went on to complete high school, followed by a college education in Nova Scotia. He became principal in the same school he attended as a boy and, after a few years, moved on to St. Francis Xavier University to earn a degree and then to a college in Rome where he studied theology and philosophy for a period of five years. All these years of study earned Coady a Doctorate in Philosophy and a Doctorate in Divinity. Coady was now a Catholic priest and chose to live and work in Nova Scotia (Alexander, 1997).

Coady regarded his first cousin, Father Jimmy Tompkins, as his mentor. It was because of this relationship that Coady "later celebrated [Father Jimmy] as the original adult educator in that part of Canada" (Alexander,

1997, p. 22). Father Jimmy advocated for adult education and self-reliance. He passionately believed that everyday people, when empowered with ideas, have the potential to contribute to significant change (Lotz & Welton, 1997). In other words, ideas must manifest into action.

Tompkins and Coady committed their life to the Antigonish movement. This work was guided by six foundational principles (Laidlaw, 1961):

1. The primacy of the individual;
2. Social reform must come through education;
3. Education must begin with the economic;
4. Education must be through group action;
5. Effective social reform involves fundamental changes in societal and economic institutions; [and]
6. The ultimate objective of the movement is a full and abundant life for everyone in the community. (pp. 97–98)

In *The Coady Connection* (March 2000), an alumni newsletter published by the Coady International Institute, Margaret, grand-niece of Moses Coady, offered a few famous quotations from her great-uncle:

No force can stop people when they organize with a just cause.
Use what you have to secure what they have not.
We must use force! The force of ideas.
Give us a people who have a sense of belonging, of taking part in the business of the country and they will learn to do difficult things. Only in this way can we build a great civilization worthy of a country of such great natural resources. Only in this way can we build a strong, self-reliant population freed from the need of continuously calling on the government for material assistance.
Freedom should mean that people have the right to set up institutions that will act as a counter-force to the anti-social elements of society who build up economic institutions to suppress the people and exploit them.

You're poor enough to want it and smart enough to do it.

If we are wise, we will help the people everywhere to get the good and abundant life. We are all our brother's keepers. (p. 2)

Some of the outcomes achieved by the Antigonish movement, and as cited by Dr. Carol Roy in chapter 4, were the creation of credit unions, producer and consumer cooperatives, and housing cooperatives.

Although there are many great texts that tell the story of Antigonish, we pay special tribute to Dr. Anne Alexander; Anne wrote the final chapters of *The Antigonish Movement: Moses Coady and Adult Education Today* (1997) in the last few months before she died. Alexander studied the Antigonish movement for many years and cited it as a story that needed retelling, over and over again, through many different lenses. Alexander maintained that, as adult educators and adult learners, the Antigonish story provided "a realistic assessment of how it might be possible, in the future, for the field of adult education to find a balance between professionalization and social service thrusts" (Alexander, 1997, p. 10).

## Adult Education and Vocational Education

The Council of Ministers of Education, Canada[3] report provided a detailed account of post-secondary education in Canada in 2008. This reported included a range of post-secondary institution types and diversity of programs offered, and disciplines and fields that sought to hire graduates from these educational institutions. Programs offered by vocation-oriented institutions spanned numerous employment-preparation education and skills training programs, apprenticeship programs, business and industry training, professional credentialing, and technical training. Many institutions described also provided literacy programs, academic upgrading, and retraining for those who needed to upgrade work skills. Types of educational institutions included public colleges, community colleges, private for-profit colleges, and institutes of technology and polytechnics (a partial list only). In reading this report, one might conclude that Canada, the second-largest country in the world, remains committed to the adult learning needs of individuals and that Canadian post-secondary institutions attend to these needs through the provision of adult education programs that span a broad and diverse continuum. It is significant to note, however, that

> participation in adult education and training is far from equal and reflects the "Matthew Effect" (i.e., those who already have more get more and those who have less get less) … There is a well-documented relationship between social and family backgrounds, educational attainment, and position in the labour market which affects adults' subjective readiness to participate, as well as actual opportunities for adult learning. (Elfert & Rubenson, 2013, p. 239)

Of additional concern is the increased role and voice of employers in guiding post-secondary agendas. In Alberta, for example, post-secondary institutions reeled with the recent news that government funding for their institutions would be significantly decreased. Decreased public funding continues to position educational institutions to rely more heavily on business and industry for financial support. We recognize the benefits when post-secondary institutions partner with business and industry in support of developing and delivering adult education programs. Post-secondary education institutions, and in particular adult educators, however, carry a role and responsibility to educate external stakeholders that education extends significantly beyond the acquisition of work-related skills. Unfortunately, citizen education, critical thinking, arts-based learning, a strengthened social consciousness, and engaging with diversity are often put on the backburner in favour of more measurable and quantifiable skills. When the main measure of program success is determined by how quickly and how many graduates are employed, the roots that inform adult education—empowerment of individuals and communities, community engagement, activism, and change— remain the poor cousin (Organization for Economic Co-operation and

Development, 2002) in the post-secondary, adult education agenda. Considering the thrust of professionalization and an advanced neo-liberal agenda that continues to impact, shape, and drive the direction of post-secondary and higher education, we are compelled to revisit concerns expressed by Alexander (1997) that "mainstream adult education practice and professionalized adult education [has] become separated from their social movement roots" (p. 11). Tom Nesbit, adult educator and past Director of the Centre for Integrated and Credit Studies and Associate Dean of Lifelong Learning at Simon Fraser University, reinforces Alexander's call to a return to our heritage of activism and community action.

 When asked about my work, I usually say something broad about having spent most of my life as an adult educator and the past 20 years or so developing and managing continuing education in a university. If the persistent go on to query what that actually means, I launch into a potted history of the adult and continuing education movements in Canada and Great Britain and the proud 100-year-old tradition of educational institutions opening their doors and providing opportunities to adult learners. Most people tend to regard this educational approach as just a way for people to land a better job or otherwise improve their personal life chances. However, I always throw in some comments about education as a way of enhancing citizenship and involvement or developing greater social awareness and providing a critique of dominant cultural and political phenomena and processes—something along the lines of "while the individual benefits of continuing education are, of course, very important, so are the confirmation of people as social beings and the recognition that education can help people become active in building a just society."

In other words, continuing education should not teach people merely to adapt to or cope with existing circumstances, but instead explore ways to confront the existing order of things or what challenges them. I often conclude with a few remarks about the essential role of universities in helping create what we now call "a learning society" by

> providing spaces for public debate about these and other issues—and
> not just for the academic elite or already privileged but for all people,
> especially those labelled "disadvantaged." No one asks twice.
>
> —Dr. Tom Nesbit, Adult Educator, Retired Professor

Grace and Kelland, in the *Canadian Association for the Study of Adult Education (CASAE): 25th Anniversary Memory Book (1981–2006)*, identified three federal legislation measures that transformed Canadian technical and vocational education: the Technical and Vocational Training Assistance Act (1960), which made unprecedented amounts of money available for vocational training facilities and programs, and made possible the creation of many of our colleges, vocational schools, and technical institutes; the Occupational Training Act (1967), which continued this development and also brought the federal authorities into a more direct role in purchasing training, and selecting and supporting students; and the National Training Act (1982), which placed greater emphasis on training on-site in industry and on high-skill vocations. (p. 12).

Employment preparation and vocational skill development continues to take centre stage at many post-secondary education institutions. In a 2013 publication titled *Adult Learning Trends in Canada: Basic Findings of the WALL 1998, 2004 and 2010 Surveys,* Livingstone and Raykov confirmed this:

On the basis of national [government] surveys conducted in 1998, 2004 and 2010, about half of Canadian adults were found to participate in further education courses annually. The vast majority of adults were participating in informal learning related to paid employment, housework, and general interests. About 20 percent express unmet demand for further education. Older and working class people may have somewhat lower rates of participation in further education courses but not in informal learning. There are also suggestions of a trend toward increasing underutilization of educational qualifications and continuing underuse of computer skills in paid workplaces. (p. 4)

These findings are significant considering that "in 1960, according to the first government survey, only about 4% of all Canadians over 17 years of age were enrolled in any sort of adult education course" (Livingstone & Raykov, 2013, p. 4). The report also noted a rapid increase of engagement in formal adult education programs by adults of all ages.

Anna Kae Todd, a voice with 33 years of experience, has witnessed the changes in post-secondary and vocational education. She speaks with heart of her philosophy and vision and her experience of reciprocity of relationship and learning that occurs between educators and adult learners within the post-secondary environment in which she works.

 In my career as an adult educator, I have come to understand that my enduring interest and involvement in the field is in no small part due to the fact that, after 33 years, I am still learning about learning and learners.

To be involved in adult education is to be involved in a journey of discovery with learners and about learning. To move from the accommodation to the assimilation of knowledge requires active and exploratory interaction with objects, people, materials, events, and processes. Effective adult educators understand that regardless of the modality of delivery or the formality or informality of a setting, the quality of the interaction and the intervention in a learning event is what will most positively impact the outcome. And adults engaging in learning also innately understand, and come to more explicitly understand, that learning requires active engagement as opposed to a passive receptivity.

As an adult educator, the key outcome for which I strive is to facilitate the development of self-initiating, independent lifelong learners. In the course of that journey, one realizes it is a two-way street; that the thoughtful interaction with the adult learners, who bring with them the knowledge and many experiences and assumptions of their lives, informs and enriches the life-wide learning journey of the educator.

As I ponder further on the question that the authors of this book have asked me, and on my subsequent reflections, I ask myself, do my beliefs—as expressed above—apply in equal measure to my journey that has taken me from direct engagement with the learners of the classroom to the less-direct realms of the administrator? As someone who was energized by—and successful in—the classroom, to someone who has by virtue of moving through various levels of administrative responsibility become more removed from direct engagement with learners, have I become more removed from the key outcome that I espouse? Admittedly, on some days it feels that way. However, I realize that I see myself, now, as an institution-builder; as someone who, in engaging with other learners (administrators, staff, faculty, and the community), is still very much in the business of being an architect of learning; and who, in doing so, is made even more aware of the iterative nature of our lifelong learning journey.

—Anna Kae Todd, Vice-President Academic, Bow Valley College

Although Anna Kae's administrative responsibilities have contributed to her being away from formal classroom teaching for a number of years, her commitment to supporting the lifelong learning journeys of adults at Bow Valley College is passionately expressed in her testimonial.

## Adult Education and Women's Institutes

In the early 1900s, when men in rural communities were forming farmers' institutes to acquire better farming skills and technologies, rural women maintained that they too would and should benefit, like their menfolk, from further education. This assertion of women's voices provided the impetus for the creation of women's institutes. Subsequently, women from rural areas organized to connect with one another and to learn and grow in skills to support their work in their respective farming communities. By 1930, women's institutes had taken up the study club method that emerged from the Antigonish movement (MacKeracher, 2009). Together they directed their focus to personal growth and development, individual and community health and wellness, and fundraising, and campaigned on socioeconomic issues and challenges that warranted collective action and protest.

In the years that followed, women's institutes became more formalized and emerged across many provinces in Canada. Half-hour National Farm Radio Forum broadcasts became a weekly staple in these gatherings. National Farm Radio Forum provided rural farm women access to ongoing, informal education to support the day-to-day challenges they faced, both individually and collectively:

> Farm Radio Forum, 1941–65, was a national rural listening-discussion group project sponsored by the Canadian Association for Adult Education, the Canadian Federation of Agriculture and CBC. Up to 27 000 persons met in neighbourhood groups Monday nights, November through March, using half-hour radio broadcasts, printed background material and pretested questions as aids to discussion of social and economic problems.
>
> Farm Forum provided an antidote to the hard times of the 1930s economic depression, and meeting and discussing new ideas in neighbours' homes helped restore rural confidence, often leading to positive group action in the community. Farm Forum innovations included a regional report-back system, whereby group conclusions were collected centrally and broadcast regularly across Canada, occasionally being sent to appropriate governments. In addition, discussion—leading to self-help—resulted in diverse community "action projects" such as co-operatives, new forums and folk schools. Farm and community leaders claimed that the give-and-take of these discussions provided useful training for later public life. (Shugg, n.d., para. 1-2)

One might be tempted to romanticize these times of women gathering with baked goods, small children, and quilting in hand, 80-some years ago, to huddle around a radio broadcast that would likely be interrupted, frequently, by static airwaves. Indeed, these gatherings would have provided a needed social connection, an opportunity to share stories, and a network from which to draw perspective from one another as they navigated the challenges of their socioeconomic reality. These gatherings would also have mitigated deep feelings of isolation and loneliness.

These were difficult times, and women, if they were to survive, needed to unite and be strong. Kechnie (2003) provided a cultural lens through which to appreciate the cultural context at that time in Canadian history, and reminded us it was very much a man's world—and in this world, the voice of men shaped and dictated policies and programs. Kechnie (2003) also asserted the likelihood that women of another class—those who lived in small towns beyond the rural areas, and those more educated and affluent—might have exhibited attitudes that posed resistance to issues experienced by farmwomen of that day.

In the province of Alberta, Canada, at the Glenbow Museum, one is invited to explore many documents—minute books, pamphlets, annual reports, and yearbooks—that provide an inside view and a deepened understanding of the development, experiences, and workings of women's institutes in Alberta. Many photographs stored within these archives are a powerful reminder of the women's plight, commitment, and courage at a time when the political landscape was not at all sensitive or responsive to the needs and perspectives of women.

## Concluding Comments

In this chapter, we chose to highlight only a few of the foundational historical adult education initiatives and movements that are referenced in the literature time and time again. These historic movements were all inspired and infused by a commitment to lifelong learning and to authentic relationship formation and deep engagement. Guided by a philosophy and vision of solidarity in support of informed action, individuals and communities came together in support of one another to make a better life and to effect change. These movements, and many others that we have failed to mention, are testimony to the *power of people and community* when we believe in and advocate for a just life and a just society.

We encourage you to explore, more deeply, the initiatives and movements highlighted in this chapter. As you make your way through the rich history of adult education, widen your lens to explore the beginnings of the YMCA, the YWCA, and the National Film Board of Canada; the onset of labour unions; the development of apprenticeship programs; and the emergence of public libraries and museums. You may be surprised to discover that you remain intimately connected with and continue to benefit from these and many other adult education initiatives that were birthed across the Canadian landscape, long before your time.

## Endnotes

1  This narrative represents excerpts from a dialogue between Myles Horton and Paulo Freire in December, 1987, published in *We Make the Road by Walking—Conversations on Education and Social Change,* in Bell, Gaventa, & Peters, 1990.

2  A continuation of excerpts from a dialogue between Myles Horton and Paulo Freire in December, 1987, published in *We Make the Road by Walking—Conversations on Education and Social Change,* in Bell, Gaventa, & Peters, 1990.

3  See the Council of Ministers of Education, Canada document titled *Education in Canada* (July, 2008) for further information.

# PART III

## Learning about Learning: Exploring the Terrain

What do I know about learning? How do I best learn? Are there some adult learning theories that resonate for me? Are all learning theories and approaches equally valued in Western society? What counts as knowledge? What is discounted? Why? Are there other ways of knowing? What are some of the implications of all of this for me as an adult learner? Are there other ways of knowing and being in the world that I would like to explore more deeply?

In part 3, we learn about learning by coming to a deepened understanding and appreciation of the theoretical foundations that have shaped and influenced the ways that we learn as adults.

# Traditional Theories of Learning

## KAREN

I started university when I was 17 years old and I have returned at various times during my life to explore different paths of this extraordinary journey. Throughout the years, my studies have evidenced conscious changes in direction and discipline, enabling me to pursue new interests, experiences, and varied career aspirations. More often, however, it was the quest for further knowledge and the intrinsic gratification of learning that served as an inspiration to continue academic endeavours in later years.

Reflecting on my learning and its relevance in my life over the past several decades, the intersection with travel immediately comes to mind. Both learning and travel are an integral part of my life. Travel provides opportunities to exchange novel ideas and experiences and to contemplate various questions, theories, and insights. In a parallel vein, learning offers a framework to explore and surface the multiple dimensions of knowledge, understanding, and ways of knowing. Learning and travel provide a means for us to examine the essence of who we are and how our identities have been shaped by different people, experiences, and learning.

In continuing to weave the tapestry of my life and learning, I draw upon threads of workplace and personal learning experiences to complement formal academic learning. The varied terrains, environments, and diversions of this particular learning focus have presented opportunities and challenges over the years. At the same time, the journeys of travel and learning create ever-changing landscapes—whether geographic or in terms of my evolving perspectives. They also provide avenues to explore the complexities and contradictions of knowledge from different vantage points, to challenge assumptions, and to reinterpret ideologies, outlooks, practice, and our self. Post-secondary studies have also sharpened my analytical skills and their application to diverse schools of thought and their cultures. This learning has similarly expanded my perspective on social justice, including the responsibility to cultivate and sustain those qualities.

On a broader level, I find it interesting to consider how the nature and purpose of learning has dramatically changed throughout the years, reflecting social, economic, political, global, and other influences. In navigating these complex changes and learning dynamics, my mature lens has increasingly relied on the relevance of previous and cumulative learning and the knowledge I have acquired through employment and from my personal interests and activities. My formerly implicit learning focus has become increasingly deliberative, purposeful, and explicit. I have also come to more frequently apply a critical perspective within the context of my learning, establishing definitive links and connections across disciplines and understandings in other areas of life.

Some things have remained unchanged throughout my lifetime of learning. In particular, I continue to value each course for the challenge and learning that it offers. At the same time, this acquisition of knowledge has enabled me to more clearly differentiate the nature and fabric of the dimensions that comprise my own life. The threads of my learning tapestry similarly maintain a strong desire to search for the concrete and pragmatic in the abstract and to realize the values and principles that serve as a guiding compass: inquisitiveness, caring, connecting with others, and creating learning synergies in my life and within the broader communities of society.

So for me, I continue the journey of integrating and consolidating my diverse learning experiences and building on and sharing this knowledge and learning with a broad spectrum of individuals ... to realize new possibilities.

—Karen Bodard, Graduate Student

## Introduction

What did you learn today? For many of us, this was a common question posed by our parents around the dinner table at the end of a school day. We may have shrugged and mumbled, "I don't know" or, if something unique had happened, we might have described an event that transpired. Fast forward to your life as an adult and think about how you would answer this same question. What did you learn today? Would you still say "I don't know" or would share what you learned from an event that you experienced? Let's ponder this further. Is learning simply something that happens *to us*, something that can be neatly packaged in a box to be unwrapped at professional development sessions, in lecture halls, or in meetings with our instructors? Like Karen, whose narrative opened this chapter, we believe that learning is so much more than these disparate, relatively passive events and that it is intertwined in the very fabric of our life. Perhaps when you are asked the question "What did you learn today?" you might describe a rich conversation with a colleague at work, a conversation about a project—and because of this conversation, you gained insight as to how to proceed with the project. Or, through your own research on the Internet, you learned how to change the oil in your car. Perhaps you were able to read a picture book to your grandchild after months of literacy tutoring. We already see, in Karen's narrative, that she understands learning as a rich and daily endeavour; a mix of the planned events through courses and travel, and the informal learning that takes place in the workplace and through her personal exploration. Like Karen, we are not saying that coursework does not promote learning, as learning often does occur in more formal settings. But the common ingredient in all of these "what did you learn today?" answers is that the response includes some sort of change or shift in our way of being in the world. When we learn, we think differently about an idea; we become unstuck and can complete a task at work; we can do something new with our hands or we can participate within our community in a different way.

In chapter 2, we linked learning with change; in particular, change that moves us toward "higher, more mature, more integrated levels of functioning

... [and] the potential for growth, for life-changing interventions bettering both individuals and society" (Merriam & Clark, 2006, p. 29). But how does the possibility for such change occur? It occurs through the "what did you learn today?" experiences of life: reading a book that sends you on a certain life trajectory; attending a lecture; becoming a first-time parent; teaching a new class; or seeing a new culture for the first time. Added to this notion of experience is the idea of engagement and movement. While we all undergo thousands of experiences every day that we may not even think about, our engagement and movement toward change through our experiences offer the possibility of learning. Learning, then, is a *process*, not an end point. Peter Jarvis (2006), an adult educator who has devoted much of his research life to understanding the complexity of human learning, arrived at the following definition of *learning*. Note how Jarvis intertwines the notions of *experience, movement,* and *change* in his definition:

> The combination of processes whereby the whole person—body (genetic, physical and biological) and mind (knowledge, skills, attitudes, values, emotions, beliefs and senses)—experiences a social situation, the perceived content of which is then transformed cognitively, emotively or practically (or through any combination) and integrated into the person's individual biography resulting in a changed (or more experienced) person. (p. 13)

The first phrase, "the combination of processes," points us to the next section: a review of explanations seeking to understand how the process of learning occurs—to *learning theories*. As we investigate the increasingly complex world of learning theories, you will see different aspects of Jarvis's definition of learning highlighted. While initial learning theories focused on the cognitive processes associated with our minds, over time additional layers have been added that include emotional aspects of learning and the sociocultural context of learning.

While we focus heavily on adult learning theories in this text, in this chapter we turn to research generated on traditional learning theories.

In this way we locate adult learning theories within a larger theoretical landscape. This theoretical landscape is a rich field of study with an extensive history, extending as far back as Plato and Aristotle. While this philosophical orientation continued to dominate the discourse and debate over the centuries, the nineteenth century marked a significant shift in the development of learning theories. At this point, the field of psychology took up the study of the mind and how we learn and behave, undergirded by the premise that we could understand this phenomenon by scientifically investigating observable and measurable behaviour. Over time, however, sociology, anthropology, biology, and ecology have also engaged the phenomenon of learning, reflecting a growing realization that we can only begin to understand learning through multiple lenses.

As we explore traditional learning theories, demonstrating the increased complexity of the field that has emerged over this past century, you will see that, over time, more and more of Jarvis's definition of learning is reflected in the growth of the field. Guided by the framework of learning theories presented by Davis, Sumara, and Luce-Kapler (2008), we begin our overview with the correspondence theories of behaviourism and mentalism. We then move to coherence theories of constructivism and constructionism, to humanism, and to cultural and critical theories of learning. We also include ecological and complexity theories.

## Correspondence Theories

Correspondence theories, the most influential learning theories for much for the twentieth century, viewed learning as a mechanical process: cause and effect processes drive learning and can be easily adjusted to achieve the desired results. In addition, this cluster of theories emphasizes processes that occur within the individual learner. The first theory within this category of learning is behaviourism. In summary, our learning focuses on a change in behaviour that is measurable and observable, as opposed to internal thought processes not visible to the eye. Secondly, it is the external environment, as opposed to internal processes within a learner, that shapes what is learned. Finally, the principles of continuity—the link between stimulus and response—and reinforcement or reward are key to explaining this learning process. The example that comes to mind for many of us, when we think of a behaviourist approach to learning, is Pavlov's experiments with dogs. Typically, salivation occurs when a dog sees and smells food. By ringing a bell every time food was given to the dog, Pavlov was eventually able to remove the food stimulus and just ring the bell, as the stimulus, in order to induce salivation.

The second learning theory associated with correspondence theories is mentalism: how the mind works. The underlying assumption is that our minds take in information from the external world. We store and organize this information. In mentalism, "learning is a matter of assembling an inner representation (or mental model) of an external world ... the head contains a map, image, or other sort of facsimile that corresponds to the real world" (Davis, Sumara, & Luce-Kapler, 2008, p. 95). When we step back and consider this statement, it is true that we often speak about the brain as a storage device. We are *taking things in, filing items into our brain, absorbing new information*, and *acquiring the latest ideas on a topic*. The dominant critique of the mentalism approach is not that the brain and the associated cognitive processes are pivotal to the process of learning; rather, it is the idea that we actually hold and store knowledge that we can retrieve at the click of a button (Davis, Sumara, & Luce-Kapler, 2008). What we are referring to here is retrieval, accessing our memory. However, a memory is not something stored within a place; rather, memory is a process. "Memories are constructions assembled, from various places in the brain, at the time of retrieval, and the information storied during the initial experience is only one of the items used in the construction" (LeDoux, 2002, p. 203). So, when new sensory input is being taken in, the brain is busy looking for connections to earlier information or memories. When the brain cannot find any previous experience or meaningful links to existing patterns, we find it difficult to retain the new information. The quest to connect new experiences into existing and meaningful links or patterns is further taken up when we explore coherence theories.

Transferring a behaviourist approach to adult learning situations, we point to several examples in current practice. For example, when you learn a new software program, you can rely on a behaviourist orientation to learning. An updated word processing program is uploaded onto the computer, changing how you can engage with the computer. As you use the online tutorial, you figure out, through trial and error, how the new program works. Positive and correct behaviour is rewarded when you press the right keys to launch commands. Incorrect choices block your ability to move forward. The tutorial might even congratulate you when you get the right answer or encourage you to try again when you make an incorrect move. Through ongoing stimulus and response, you will gradually adapt your behaviour and, ultimately, you will be able to successfully use the new word processing program. In addition, we may see behaviourist approaches used in some weight-loss and smoking cessation programs. The key tool applied in these programs is immediate feedback, rewarding positive results and not rewarding negative or undesirable results. According to Merriam, Caffarella, and Baumgartner (2007), evidence of correspondence theories of behaviourism and mentalism within more formalized learning are typically seen in human resource development and adult career and technical/vocational education. Within vocational education, the emphasis is on acquiring technical skills needed to perform a specific occupation at a certain standard level of competency. Human resource development departments often focus on introducing new concepts and developing specific skills and competencies where there are specific and measurable performance outcomes that will enhance the effectiveness of an individual, department, and, ultimately, the organization. Turning to your own place of work, do you agree with this claim? When this approach to learning is used, when is it effective? When and where does it fall short? Can you see evidence of this approach in your own informal learning?

## Coherence Theories

Returning to Karen's narrative, she drew a wider circle around the influences that informed her learning journey, as she noted critically the importance of social, economic, political, global, and other influences. Her narrative reflects an underlying assumption highlighted in the next phase of learning theories. We refer to coherence theories, which include wider and deeper aspects of the self and the world around the self that are involved in learning processes. These wider and deeper aspects include the body, the mind, self and others, individuals and collectives, knowers and knowledge, and humans and non-humans (Davis, Sumara, & Luce-Kapler, 2008, p. 98). This advancement, occurring over the past 40 years, is a dramatic jump from the correspondence theories of behaviourism and mentalism that had little interest in how the body—with the associated dimensions of emotions, spirit, and physical experiences—informed learning, or how others—beyond the individual—informed learning. The underlying principle for these theories is the focus on an internal fit (coherence) with our internal selves. This means that when we are learning, we are continuously trying to make sense of what is going on and trying to maintain coherence with our existing memories, perceptions, and our own sociocultural contexts. In other words, we are continuously "relationship making"—asking ourselves how this new experience, idea, or observation relates to ourselves and to the way we locate ourselves in the world.

Coherence theories include humanism, constructivism, cultural and critical theories, and ecological theories. Beginning with humanism, learning is viewed as a function of the whole person and it cannot occur unless cognitive and affective domains are involved. Humanists also believe that people can control their own destiny, that they are inherently good, that they have the potential for growth and development, and that learning from their experiences is pivotal to their growth. Maslow (1970) and Rogers (1961), most associated with introducing humanistic psychology to the world, heavily influenced the early theoretical development in adult learning with their emphasis on self-directed growth and self-actualization. However, you will learn—when we look at these earlier theories of adult learning in the next chapter—that critiques of the humanistic orientation to learning argued that this approach focused almost entirely on individual learners and their own growth, and did not recognize the broader sociocultural contexts of learners.

Constructivism focuses on how individuals make sense of the world and their experiences. Piaget (1973), a central educational theorist introduced in chapter 2, said that learning is an ongoing process of updating one's sense of the world based on new experiences. We are constantly reworking and revising in order to have a coherent understanding of our world. Of particular note is that this theory maintains that we each inhabit a world that is made up of our own histories, narratives, emotions, physical sensations, thoughts, and beliefs and that two people can have the same experience and interpret it in very different ways. A case in point might be discussion of a novel at a book club. All members come to the discussion with their own perceptions of the novel and how it connects with their own story, to the point where one might wonder if they all read the same book. What this means for us as educators is that while we may design a learning experience and hope for the achievement of certain learning outcomes, the results will be unpredictable, and learning for each individual will vary.

While constructivism focuses on the experiences and process of engagement *for the individual*, social constructionism, while still focused on meaning making, shifts its attention away from the individual and explores how culture shapes the way individuals perceive the world around them. Social constructionism is concerned with interpersonal dynamics and collective activity across learners; therefore, social status, gender, and cultural background play a central role in how we make meaning. "In this frame, 'mind' is understood not as an individual possession but as a product of shared human interest that arises in an environment that is both social and physical" (Davis, Sumara, & Luce-Kapler, 2008, p. 102).

In terms of designing learning experiences, social constructionists are interested in learning that emerges within small groups as shared understandings are developed. You may have had an experience in which, through deep dialogue, you and your colleague together arrived at a place of new understandings and insights. Your thoughts coalesced and together you came up with something that you knew you would not have been able to do on your own. Vygotsky (1978), the key educational theorist associated with this approach, developed the theory "situated cognition." Situated cognition combines the individual and the social in order to learn. A common approach associated with this type of learning in an adult education context would be apprenticeship, a dominant approach to learning within post-secondary institutions that focus on vocations and trades. An example would be a learner who aspires to being an auto mechanic enters an established group of automechanics and learns through co-participating within a collective of other learners who have their sights set on this same career goal.

Cultural and critical theories of learning also fall into the category of coherence theories. During the 1960s and 1970s, a counter-movement emerged and became increasingly critical of the dominant discourse regarding individual learning and social contexts that drew primarily from the disciplines of psychology and sociology. Researchers from anthropology, philosophy, and political science began to enter into the conversation to consider the cultural context of learning and the social implications of our educational systems. We began to explore privilege within society—by looking at such factors as gender, race, class, sexual orientation, and disability—in order to ask whose voices and ideas had power, who was pushed to the margins, and how this shaped the world and experiences of the individual. In adult education, we often point to Paulo Freire (1970) as a seminal figure who introduced the notion of conscientization, "the effort to render explicit the cultural conditions that delimit possible worlds and acceptable identities" (p. 54). Freire believed that we all hold myths about society, myths that typically reflect the dominant discourse. Freire maintained that critical learning was about uncovering these assumptions and working toward change at multiple levels, from the individual to the larger society. Brookfield (2005a) indicated that there are several tasks we need to engage in when taking up a critical-theory approach to learning: challenging ideologies, contesting hegemony, unmasking power, overcoming alienation, learning liberation, reclaiming reasons, and practising democracy.

Turning to adult learning, theorists in the 1980s also began to push against the dominant research trends that focused only on individual learning and learning within professional contexts. These theorists argued that we were forgetting our social justice roots by simply complying with the existing economic structures. If you remember, when we explored the historical underpinnings of adult education in chapter 5, we highlighted social justice as a theme foundational to our work. The primary goal of many programs guided by a social justice mission and vision is to provide access to learners typically denied entry into traditional learning programs and to question existing political and economic structures and power differentials.

We now turn to a voice from the field, Nancy Taber, an adult educator and researcher interested in learning within military contexts. In her brief sketch, she provides a powerful example of how a critical lens, when applied to a particular social institution, can expose some profound implications for adult learning in a highly gendered environment.

 The key point to consider in exploring learning in military contexts is the fact that militaries are gendered societal institutions. Men are expected to act in accordance with hegemonic masculinity while women are expected to embrace certain aspects of masculinity while retaining their femininity. These expectations persist, regardless of the ways in which the actualities of military members' lives may challenge these gendered discourses. As such, learning goes beyond simply training in a specific military trade, but encompasses learning to enact military masculinities and femininities. Furthermore, learning gender within the military is connected to learning gender in other contexts, such as those visibly linked to the military (e.g., military families, private contractors deployed for defence purposes, weapons manufacturers) and those which are linked in less obvious ways (e.g., mass media, popular culture, industry, education, and society as a whole). Gendered militarism thus permeates learning in various aspects of life, valuing violent discourses that rely on binary under-standings of good/evil, protector/protected, and masculine/feminine, with the former in each relation privileged over its latter counterpart. Thus, educators working for social justice should consider and critique the ways in which gendered militaristic discourses interconnect with learning in multiple contexts.

—Dr. Nancy Taber, Associate Professor, Brock University

Nancy's concluding statement is particular noteworthy, reminding us that applying a critical lens to a particular social construct of learning is intertwined with the larger quest for change: changing the gendered militarism within this context in order to address a larger problem of societal violence.

We now turn to ecological theories, learning theories located within coherence theories. Typically, an ecological focus is associated with and located within environmental studies. As Davis, Sumara, and Luce-Kapler (2008) pointed out, however, *ecology* has a much broader meaning, as it is really about a study of relationships. While relationships are pivotal across all coherence theories, ecological theories of learning broaden the notion of relationships to also consider those we hold beyond the human world: interspecies relationships and planetary relationships. A pivotal shift in ecological theoretical work is that our cognitive processes and actions are no longer separate from each other or from the natural world. Rather, "our habits of thought/action are entwined with and implicated in the evolving structures of many other systems" (Davis, Sumara, & Luce-Kapler, 2008, p. 107). Noting that studies over the past 50 years point to the profound implications and deepening ecological crisis of seeing ourselves as separate and distinct from the natural world (Macy & Johnstone, 2012), ecological theories of learning are gaining more importance and momentum. Indeed, probably the most important work of environmental educators is to guide learners, particularly within the Western world, in making this deep change from being apart from nature to being deeply intertwined with nature. Darlene Clover, an adult education scholar engaged in environmental adult education, affirms that embracing this focus and embracing this agenda is a daunting mission.

 The theory and practice of environmental adult education began with the 1992 United Nations Conference on Environment and Development—the Earth Summit—held in Rio de Janeiro. Until that time, there was in fact no emphasis in adult education on environmental issues. Yet the world was faced with an unprecedented problem—an environmental crisis that was multifaceted: local, yet global, touched every aspect of people's lives, was about our physical health, our cultural and spiritual relationships and identities, our livelihoods and economies, and our politics and daily practices. It was about gender equity, about race and class.

Environmental adult education is an amalgam of methods, theoretical perspectives, discursive lenses and epistemological understandings. Given the breadth, depth, and scope of environmental problems, it is a practice that is highly political, recognizing that environmental problems have emerged from industrialization and the mad game of maximizing global profit. Key to environmental adult education is the concept of ecological knowledge: cultural, spiritual, and everyday ways of knowing and relating to the land of Indigenous peoples, women, and farmers. Environmental adult education employs the arts and creativity; it is hopeful, fun, and engaging. It aims to make people feel powerful, energized, and strengthened in the struggle for socio-environmental justice. It allows the rest of nature to teach, to lead, to tell stories, to hold truths, and to guide in a quest to fundamentally transform human/Earth relations.

—Dr. Darlene Clover, Professor, University of Victoria

As we close our exploration of coherence theories of learning, we are reminded that the underlying principle across these theories is that when we are engaged in an experience and in the process of learning, we are continuously striving to make sense of what is going on. We are also striving to maintain coherence within our memories, perceptions, sociocultural contexts, and/or interspecies relationships and planetary relationships.

## Complexity Theories

Let's take a moment and return to Peter Jarvis's definition of learning:

> The combination of processes whereby the whole person—body (genetic, physical and biological) and mind (knowledge, skills, attitudes, values, emotions, beliefs and senses)—experiences a social situation, the perceived content of which is then transformed cognitively, emotively or practically (or through any combination) and integrated into the person's individual biography resulting in a changed (or more experienced) person. (2006, p. 13)

What is striking about his definition and about coherence theories is that there is no separation between the physical and the mental, the "me" and the "other," beliefs and knowledge, and so forth. Building upon the idea that such separations are artificial, complexity thinking recognizes that the multi-level dynamics at play in any learning situation can shift; in other words, there is an ever-changing emphasis on different domains of the learning process, depending on the learner, the situation being experienced, and the broader context. Complexity theory is a form of systems thinking drawn from biochemistry. In essence, this theory describes systems as "living organisms and social systems, integrated wholes whose properties were determined by the relationships among their parts. Systems thinking meant contextualizing so that an organism was always understood as existing through relationships with the greater whole" (Swartz, 2008, p. 1). Therefore, everything described within coherence theories applies to complexity theories; they are specific examples of complexity thinking:

> What complexity thinking adds however, is an insistence that these theories and their foci should be addressed at the same time. That is, education is a *transphenomenon* and, as such, requires a *transdisciplinary* attitude ... education simultaneously affects and is affect by many overlapping, intertwining and nested learning situations. (Davis, Sumara, & Luce-Kapler, 2008, p. 107)

Transphenomenal dimensions of learning move from the bodily subsystem, to the person, social groups, culture, species, and biosphere. Transdisciplinary dimensions draw from medicine, psychology, sociology, anthropology, biology, and ecology. When you stop and consider these intersecting dimensions, you will realize that we have touched on all of them in some way in our description of the chronological unfolding of educational theories over this past century. What complexity theories suggest is that learning is an intricate web that involves all of the dimensions, with various dimensions moving into the forefront or receding into the background in a responsive manner as learning unfolds. The meaning of *learner* extends beyond the individual and can be represented at many system levels, perhaps even several at the same time. To elaborate, within a community of practice (CoP), individuals themselves may be a learning entity at the same time that the CoP is an entity of learning; they can be learning as individual systems *or* as part of a complex interacting system (Davis & Sumara, 2006; Doll et al., 2005). Swartz (2008) is also taking up complexity theory, arguing that we are connected to ourselves through self-reflection, to each other, and to the world as co-creators. By making these multiple-system connections, we can generate improvements within our workplaces and our own wellness. Finally, turning to our role as adult educators, "By using one's own connectivity with students, revealing connections to self, [we strive to help] them understand this web of life and explore perceptions that tell us how to navigate it" (Swartz, 2008, p. 7).

## Concluding Comments

As we revisit the question "What did you learn today?" we are beginning to realize what a complicated and multi-faceted question it is! Now, as you ponder this question, we hope that you are also mindful of the multi-faceted learning processes that have been called upon in order to arrive at this new place of understanding and knowledge. Over the past century, we have moved from a behaviourist approach to learning, to coherence theories of learning, and now to complexity theories—gradually adding additional layers to the process of learning that locate us as learners within a deeply interconnected world. Now, as we move into a chronological exploration of adult theories of learning in chapter 7, you will see that this specialized field of study reflects the evolution of the broader field of traditional learning theories, drawing on this research to gain a deeper understanding of how adults learn.

# The Big Four Adult Learning Theories

## MATT

 These days I find myself in graduate school researching the topic of "callings in the workplace" at the University of Calgary. My journey here would hardly appear linear. For example, my cornucopia of a resumé includes experiences as diverse as real estate, hospitality, retail sales, mobile marketing, and other tech/website startups. It is only when I infuse my narrative with emotional context that this non-linearity irons itself out.

When I was 10 years old I was introduced to speech arts, and I immediately excelled in it. I won nearly every competition at the time, and by the age of 17 I had transcended the amateur world of acting with several professional acting credits in theatre, TV, and film. I felt my calling was musical theatre and I dreamed of performing on Broadway. However, when it came time for university I was too scared to audition for The Juilliard School's drama program. Conveniently, I felt it was "smarter" to obtain a backup degree first so that I would not have to endure long hours as a starving actor in case my dreams did not pan out. To make the best of my backup plan, I thought it would be fruitful to complement my artistic and creative talents with thinking skills. Thus, mathematics seemed to be the best choice for this rationale, but I paid the price in stress and anxiety. Notwithstanding the overwhelming difficulties I faced in school, I thought that instead of transferring out of the program, I should persist so I could confidently affirm that I had the ability to overcome anything.

Soon after I graduated from university, my mother succumbed to her long, hard-fought battle with cancer. I immediately cast myself in her light and saw my own fate shortened to the same age of 55. This would mean that despite being only 22 years old I was almost "middle-aged," and endured what I believe to be a mid-life crisis. With what small amount of life I felt I had left, I thought it would make the most sense to make it rich first, get married, have kids, live off the interest of my fortune, and then develop my acting career in security and comfort. What ensued was five desperate years of the aforementioned get-rich-quick schemes (commercial real estate, hospitality, etc.) that all ended in failure. Suffice to say, I was a mess by the end of it all and asked, "Why am I failing when I previously proved that I have the ability to overcome anything?"

Eventually, I gave up on the idea of getting rich quickly, and settled on the idea of being a speech and drama teacher. The idea grew on me, and I started to read—and read I did. My family watched in astonishment as the social butterfly, who once hated to read, morphed into a voracious bookworm. When I reflected on this personal transformation, an epiphany struck: Success was not about one's ability, but rather one's commitment to doing the job "correctly" for its own sake and not personal gain. But this is something my parents tried to instill in me continually growing up; so why am I only doing this now? In short, it is more than just passion that enables us to overcome ourselves (i.e., our attitude, pride, fear), but rather, it is our "calling" furnishing us with a kind of passion. My new calling is to argue that there is merit and room to bring these passions into the workplace. What's more, I am finally starting to realize success!

—Matt Cohen, Graduate Student

## Introduction

By now, you have probably realized that the role of experience on the learning journey of adults has been a constant theme in this book. You can see that the importance of experience also features in a big way in

Matt's story on his understanding of callings. The key, however, was not the experience alone, but Matt's quest to engage and learn from those experiences. As result, Matt's life was hardly linear; it was almost like a zigzag as he lived his life, reflected on those experiences, and then made a left or a right turn in response to the "learnings" offered to him. Right from the beginning of the research on how adults learn, the role of experience has been taken up, beginning with early pioneering work of Malcolm Knowles, who coined the term *andragogy*, on to Allen Tough, who introduced the notion of self-directed learning. From there, other theorists have deepened the exploration of experience in the learning of adults through the development of experiential learning and transformative learning. In this chapter, we will introduce you to what we have identified as the "big four" theories of adult learning, both returning to and broadening our understanding of how experience plays a role within our understanding of how adults learn. While we recognize there are multiple theories on how adults learn, we chose these theories as they mark the emergence of adult education as a distinct area of scholarship, and they still play an important role in research on adult learning theories.

As we delve into the evolution of adult learning theories, it is important to place this story in the broader picture of education theories. If you remember, in the previous chapter, we learned that most educational theories that developed in the earlier portion of the twentieth century drew heavily from the field of psychology, particularly behaviourist and constructivist orientations. Theories of adult learning follow the same path, with earlier research relying heavily on psychology with strong constructivist and humanistic orientations and then, gradually, bringing in ideas from the fields of sociology, anthropology, critical theory, feminism, and environmental studies. Finally, you will note, particularly as we move into the work of Knowles, that in our earlier years of theory development, we were preoccupied with trying to distinguish adult learning and adult education from the ways children learn and with separating ourselves from pre-adult schooling—typically kindergarten to grade 12.

## Andragogy

The best-known and earliest framework that was developed to understand adults as learners is called andragogy. In the 1960s, Malcolm Knowles took up this framework and developed it further. The terms *andragogy* and *pedagogy* share the same root—*gogy*—a Greek word for leading, which has now been modified to mean teaching or instruction. *Peda* is translated as "child" and *andra* is translated as "adult." Therefore *andragogy* is described as "the art and science of helping adults learn," which is in contrast with *pedagogy,* described as the art and science of helping children learn (Knowles, 1980, p. 43).

Knowles (1980) identified six key assumptions of andragogy and four perspectives of what it means to be an adult. First, from a *biological* perspective, we become adults when we can reproduce. Second, from a *legal* perspective, we become adults when we can vote, get a driver's licence, get married, and so forth. Third, from a *social* perspective, we become adults when we start performing adult roles such as maintaining a full-time job, being a spouse, and being a parent. Finally, from a *psychological* perspective—and located within a humanistic orientation, the view that Knowles felt was the most crucial to the development of andragogy—we become adults when we gain the self-concept of being responsible for our own lives and for being self-directed. While he recognized that this process is ongoing throughout childhood and adolescence, he argued, "Most of us probably do not have full-fledged self-concepts of self-directedness until we leave school or college, get a full-time job, marry and start a family" (Knowles, 1980, p. 57). Based on this understanding of adulthood, Knowles developed six assumptions about the way adults learn and outlined their implications for educators of adults:

1. *The need to know*: Adults need to know why they need to learn something before they invest in the endeavour.

2. *The learners' self-concept:* Adults have a self-concept that assumes responsibility for their decisions and their own lives. As a result, it

is critical to develop learning situations in which adults are viewed as being self-directed and responsible for their own learning.

3. *The role of the learners' experience:* Adults come into learning situations with an increasingly rich reservoir of experiences. As educators, it is important to recognize the pivotal role of those experiences in a learning situation.

4. *Readiness to learn:* The readiness to learn for adults is closely associated with real-life situations and experiences. For example, learning about hypothermia would be extremely timely and relevant for someone preparing for a backcountry canoe trip.

5. *Orientation to learning:* Adults are life-centred in their orientation to learning. Is the learning relevant to their lives? Will this learning help solve a real-life problem? Will it address a task that needs to be attended to?

6. *Motivation:* The most crucial motivation for adults to learn comes from within (e.g., self-esteem, quality of life) and not from external pressures (e.g., a job promotion). (Knowles, 1980, pp. 57–63)

While there are numerous critiques on Knowles's "model of assumptions," which we will explore shortly, his model provided adult education theorists and practitioners with an identity; a place that located the theory and practice of teaching adults as being separate from other areas of education, particularly the instruction of children in the formal kindergarten to grade 12 context. As Merriam, Caffarella, and Baumgartner (2007) indicated, andragogy became almost a rallying cry to help scholars and practitioners define adult education as being separate from other areas of education.

However, two critiques of andragogy quickly emerged: first, the notion that andragogy was a "theory of learning" and second, that andragogy and pedagogy were distinctly different from each other. Turning first to the debate surrounding andragogy as a theory of adult learning, scholars were quick to point out that Knowles's assumptions were really just his guidelines for effective teaching and learning practice; they were not developed as a result of extensive research on the process of adult learning. In summary, andragogy was closer to a philosophy of learning and not an emerging theory on how adults learn. Hartree (1984), in an article critiquing andragogy, stated that a full theory of adult learning would have three dimensions: "how adults learn, what they learn where this is distinctive, and why they learn. Because Knowles' assumptions centre on the learner rather than the learning process, these dimensions do not emerge clearly" (p. 207). Indeed, even Knowles came to this conclusion, indicating that he "prefers to think of [andragogy] as a model of assumptions about learning or a conceptual framework that serves as a basis for an emergent theory" (1980, p. 112).

Turning to the second point of contention—that andragogy and pedagogy are distinctly different from one another—Knowles (1990) waded into the debate in the fourth edition of his book *The Adult Learner: A Neglected Species*. He informed his audience that during the decade following the first publication of this book in 1970, numerous teachers in elementary and secondary schools, as well as college instructors, told him that they were experimenting with the andragogical model in their classrooms and that their students seemed to be more effective learners in many circumstances. Conversely, many educators and trainers of adults were telling him that the andragogical model was not working in their context. In response, Knowles suggested that there is a continuum of learning, where on the one end of the continuum is the dependent learner who needs direct instruction—pedagogical approaches—and on the other end of the continuum is the independent learner who would prefer a self-directed pathway to learning—andragogical approaches. So, while he argued that children are generally more dependent learners, relying on pedagogical approaches to learning, and adults are more self-directed, relying on andragogical approaches to learning, he readily agreed that a clear distinction could not be made. Indeed, we are the first to admit that both of us would need a great deal of direct instruction if we decided that we want to learn how to pilot an airplane. Neither of us has any direct experience in this situation. We have no previous knowledge to draw from, nor do we have an internal need to become pilots. Conversely, we can easily identify children who, passionately driven by a love of dinosaurs, can easily tell us about the various types and all of their habits in minute detail, all of this knowledge developed of their own volition because of their passion for this topic. In closing, Knowles reminds us that andragogical assumptions for teaching bestow value, regardless of the context or age of the learners, by "providing a climate in which the learners feel more respected, trusted, unthreatened, and cared about; by exposing them to the need to know before instructing them; by giving them some responsibility in choosing methods and resources" (1990, p. 65). Turning to your own experiences as a learner—as a child and now as an adult—can you see that you have gradually become more self-directed and autonomous as a learner? Were there learning situations, as child, in which you felt quite independent, and conversely, are there learning situations now in which you feel dependent on the instructor?

Considering other critiques of Knowles's assumptions about adult learning, one quickly realizes that Knowles was almost totally focused on the individual learner, without recognizing the power of historical, economic, and cultural forces in shaping learners' lives and the possibility of learning. Sandlin, in her review of several journal articles critiquing andragogy, summarized five critical issues that emerged:

1. Andragogy assumes wrongly that education is value neutral and apolitical.

2. Andragogy promotes a generic adult learner as universal with white middle-class values.

3. Andragogy ignores other ways of knowing and silences other voices.

4. Andragogy ignores the relationship between self and society.

5. Andragogy is reproductive of inequalities; it supports the status quo.

(Sandlin, 2005, p. 27)

It is important to be reminded that when andragogy emerged, Sandlin's critiques probably could have been applied to most of the educational theory emerging in the middle of the twentieth century. As Grace (1996) pointed out, andragogy emerged in the 1960s—a period of time when the majority of the research in learning came from psychology, where individual experience was pivotal and the quest was ongoing self-development. Knowles, like many of his colleagues, "never proceeded to an in-depth consideration of the organizational and social impediments to adult learning; he never paints the 'big picture.' He chose the mechanistic over the meaningful" (Grace, 1996, p. 386). And yet, andragogy has left its mark on the field of adult education. For many adult educators, it is one of the first concepts explored in a course on adult learning and education, and practitioners from around the world have taken up its assumptions as a useful set of guidelines in order to frame their practice. It is interesting to note, however, that while andragogy has been taken up as a series of guidelines for practice, it has not really contributed to our understanding on the process of learning nor is it really a theory of adult learning (Pratt, 1993).

## Self-Directed Learning

Before we move into the next significant model of adult learning, we want you to think about a time and a space when you initiated, on your own, the process to learn something. It should be something that was not prescribed or assigned to you. Perhaps you decided to take up a new hobby or perhaps you took up a new role in your life that compelled you to deepen your understanding of a particular facet of that role or maybe something at work has piqued your curiosity. Now that you have this event in your mind, think about why you took this interest up, what goals you set for yourself, the steps you undertook, the challenges along the way, and the final results. The learner experience we are asking you to consider is an example of self-directed learning, so retain this experience as you review the next section to determine whether the following description reflects your learning experience.

At around the same that Knowles introduced andragogy, Allan Tough (1967, 1971) was developing another model to distinguish adult learners as separate from children. As an aside, it is interesting to note that Knowles alluded to the idea of self-directed learning (SDL) through his view of adults as being increasingly responsible for their own lives and for being self-directed. However, it was Tough—who became particularly fascinated with how adults learn on their own—who was the originator of self-directed learning. In his early work, Tough began to realize that individuals take up many of the typical program planning steps to shape their own learning: they set their goals, they determine how to learn, they get the needed resources, and they evaluate their own progress. In his PhD thesis work, as he asked people to describe their own learning, he began to realize that SDL did not necessarily mean working in isolation; it can be very social with lots of interaction with other people. We turn to Alison Brophe, Coordinator of Continuing Education Programs at the University of Victoria, to make the point that self-directed learning often occurs in community—in this particular instance, the community being one's classmates in a post-secondary context.

 "I learned as much from my classmates as I did from the instructor!" As an adult education program coordinator, I'm always pleased when I see comments like this one on course evaluations. They remind me of the value of adult education and its unique ability to develop capacity in individuals and collectively. Whether in the classroom or online, adult learners gain so much for the interaction they have with their peers. They form informal communities of practice and they rely on each other as resources when they develop, deliver, and evaluate their own work as adult educators.

Although I'm intrigued by the concept of self-directed learning, I'm curious about how a self-directed learner experiences the learning that comes through connecting with classmates. I understand that, as adult learners, we often lead busy professional and personal lives, so naturally we gravitate towards the convenience of self-directed learning opportunities, and I think it's important that, as adult educators, we respect the learner's needs. I also believe that adult education program

> developers and instructors need to consider how we contribute to balancing the individual's need for self-direction with the value that comes from learning together. Being on your own, but not alone ...
>
> —Alison Brophe, Coordinator of Continuing Education Programs, University of Victoria

The distinctive quality of SDL is not independent learning; rather it is about learners having the opportunity and responsibility to make choices and decisions about their learning. At this point, it is important to tease out two dimensions in SDL; specifically, SDL refers to a *process* of learning, in which learners have the primary responsibility for creating their own learning pathway (Tough, 1967, 1971) and SDL can also refer to an *end point* or a *product* that we aspire to when we think about adult learners: the goal is to develop self-directed learners (Brookfield, 1985) who are inner-directed and inner-motivated, self-operating learners.

Patricia Cranton (2013), in her overview of adult learning theory, pointed us to the work of two other researchers, Candy and Garrison, who built upon the work of Allen Tough to deepen our understanding of the dimensions of self-directed learning. Turning first to the work of Candy (1991), he built on the notions of *process* and *product* in his determination that four qualities needed to be in place for SDL to occur. The first two dimensions refer to *product* (being self-directed) and the latter two dimensions relate to *process* (self-directed ways of learning):

1. *Personal autonomy* relates to our ability to think and act independently.
2. *The willingness and ability to self-manage one's education* refers to our ability to find the resources we need (e.g., books, seminars, courses, websites, instructors).
3. *Learner control* refers to the way instruction is organized within a formal setting. In other words, despite the formal constraints of a course or seminar, there are choices that allow learners to

determine how they will learn (e.g., individual learning, group work, self-selected topics, self-evaluation).

4. *Autodidaxy* refers to the individual, non-institutional pursuit of learning opportunities and projects.

Loop back to your own example of self-directed learning and consider the four dimensions outlined above. Think about yourself as a learner and what contributed to your ability to *be* self-directed in this situation. Secondly, reflect on the *processes* of learning undertaken in this instance. Related to the notions of *product* and *process* are discussions about the internal and external aspects of SDL. The external dimension refers to the extent to which adult learners are able to take control of, and responsibility for, their learning environment. The internal dimension refers to personal attributes we need in order to be self-directed learners—qualities such as being internally motivated, self-initiating, and being responsible for making meaning of our own experiences (Leach, 2005). Turning to Garrison's (1997) model of self-directed learning, he argued that SDL is a personal attribute as well as a learning process, with three dimensions interacting with each other: self management, self-monitoring, and motivation. Self-management refers to learners' control of the learning situation in order to achieve their own learning goals, with the focus being on collaborative learning situations, as opposed to learning independently. Self-monitoring refers to the ability to assess progress toward reaching the learning goals and, finally, motivation focuses on the learners' quest or desire to participate in learning activities that close the distance in achieving the learning goal.

It is interesting to note that several instruments were developed—such as Guglielmino's Self-Directed Learning Readiness Scale, the Oddi Continuing Learning Inventory, and the Self-Directed Learning Perception Scale—to assess people's perceptions of having the necessary skills, attributes, and attitudes typically associated with self-directed learning. While there have been numerous concerns regarding the validity of these instruments, they are still in use today.

Finally, turning to critiques associated with SDL, some mirror those associated with andragogy: in particular, early debate centred on whether or not SDL could only apply to adults. Conversely, debate also focused on whether or not adults are automatically self-directed learners or if it is something that can be developed. We now turn to a voice from the field, Tara Hyland-Russell, who has engaged in extensive research with Janet in the learning journeys of marginalized adult learners enrolled in an entry-level university program focusing on the humanities. Her entry allows us to see how contextual challenges can have a profound impact on our capacity to be self-directed learners.

 Working with adults who have felt left out of society challenges us as educators to imagine new ways of being and teaching. Many adults have been marginalized and excluded from learning through experiences with poverty, interrupted or negative educational experiences, unstable housing, trauma, discrimination, immigration, or illness. Despite a passion for learning, one of the powerful impediments for these adults to engage in education is an internalized script of self-doubt and lack of ability. Inviting marginalized adults into a relationship with learning requires extending a deep and genuine hospitality. A hospitable stance positions us as co-learners, open to mutual dialogue and attuned to the strengths and resiliency of people who have maintained curiosity in the face of adversity. If we are intent on building capacity, we recognize our own need for growth, and learn alongside all those who join a circle of learning. Hospitality offers generosity, patience, and humility and is attentive to dynamics of power and authority that can hinder learning. At the same time, hospitality accepts the responsibility of teaching and respects the transformative potential of learning—for all who gather together.

—Dr. Tara Hyland-Russell, Associate Professor,
St. Mary's University College

Indeed, Tara reminds us that we are not autonomous learners involved in a linear process of learning; rather, we come to our learning with a complex personal narrative about our ability to learn, in addition to multiple contextual factors that can often inhibit our ability to engage in the SDL process. Finally, Usher, Bryant, and Johnston (1997) reminded us that we need to challenge a Westernized notion of SDL where the "notion of self" is individualistic, unitary, rational, and decontextualized from historical and cultural forces. There are many cultures that do not uphold SDL as an ideal "product" for adult learners, preferring relational learning where interdependency, shared interests, and collective action are valued.

## Experiential Learning

Boud (2005) stated that experiential learning in its broadest form is both a philosophy and a practice. Its philosophical origins go back to the work of John Dewey (1938) in his book *Experience and Education*, in which he linked together life experiences and learning, ultimately arguing that all learning comes from experience, with the caution that not all experiences lead to learning. Returning again to Matt's story at the beginning of this chapter, we see, at the end of his narrative, that Matt had a profound learning moment after multiple experiences throughout his life journey. His definition of success shifted from outward manifestations of riches and external affirmation to inward indicators of passion, meaning, and purpose. Matt was able to connect what he had learned and experienced in the past to his current experiences and perhaps even to his future, where his changed notions of success may influence experiences yet unknown. The philosophy of experiential learning is as follows:

> Learning must take account of the learner and what he or she brings with them from all earlier experience as these not only provide

the foundation for dispositions, expectations and motivations, but also establish the base of knowledge and expertise on which new knowledge must build. (Boud, 2005, p. 244)

Turning to the *practice* of experiential learning, research began to emerge in the 1980s, with the common reference point being the work of David Kolb (1984), who drew on the work of Kurt Lewin, Jean Piaget, and John Dewey to shape his definition: "Experiential learning is the process of gaining knowledge from experience and applying it to education, work, and development. It occurs when the learner directly experiences the realities of the theory, concept, or fact that they are learning" (1984, p. 40). In turn, Kolb broke this process down into a four-part model of learning: concrete experience, reflective observation, abstract conceptualization, and active experimentation. The following is an illustration of Kolb's experiential learning cycle (1984, p. 21) with an elaboration by Dorothy MacKeracher (2004, p. 57) of each phase.

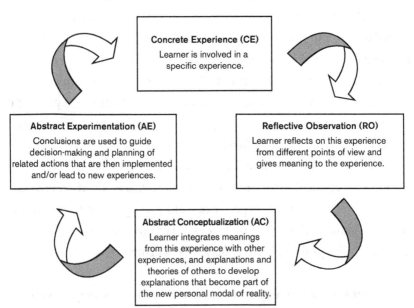

FIGURE 7.1: Kolb's Experiential Learning Cycle

Connections to our own lives and the potential for learning, using this model, can be easily made. Turning to the first step in Kolb's experiential learning cycle, concrete experiences (CE), we draw on experiences that occur in our daily life through our workplaces, in our families, via our volunteer work and community engagement, and in our places of learning. In addition, CE can also be associated with experiences in a formal learning setting that have been deliberately designed to launch learners into a specific space of learning, such as case studies, simulations, and role plays. The second phase of the cycle, reflective observation (RO), has the learner revisit this experience and draw out meaning and significance from it. Within our classes, this might be done through small group dialogue and/or journaling. In the third phase, abstract conceptualization (AC), similar activities would apply, but we would prompt our learners to consider how the meaning derived from the experience might generate new ideas, concepts, and ways of thinking and living in the world. Finally, it is in the final phase, active experimentation (AE), where we test how these new ideas apply to our lives. Again, returning to Matt's story, it would be interesting to follow up with him to see how his newly internalized views of success are playing out. Have his lived experiences with the new notions of success gone well? Has he modified them somewhat? Have his ideas shifted again due to new experiences? And so cycle plays out over and over again.

Much like previous critiques for andragogy and SDL, this model has been assessed as being too rational, autonomous, and linear. In particular, the cycle portrays the learner as moving through the cycle in a systematic manner. The cycle does not account for the role of others within the learning process; that learning can be confusing and anxiety-producing; and that we may not go through the stages in a predictive way. However, despite all of these concerns, Boud (2005) indicated that this model is used in multiple contexts such as business, nursing, and continuing education.

Moving beyond the experiential learning cycle, the underlying agenda in the *practice* of experiential learning is to move away from classroom-based, strictly cognitive activities to multi-faceted experiences that have the potential to be a rich reservoir for learning. Typical examples would include participatory activities, reflective activities, action-oriented approaches, challenge-based or adventure-based activities, and approaches that are holistic in nature, which draw on our emotions, feelings, physical sensations, and spiritual connections. For example, still 30 years later, after an unplanned experiential learning activity, Janet can easily describe the symptoms of hypothermia and the needed first aid. She is drawing from her experience as an outdoor education student as she assisted in a rescue of a co-learner from a river after he tipped his canoe over in the frigid early May water. Pivotal to her ability to accurately describe hypothermia and follow-up care was the guided facilitation of the outdoor education instructor as he led a powerfully reflective group dialogue on the event, the rescue, the feelings experienced by everyone involved, and the key learnings that could be drawn from this accident.

While there is agreement on the types of activities typically associated with the practice of experiential learning, there are differing opinions on the desired end point or goal of this particular approach to learning. Boud (2005) drew on the work of Weil and McGill (1989) in their creation of four interacting and overlapping "villages" of experiential learning to highlight the variances in this particular theory of learning. Village One is concerned with the assessment and accreditation of experiential learning through prior learning assessment processes; Village Two locates experiential learning with catalyzing change through education by emphasizing learning that occurs through relevant and hands-on experiences; Village Three focuses on the importance of experiential learning for consciousness raising, community action, and social change; and Village Four concentrates on using experiential learning to focus on personal growth and development to increase self-awareness and group effectiveness (Boud, 2005, p. 244). Fenwick (2003) also offered five conceptualizations of experiential learning, mirroring several aspects described in the four villages. The first conceptualization reflects the common and dominant thread of experiential learning offered through

Kolb's model: that knowledge is constructed by reflecting on concrete experience. The remaining conceptualizations address some of the criticism directed toward experiential learning, offered earlier. Specifically, experiential learning can be conceptualized as knowledge developed in groups; it can also happen when we attend to unconscious desires and fears; it can emerge when we resist dominant ideas; and finally, it can happen when we engage in learning that addresses ecological relationships emphasizing our interconnectivity with each other and the natural world (Fenwick, 2003, p. 21).

Experiential learning, like andragogy and SDL, received significant attention during the emerging years of research and practice in adult education; but now it is becoming a less distinct area of focus and is becoming more common in mainstream educational research and practice. Finally, it is important to distinguish various terms that are emerging out of experiential learning. Usher (1993) argued that "learning from experience" happens within everyday life, but "experiential learning" refers to a specific learning experience that is created by instructors to create a particular type of learning.

## Transformative Learning

When you hear the word *transform*, you probably connect it to the idea of change—not just superficial change, but substantial and deep change. As an aside, not all learning is about "significant change." We often add knowledge to our existing meaning schemes and learning schemes—perhaps adding jazz to our repertoire of music we play on the piano, or learning a how to use a computer software program. While we mentioned at the outset of this chapter that the thread of experience was going to be interwoven throughout our exploration of the big four adult learning models and theories, we have also been talking about substantial change—change that causes us to see ourselves and the world differently.

Taking up the idea of substantial change, transformative learning theory has become the most researched area of adult learning and education over the past 40 years. This theory is based on the premise that there are no enduring truths in the world and we are always changing (Taylor, 2008). As part of this change, we are constantly renegotiating and revising our beliefs, based upon new experiences, in order to guide our future action (Mezirow, 1996). Therefore, transformative learning occurs when we shift from uncritical engagement in the world, toward learning "how to negotiate and act upon our own purposes, values, feelings and meanings rather than those we have uncritically assimilated from others" (Mezirow and Associates, 2000, p. 8). Transformative learning theory then is focused on understanding the learning process that we undergo as we construct and appropriate new and revised interpretations of meaning regarding our experiences in the world.

Jack Mezirow first introduced the term *transformative learning* (1978) when he explored the learning journeys of a small group of middle-aged women, including his wife, as they re-entered college as mature students. As they engaged in their studies, they found that many of their own assumptions about their roles in the world were being challenged. In summary, their perspective was being transformed; they were undergoing "a structural reorganization of the way a person looks at himself" (Cranton, 2005, p. 631). Mezirow delved into the learning process we undergo as we experience such a perspective change or paradigmatic shift within our current perspectives or *frames of reference,* defined as "structures of assumptions and expectations that frame an individual's tacit points of view and influence their thinking, beliefs, and actions" (Taylor, 2008, p. 5). Specifically, Mezirow (2012) suggested the transformational learning process involved in shifting our frames of reference moves through the following 10 phases:

1.  A disorienting dilemma
2.  A self-examination with feelings of fear, guilt, or shame
3.  A critical assessment of assumptions
4.  Recognition that one's discontent and the process of transformation are shared

5. Exploration of options for new roles, relationships, and actions
6. Planning a course of action
7. Acquisition of knowledge and skills for implementing one's plan
8. Provisional trying of new roles
9. Building of competence and self-confidence in new roles and relationships
10. A reintegration into one's life on the basis of conditions dictated by one's perspective

(Mezirow, 2012, p. 86)

## *Jeff*

We now offer Jeff Kawalilak's narrative of returning to graduate school. As you read his story, we invite you to reflect on his journey and how Mezirow's phases of transformative learning are animated throughout.

Throughout my K–12 years and my undergraduate studies, I had never considered myself to be much of an academic. As a result, enrolling in a Master of Education program stirred up quite an imposter complex within me as I felt this level of education was a bit out of my league. I was convinced everyone in the graduate program would be far more qualified than I was. People choose not to return to school in their adult years for a number of reasons such as family commitments, children, work, and money. However, my hesitation and fear stemmed from feeling that I was somehow unworthy of the task.

Over several years, prior to taking my Master's Degree, I experienced quite a transition in my life. Thoughts, goals, ambitions, hobbies, and dreams had all taken on a different shape and began to change. I experienced such unfamiliar territory and, to be honest, I found it all very frightening. Where I wanted to be was no longer where I thought I wanted to be and I began to question my place in life, where I was, what I was doing, what my passions were, and where I was going.

However, as I reflected on the terrain and these unfamiliar waters I was attempting to navigate, I embraced the journey. I chose to face this new pathway head-on and, as a result, I realized that what brought me a huge sense of comfort and ease was the realization that continuing my education and returning to school was what I really wanted. This was a bit odd considering that this very thought was what had initially created a tremendous amount of anxiety for me in the many years prior.

As my fears began to subside, the thought of returning to school excited me; I was reconnecting with a deep sense of motivation and this rekindling of my passion for learning was becoming stronger than any anxieties I was harbouring. Sometimes, I still sit back and have a laugh at this, considering that when I completed my undergraduate degree, I swore that I was finished school forever—I had vowed never to return! Needless to say, my perspective toward furthering my education and the value I placed on lifelong learning changed significantly. As I began my new learning journey, I embraced my new role as an adult learner; my imposter complex started to fade and I began to feel more worthy and able. It became clear to me that I did deserve to be there and that all the life experiences I had accumulated along the way, formal and informal, experiences I had once thought to be irrelevant, would become the very foundation and bedrock upon which to anchor and inform new learning.

Those few years that I spent reflecting on my past and my future are what led me to my present ... teaching in an adult learning, post-secondary education environment. Needless to say, in the beginning, I deeply underestimated my ability and potential as a learner. Since then, I have cherished and embraced the learning process as a daily practice on both a personal and a professional level. I now realize that every experience, every relationship, every success and challenge has the potential to teach me something. It is all of this that has contributed to where I am now standing. The journey never ends!

—Jeff Kawalilak, MEd, Adult Educator, Bow Valley College

We see that Jeff underwent a perspective transformation, shifting from a fearful learner holding onto an imposter syndrome to one who began to love learning and the dynamics associated with the process. His experience mirrored many of the phases Mezirow outlined, right from the experience of disjuncture at the beginning of graduate school, to critically reflecting on his experience, engaging in the opportunities of dialogue offered through the coursework, and gradually assimilating those experiences to develop a new construct of himself as a confident learner and ultimately an adult educator.

While Jeff's story highlights many phases of transformational learning, these phases are widely debated and, indeed, Mezirow's psychocritical orientation to transformative learning theory shares many of the same critiques associated with the other adult learning theories we have explored: it is highly individualistic, focusing on individual change; it emphasizes a cognitive process of changing thinking; and the goal is autonomous thought, free from the influences of others. In addition, learning activities focus on analytical discussion and probing rational assumptions, and outcomes are expected to be progress- and growth-oriented (Lange, 2013, p. 109). However, recent developments in transformative learning theory have moved beyond Mezirow's approach. Taylor (2008) indicated that, beyond the initial psychocritical perspective on transformative learning, there are six additional theoretical perspectives emerging (pp. 7–11). Below, we briefly highlight the key components of each one, including the psychoanalytic approach:

The psychoanalytic view refers to the process of individuation, which is a lifelong journey of coming to understand one's self by reflecting on our psychic structures. The focus is on the individual.

The psychodevelopment view looks at transformative learning across a lifetime, focusing on continuous and gradual change and growth. In this view the focus is also on the individual.

The social-emancipatory view moves away from an individual-perspective change to social change. The gaze of individuals turns outward to reflect and act in order to transform the world so it can become a more equitable place for all to live.

The cultural-spiritual view probes the rational analytical approach to the learning process and emphasizes culturally and spiritually relevant approaches to learning. Storytelling, cross-cultural relationships, and developing spiritual awareness are fostered in this approach.

The race-centric view offers a non-Eurocentric view of transformative learning, in which the focus is on race and sociopolitical dimensions of learning. Key to this approach is the promotion of inclusion, empowerment, and learning, negotiated effectively across and between cultures.

The planetary view moves well beyond the individual and fundamentally recognizes the interconnectedness among all aspects of our world: each other, the natural environment, the planet, and the universe. The transformative learning process not only includes how we relate to each other, but it challenges us to consider how we, as humans, relate with the physical world.

(see Taylor, 2008, p. 7–11)

These recent views of transformative learning parallel the widening circle of disciplines that infuse and inform both traditional theories of learning and those residing in adult learning. We have embraced the fields of psychology, sociology, cultural studies, feminist studies, and ecological studies—to name a few—to deepen our understanding of how we learn. We now realize that transformative learning is a multi-faceted endeavour that has moved well beyond the psychoanalytic approach.

## Concluding Comments

In this chapter we explored what we refer to as the big four adult learning theories: andragogy, self-directed learning, experiential learning, and transformative learning. As indicated at the onset, while there are numerous theories of adult learning, we chose these four as we believe they reflect the evolution of our understanding of adult learning over the past 40 years. If you remember, part of the agenda in the earlier research on adult learning theories was to develop a distinct area of research and scholarship in adult education, separating the field from research focused on learning located within the kindergarten to grade 12 school system. Of course, we now realize that this agenda was too simplistic, as it is impossible to tease out absolute and distinct approaches to adult learning.

What has become apparent over the past four decades is that experience and awareness of and reflection on these experiences are constants in adult learning processes. We also understand that learning through experience is a multi-faceted endeavour. Learning no longer resides with autonomous and isolated individual learners who systemically reflect in a linear fashion on those experiences. Rather, the evolution of adult learning theories recognizes that we are learners embedded in a complexity of relationships with ourselves, with each other, with a particular sociocultural context, and with the planet. In turn, we are also realizing that learning is not just a cognitive process; we are engaged through our emotions, through our bodies, and through our souls. We also recognize that music, dance, and art play a critically important role in how we learn. In this next chapter, we explore these "other ways" of learning, revisiting how they deepen our understanding of experiential learning and transformative learning processes.

# CHAPTER 8

# Other Theories of
# Adult Learning

## LAUREL

 I recognize that my visual art practice stems from what Umberto Eco (1989) referred to as open questions. In my most recent body of art, I was inspired by the question, "What is the right red?" I started exploring this as a continuation of my abstract painting practice. However, my search led in unexpected directions. I began collecting books with the word red in the title. I then considered what our world might be without red and designed a model rocket prototype to ship all red objects in the world to Mars. The rocket inspired me to make other works, including an artist book of rocket fonts, souvenir lapel pins for viewers to take off the gallery wall, and a rocket launch performance. The material changes caused by my viewing red in several ways transformed the focus of my painting practice.

Butler-Kisber (2010) called this approach arts-informed inquiry. Arts-informed inquiry recognizes that learning may be led or informed by artistic research. In my example, the reflection upon my art practice, research about Mars, and investigations regarding the colour red sustained ongoing modifications of my original research question regarding the right red. As an artist and scholar, I wanted to remain open to these changes to allow my artistic practice to continue its evolution. In other words, from a learning perspective, art presents opportunities to engage emerging questions that often produce unpredictable results.

Early on, I didn't have the language to describe my continual interest in learning and taking classes, and it was only later, after identifying myself as a professional visual artist, that I came across terminology that caused me to also identify as an adult learner. Adult learning helps me to define my artistic activities as being educative. Adult learning refers to lifelong learning practice (Lindeman, 1961) that positions learning as an evolving creative process. When art is considered through the lens of adult learning, artistic creations can be perceived as evidence of learning and potential inspiration for new questions to emerge. As I consider the dynamic perspectives of artist and adult learner, I see that both reflect a shared love of inquiry and critical reflexivity. This inspires and sustains my learning within and beyond my artistic career. The impetus for learning, like my art praxis, is to expose and launch questions that lead to new possibilities that I cannot foresee.

We all have unique viewpoints and art invites us to contribute our insights to our collective cultural knowledge. As Nishida Kitaro, founder of the Kyoto School, said to his students, "Each of us is one of the focal points for the world's creative self-awareness. In giving birth to an infinite number of such focal points of self-awareness, the world reflects itself through them and becomes creative in the process" (Nishitani, 1991, p. xvii). Adult learning invites us to appreciate that learning is acquired through many lenses. Art provides spaces in which dynamic learning processes can occur for artists and viewers.

—Laurel Smith, PhD, Adult Educator, Contemporary Minimal Artist

## Introduction

Virginia Griffin (2001), in her article on holistic learning, used the metaphor "playing a one-string guitar" to tell us learning that only relies on our rational individual mind would quickly become monotonous. And yet for many of us, this is what we think learning is. By extending her metaphor, we are reminded that is it only by playing all six or twelve strings on a guitar that we are able to play beautiful and complex music. And so it is with learning; only by drawing on other capabilities that we hold as learners are we able to make "limitless music in our learning and can then go on to help our students do the same" (Griffin, 2001, p. 108). For example, turning to the narrative of learning just offered to us by Laurel, she eloquently articulated the power of art as a rich source of adult learning. Within this chapter, we explore the other strings on the guitar to create a more holistic understanding of adult learning theories. As we explore these other theories of adult learning, we invite you to explore your own learning processes. What does the learning process feel like when you learn through your body, through artistic expression, by attending to your emotions and imagination, by going deeper to draw on spiritual ways of being, or through insights developed through relationships? Finally, reflecting on the one-string guitar metaphor, it is critical to draw on other ways of knowing in cultures located beyond Western perspectives. Indigenous ways of knowing and being in the world are a powerful example of leaning into perspectives and epistemologies that reside *beyond* the Western, Eurocentric paradigm. By adding to the strings of the guitar, we recognize and value *other ways of knowing and being* in the world.

## The Body and Learning

Probably the type of learning we most associate with the body is *kinesthetic learning*, in which we learn to "do something." We learn how to ski, we learn to swim, we learn how to frame a house, we learn to chop garlic; all these examples require our bodies to learn how to move in specific ways in order to engage in a task. The body is actually doing the learning. However, there is much more to notion of the body and learning. For example, when Janet attended a yoga retreat, she began to really look forward to the part of the class when the instructor offered a guided meditation in which the class focused on different parts of the body: "place your focus on the toes of your left foot; now wiggle them. Okay, move your focus up your leg to your knee ..." What she was experiencing was an example of *somatic learning*; learning that occurs through purposeful bodily experiences like yoga, dance, and tai chi (Freiler, 2008).

The focus of learning is actually on the body itself—bodily awareness and sensations experienced during a purposeful learning event. Returning to Janet's experience in yoga, she became very aware of her body and what it was telling her. She felt her tight shoulders, as a manifestation of stress, and in turn, she realized how important it was to drop her shoulders when anxious and also to roll her shoulders throughout the day, particularly when she was working at her computer for long stretches.

Two other terms—also under the umbrella of the body and learning—*embodiment* and *embodied learning*, refer to "a broader, more holistic view of constructing knowledge that engages the body as a site of learning, usually in connection with other domains of knowing," (Freiler, 2008, p. 39) such as spirituality, and symbolic and cultural learning. While this definition may sound complex, embodied learning is something that many of us live with every day when we have a "gut feeling." We can walk into a room of people and feel tension in the air. Or we can have the sense that we shouldn't trust what is being said or, conversely, we can have an instinctive or intuitive feeling regarding the next step we should take. Our bodies are telling us something in the moment, and then the rest of ourselves catch up. Our question to you is, "What do you do with this gut instinct?" Do you pay attention to what is going on in your body as an important site of learning or do you dismiss it as not being valid? The notion of embodied learning or embodiment is only recently being acknowledged as a significant site and source of knowledge and learning. As Clark (2005) pointed out, Western culture has a complicated and conflicted relationship with the body, with a dominant focus on objectifying it in order to fit a predefined notion of beauty. As a result, many of us have become increasingly uncomfortable with our bodies, living and learning within our heads. However, Berman (1981) reminded us that during the Middle Ages, before the time of Enlightenment, learning was more holistic and people saw themselves and their bodies as being deeply connected to nature. Turning to the present, we can also point to many existing cultures, including Indigenous cultures, that value the body as a site of authentic learning, something we will explore later on in the chapter.

Relating the body and learning to broader educational theories, we see that tacit knowledge actually begins with the body. Polanyi (1969) suggested, "Every time we make sense of the world, we rely on our tacit knowledge of impacts made by the world on our body and complex responses of our body to these impacts" (pp. 147–148). Turning to experiential learning theory, Fenwick (2003) cautioned we are too quick to set aside the actual embodied experience in the learning process, placing too much emphasis on the reflective process that occurs after the embedded physical experience in which the complexity of sociocultural conditions actually produce the knowledge. According to Michelson (1998), the reflective processes are "the moment in which [our] mental processes caught up with what [the] body already knew" (p. 212). Finally, numerous connections have been made between embodiment or embodied learning, experiential learning, transformative learning, and women's learning.

We now turn to another string of learning, one that is beginning to be acknowledged as playing a critical role in our processes of learning: our emotions. It is often by paying attention to embodiment and embodied learning that we access our emotions. The tightening of the shoulders or the jaw can signal a state of stress or anxiety; the smile we can't wipe off our face represents the absolute joy we are feeling.

## Emotions and Learning

When our newly admitted graduate students arrive on campus for their orientation, they typically experience a wide range of emotions, moving from anxiety, to excitement, to fear, and to uncertainty throughout the day. Deeper into the term, one of these students might express total frustration with his team as he works toward meeting the deadline for a group project. Another graduate student may feel absolutely out of her element and begin to panic as she feels little affinity for the courses she is taking that term. Finally, there is the graduate student who has just passed his candidacy, and feelings of relief, euphoria, and accomplishment wash over him. These are all examples of conversations both of us have had with our graduate students, representing the deeply inter-twined nature of learning and emotions. While we may talk about the "content" of our graduate students' courses and their thesis work, it is not possible to separate emotions from these conversations; nor should we try. Emotions, like embodiment, are an integral part of the process of learning and their inclusion allows us to learn in more holistic ways. John Dirkx (2008), a scholar engaged in research on the centrality of emotions in adult learning, pointed out that we have begun to have a more holistic idea of learning that recognizes the positive and important role emotions have in our lives and in our learning. Turning to the work of Solomon (2007), he suggested, "We live our lives through emotions and it is our emotions that give our lives meaning" (p. 1).

As we consider how emotion is manifested in adult learning, Dirkx (2008) indicated learners experience a range of emotions from positive and energizing to negative and distracting. For all of us, these feelings can arise almost unconsciously from within ourselves, from the actual dynamics within the learning environment itself or due to a struggle with personal issues at home and/or at work. Taking a longer view, "learning-related emotions among individuals often reflect a history of emotional experiences or trauma … being humiliated by certain teach-ers … or experiencing physical, sexual or emotional abuse by persons in authority" (p. 9); potentially resulting in an avoidance of learning or *non-learning*, a concept we explored previously, in chapter 2. Both Dirkx (2008) and Griffin (2001) pointed out emotions are always close to the surface in adult learning situations, and helping ourselves as learners and as instructors make sense of emotion-laden experiences within a learning situation is probably one of the most important and challenging tasks for adult educators to incorporate into their practice.

Looking specifically at emotions typically labelled as "negative"—frustration, fear, guilt, hurt, rejection, confusion, and anger—Griffin (2001) believed they could block learning if we, as learners and instruc-tors, don't recognize and address them. For example, Janet's challenge is working through conflict, both personally and as an instructor. But avoiding conflict doesn't help anybody and confronting the difficulty of addressing conflict offers a significant learning opportunity for her. Important to our learning process is recognizing, naming, and accepting our negative emotions, especially since they can lead us to important learning and change. In particular, "chief among negative emotions in adult learning is one often labeled as resistance to accepting new ideas or change" (Griffin, 2001, p. 111). Learners can be fearful of the unknown consequences of their learning, and it is the role of the instructor to encourage learners to be actively engaged in their own learning and to reassure learners that they, themselves, are the ones who decide how to move forward.

We also experience a myriad of positive emotions when we learn, cueing us to those learning experiences that have personal meaning for us. Colleen experiences a deep sense of calm, quiet, and connectedness when playing with colour to design a new quilt creation. Janet is energized when challenged to learn a new piece of music for her choir. In addition, positive emotions are the reward we give ourselves when we are moving toward a desired goal and when we have accomplished something that required significant learning. "When we feel the high of accomplishment, we should reflect on what enabled it to happen, what we've learned about ourselves in the process, and how we like to learn" (Griffin, 2001, p. 11).

Turning to the adult learning theories of experiential learning and transformative learning, scholars (Boud & Miller, 1996; Beard & Wilson, 2002) recognized the centrality of emotions in these learning situations, emphasizing the importance of acknowledging and working through feelings arising during and after experiences, and the ongoing change process. In summary, the central message we derive from emotions and learning is that the full range of feelings we experience are part of the learning process, including those that are uncomfortable. In turn then, we should not push those emotions down but, as in embodied learning, recognize them as a valuable source of knowledge about the process of learning and about ourselves.

## Spirituality and Learning

Much like embodied learning and emotions and learning, spirituality and learning reminds us to draw the circle wider still to incorporate multi-faceted ways of being and knowing in the world. Even though research into understanding spirituality and adult learning has only really begun to emerge in the past few decades, we can go back to 1925 and Basil Yeaxlee, an adult educator, who argued that "education cannot escape the universal, the metaphysical dimension to the quality and meaning of life … on this point he further argued that adult education could be envisaged as a spiritual activity" (Cross-Durant, 1984, p. 283). We can also see glimmers of an emerging recognition of the importance of spirituality and adult learning in the earlier work of Dirkx (1997), where he stated that transformative learning is not only about the recognition of the emotional process, but it requires us to go deeper and delve into spiritual and soulful dimensions of learning. "Our journey of self-knowledge also requires that we care for and nurture the presence of the soul dimension in teaching and learning … learning through soul fosters self-knowledge through symbolic, imagistic and contemplative means" (Dirkx, 1997, pp. 80–83). In order to illuminate this powerful statement, we turn to Monty Smith, a former principal who had taken a graduate course at the University of Calgary entitled Spirituality and Emotional Leadership. In the following quotation he tells us why the soul dimension in teaching and learning is so important in his professional practice.

 I think we need that [spirituality] as a counterbalance to a world that is getting more and more consumer-oriented, more materialistic, more technological, and more complex. We need that counterweight on the other side to ground us in who we are and to help us navigate through that. To make it more specific, our work as educators is also getting to be more and more complex; there are more demands on us. For our own sanity, peace of mind, and relationships with our loved ones, our students, and our colleagues we need to also find some oasis of peace within us.

—Monty Smith, MEd, Retired Educator

Janet (Groen, 2012) has been exploring spirituality and adult learning within a variety of contexts including the workplace and higher education. Through her research she aligns herself with Tisdell (2003), who argued that this type of learning does not need to be not associated with a religious upbringing or orientation. Typically, spirituality and learning is about being aware and honouring the wholeness and interconnectedness of all things; it is about seeking a sense of purpose and ultimately making meaning in one's life; it is always present in the learning environment; it values the construction of knowledge through symbolic processes; and it is about action and an outward response that challenges inequities, works toward social justice, and asks difficult and uncomfortable questions.

While we are seeing spirituality as being an increasingly important aspect of adult learning, it is important to be aware of approaches that can help us nurture this quality within our own learning journey and to support this aspect of learning as an instructor. Meditation and contemplation, journaling, storytelling, and bodywork through a practice such as yoga are both individual pathways to cultivate spirituality and potential approaches for incorporating spiritual dimensions within a more formal classroom setting. For example, even though Janet has had the good fortune to teach a course explicitly focusing on spirituality and adult learning, she has not relegated "spiritual activities" to these courses. Like Miller (2012), she has introduced a meditation practice into her teacher preparation courses and her graduate courses. In addition, she has taken up Tisdell's (2003) suggestion to incorporate the symbolic domain into her classroom work. "Participants might bring a symbol or create or share an art piece, a poem, a drama, or music that encapsulates their learning ... creating learning experiences that are more holistic might be experienced, as ... the spiritual for some"(p. 214). We now refer to Shauna Butterwick, an adult education professor at the University of British Columbia. In her vivid description of symbolic learning activities in her graduate classes, she demonstrates the power of tapping into holistic ways of learning and how they open up the possibility of spiritual learning for some of her students.

A student comes to the front of the class and assumes the role of artist/sculptor by moving my head, arms, feet, mouth, and eyebrows, creating an image illustrating her response to an assigned reading; another student follows her and moves me into a different image. A rich discussion follows illuminating the diversity of students' understanding and response to the readings. In another course on adult learning theory, students are invited to use fabric of various colours and textures to create images. One group wraps yards of fabric atop one student's head, who walks carefully and slowly to ensure the fabric stays in place, illustrating the idea of banking education. Another group drapes different coloured fabrics loosely on one of their group members, which ripple and shift as she walks around the room, illustrating that group's notion of transformative learning. As with the first example, there is full participation in the discussion. Students who have been reluctant to participate are eagerly sharing their views. These are examples of using creative expression in my teaching. These aesthetic approaches bring the heart, mind, spirit, and body to the learning process, enabling a more holistic approach and a more inclusive learning environment. The arts tap also into our imagination and subconscious knowledge.

—Dr. Shauna Butterwick, Associate Professor,
University of British Columbia

## Relationships and Learning

An ongoing theme in this chapter and throughout this book is that our experiences are located at the centre of our learning and that we, as adult learners, are *not* autonomous and isolated individuals. As we each live out our ongoing and shifting narrative in a particular time, place, and space in history *and* within a particular social and cultural context, this all occurs within a web of relationships. Transferring this idea to relational adult learning, we believe that when we learn we are engaged in multiple and simultaneous relationships: with our ongoing narratives within ourselves, with other learners, with our instructors, with the ideas and concepts being explored, and with the larger community, including the natural environment.

According to Rossiter (2005), the origins of relational learning come from the relationship philosophy of Martin Buber (1970). Buber believed we enter into two types of relationships with the world: I-It and I-You (or I-Thou). In the I-It orientation, we relate to people, knowledge, and the world as an object, and we remain apart. In contrast, I-You moves away from being separate, into full relationship. Returning to one of the core qualities of spirituality and adult learning—interconnection with each other and the world around us—we would argue a rich and satisfying life is only possible through I-You relationships. When this fundamental need to be interconnected and in relationship with others is not present, Palmer (2002) believed the ensuing isolation we experience is dangerous, even toxic. In making this case, he pointed out a faculty member within his university who had recently quit her job because it was so lonely. Conversely, when he developed a series of seminars in his newly created teaching and learning centre, he created spaces where faculty could relate to each other about their experiences. "Above all, they wanted to connect, and teaching was what they all had in common ... [it] was a chance to interact with colleagues from other departments which created a sense of belonging to the university community" (p. 205).

Rossiter (2005) posited that relational learning has been implied, if not specified, in much of adult teaching and learning. Relational learning, often associated with feminist theory and women's ways of learning and knowing, refers to connected knowing—to self in relationship and to empowerment (Belenky, Clinchy, Goldberger, & Tarule, 1986). As women, our ways of knowing are also deeply impacted by our positionality—to our cultural, socioeconomic, family structure, ability, and sexual orientation (Tisdell, 1995). All of these positionality factors and influences impact and shape who we are, what our roles and responsibilities are, how we respond, and how we are responded to in the world. Positionality factors and influences are intimately interconnected with the formation of our identity as women and to how we interpret and make meaning of our experiences.

Having recognized the centrality of relationships within learning, we also recognize the nuances and challenges of this within adult learning situations. As Griffin (2001) rightly indicated, part of any learning situation should also involve time spent in relationship with "self" in silent reflection. "There are times ... when people need to talk to others to explore their feelings and ideas, and times when they need silence to centre themselves, to knit together their thoughts, and reflect on personal meanings in the experience" (p. 114). She called this the "rhythmic pulsations in learning with others" (p. 114). Finally, we also need to acknowledge that power dynamics and potential disharmony are embedded within relational learning. We should not assume it is all smooth sailing. As we have already realized in the section on emotions and learning, learning in relationship raises the spectre of interpersonal conflicts and power struggles.

Having acknowledged the challenges, we can engage in or facilitate intentional processes, both formally and informally, to navigate the challenges and deepen the benefits derived from relational learning. Our discussion on dialogue in chapter 1 identified dialogue as a powerful pathway to seek a deepened understanding and appreciation of another's perspective and interpretation of experiences. We also suggested dialogue is *not* the same as conversation. In the latter, people come together with a particular point of view or agenda. Conversation often involves a quid pro quo, an exchange of information. It is often the hope that through clear communication, we will convince, persuade, or nudge the other to adopt our point of view. Dialogue, on the other hand, requires a letting go of tightly held agendas in order to enter a space with an authentic willingness and desire to view and understand a situation, tension, event, or topic through the eyes and interpretation of another. There is no place for hierarchy or power differentials in dialogue (Bohm, 1998). In fact, when there is an imbalance of power amongst those participating in a dialogue, the open expression and exchange of participants' thoughts and feelings will be significantly hindered and inhibited (Bohm, Factor, & Garrett, 1998). In an online class that Colleen recently facilitated, the power of dialogue was made evident when attempting to support and guide a group of adult learners who were experiencing extreme tension and conflict when working through a small-group assignment.

The course seemed to be going well. Participants were engaged, actively posting online, and were working hard to prepare a small-group assignment that involved developing a presentation on a particular topic and then facilitating an online discussion in the large-group forum. I then received an email from one of the small-group members indicating there was great conflict mounting in the small group and that any attempt she had made to work through the tensions with her peers only appeared to trigger more resistance and conflict. In short, the small group had "fallen apart" with little chance of achieving the assignment goals. Shortly thereafter, I received an email from one of the other group members saying the very same thing. What was interesting was that each of these individuals believed that they were doing all that was humanly possible to resolve the tensions. I was then invited to review the email exchange that had taken place between them and asked to help "sort out" what had transpired and to provide guidance and direction as to "next steps."

As the course instructor/facilitator, I needed to resist my tendency to rush in to "fix" the problem. When presented with this type of situation, it is human nature to want to take control and provide clear direction as to what is needed to accomplish the task at hand. Instead, through a deluge of back and forth emails, I gained the commitment of each group member to set their personal agendas (the direction they each maintained their presentation should take) aside, and encouraged them to take each person's idea and to only discuss the value and benefits of that particular perspective. Then, they continued with this same process until each small-group member had been "heard." Indeed, this was a challenge for all involved. It required that they take up "the dance" in step with the "other," rather than trying to persuade one another to dance to the rhythm that they felt was best. In doing this, new insights and appreciations were gained. The end result was that they decided, as a small group, that they would still present their different points of view when designing their small-group presentation for the large group. This would ultimately read, however, as different perspectives versus three different presentations. They then came together to formulate some cohesive discussion questions/activities that would invite engagement of the larger group. It was also decided that there was value in sharing the tensions they experienced while designing their presentation with the large group, as there was great potential for learning here.

This type of relational learning emerged and evolved on many different levels. Small-group participants continued to hold the power of designing their presentation; Colleen did not step in as instructor/facilitator to fix the problem. Small-group members reflected on how tightly they were each holding on to their personal agendas, and insights were gained pertaining to fear of failure, fear of being perceived as inadequate, and fear of having no voice. It is also important to note gender and cultural differences play a role in the tensions that emerged in this small group. A dominant male voice left a young woman feeling it would be disrespectful to challenge; she grew up in a culture where elders and men held more power and privilege than women.

Relational learning takes many shapes and forms and is expressed or suppressed in a number of different ways. When we recognize our learning narratives are connected to significant moments and others we have experienced along the way, and to moments we have yet to experience, we need not feel that learning is an isolated activity or event, one that we need to handle, control, or navigate alone.

Finally, as we close this section on relational learning, we also note its presence in key theories of adult learning. In both transformative learning and experiential learning, a central process in understanding experiences and working toward change is in engaging in reflective dialogue with others. Even in self-directed learning, we are reminded that Tough recognized that this process of learning did not entail working in isolation from others; in contrast the majority of chosen learning approaches involved engagement with others.

## Aesthetics and Learning

Quiet settles in the room as Janet's students each create a collage to introduce themselves to their classmates. While there is some initial hesitancy in picking up the glue sticks, scissors, pencil crayons, magazines, and construction paper, eventually a contented energy fills the room. As students reflect on this experience, they often express surprise at how much they enjoyed it. Some students will also tell Janet and other classmates that since they do not think of themselves as artistic or creative, they haven't created art since they were in elementary school. We have already seen, through Laurel's narrative at the beginning of this chapter and Shauna's example of aesthetically based learning, multiple forms of art such as painting, drama, and music allow us to delve into learning and knowledge that otherwise may not be accessible. "Art not only engages us at an intellectual level; it evokes feelings, intuitions and even bodily sensations. Paying attention to these modes of experiencing can result in a deeper knowledge" (Lawrence, 2005, p. 7)

Darlene Clover and Shauna Butterwick (2013) are passionate about the power of arts-based activities, not only for individual learning and development, but also as a pathway for social commentary and protest. Turning to an example of arts-based activities within her classroom, Shauna also described the creation of collages, in this case to describe an understanding of community as a space of rich learning. An incredible diversity of images emerged and, as the learners presented their collages, stories of hope, connection, pain, and exclusion breathed life into the idea of community. "This was serious play, playful seriousness. The creative expression created a space for sharing experiences and respectful listening. Students indicated that this process tapped into long-held stories and experiences that they had not thought about for some time" (Clover & Butterwick, 2013, p. 74).

Darlene (Clover & Butterwick, 2013), in the same article, explored three pathways to arts-based teaching and learning within her classroom. Her first approach provides creative space for students to reflect on assigned readings. While typed reflective journals are acceptable, poetry, wood-working, rug and quilt making, and painting are just a few examples of mediums that have been used. Her second approach moves beyond individual responses in order to address her wariness "of reinforcing academic and aesthetic theory that prioritizes individualized learning and art-making" (Clover & Butterwick, 2013, p. 74). Students present their findings from small-group discussions on power, social movements, and citizenship using poetry, skits, or songs. She argued that the use of art to communicate complicated theory humanizes these ideas and students "truly grasp and retain the power and complexity of the ideas they perform or re-visualise" (Clover & Butterwick, 2013, p. 74). Finally, Darlene draws on community artists to push her students and herself to not only deepen their understanding of a particular issue but to extend their technical artistic ability; they deepen their ability to paint, to take photographs, to write poetry, or to quilt when they are guided by an expert.

Laurel, Darlene, and Shauna are such important mentors for us all in encouraging growth in the arts, both as learners and as instructors. While our daily lives are infused with images, music, dance, and drama, we often view these as forms of entertainment that can only be created by the "experts." Rarely do we see ourselves within the actual process of creation; not only can we critically engage in what is offered to us, we can also create images, music, dance, and drama ourselves. Arts-based activities connect us with our minds, our souls, our bodies, and our emotions. In addition, they offer a powerful entryway into experiential learning, providing an alternative and powerful concrete experience that in turn bridges into reflection and response. "They interrupt the ingrained power/knowledge discourse—the Kantina mind over body dynamic ... —and help students to ground theory and concepts in relation to their own lived experience" (Clover & Butterwick, 2013, p. 77).

At the beginning of the chapter we used the metaphor of guitar strings to remind you the process of learning is a holistic endeavour. We explored five additional "strings" of learning: the body and learning, emotions and learning, spirituality and learning, relationships and learning, and aesthetics and learning. We now widen our exploration beyond the instrument we used for this metaphor—the guitar—to consider multiple instruments of learning: learning within cultures located outside Western perspectives.

## Other Ways of Being and Learning

> How might your life have been different if, once, as a young girl ... when you wandered alone in the woodlands not far from your mother's house ... you had come upon a small glade you had never seen before? If, as you listened to the wind blow mysteriously ... you had seen, there in the shadows, a circle of rough-hewn stones? And, as soon as you saw the stones, you sensed the wisdom waiting there ... knew that this was a place where women had gathered throughout the ages to reflect upon their lives. And you sat down quietly on one of the stones ... as if the stones, themselves, would teach you what you needed to know. How might your life be different? (Duerk, 1993)

Others ways of being and learning refer to other ways of knowing—to alternative knowledge acquisition traditions that are often referred to but *not* fully integrated into the learning literature. Alternative ways of knowing are also often informed by and connected to spirituality and learning. In the words of Vogel (2000)

> When [we] invite learners to journey toward wholeness by entering into a "spirited epistemology" that seeks a more just and

compassionate way of being in the world, horizons are expanded and all are invited to share in the benefits of that work. (p. 26)

We take up Vogel's invitation to practise in whatever work and learning context we are in, by bringing our "whole person" to the process, as by doing this, "[we] reckon with [our] own spirituality [and this] becomes an act of caring" (2000, p. 26).

Others ways of knowing recognize a connectedness to something beyond "self" and encourage "moving away from the focus on the individual self towards the collective [and to] explore more deeply in another direction" (Bratton, Mills, Pyrch, & Sawchuk, 2004, pp. 149–150). *Beyond self* and *another direction* have deep implications for how we view the world, and locate ourselves in and respond to the world, regarding communities that we are more intimately connected with—family, social networks, and our work, learning, and professional communities. This invitation also calls us—as thoughtful citizens—to be aware of, participate in, and contribute to issues, initiatives, and discourses that present and unfold beyond our immediate communities; a beyond*ness* that unfolds nationally and globally. To extend ourselves in this way, then, becomes testimony to our recognition that we are all connected and to a deepened appreciation and understanding that learning, knowledge construction, and knowledge sharing takes place and unfolds in ways that may not always align to what we think we know and to what we have become accustomed to. To extend beyond self and to explore in another direction invites and supports a more expanded and deepened world view. Olsen, Lodwick, and Dunlap described world views as mental lenses, "cognitive, perceptual, and affective maps that people continuously use to make sense of the social landscape and to find their ways to whatever goals they seek" (Hart, 2010, p. 2). Olsen, Lodwick, and Dunlap (1992) referred to the importance of recognizing that our particular world view is shaped and formed within a particular social and societal context and that, consequently, the individuals who espouse the dominant mindset and perspective are typically held up by the majority in that society. Indeed, although diversity is represented within any given society, due to the "encompassing and pervasive ... adherence and influence [of the majority] ... they are usually unconsciously and uncritically taken for granted as the way things are" (Hart, 2010, p. 2).

Indigenous epistemology and perspectives are a powerful example of "exploring more deeply" in another direction, in recognition of other ways of knowing, being, and doing. While recognizing diverse perspectives, practices, norms, and traditions within and across Indigenous communities, cultures, and societies, there is much common ground that unites Indigenous world views (Rice, 2005). A common connection uniting Indigenous communities and groups is that Indigenous knowledge is personal, shared in the oral tradition, experientially based, holistic, and often expressed metaphorically (Castellano, 2000). Sefa Dei, Hall, and Goldin Rosenberg (2000) defined Indigenous knowledge as knowledge that referred to

> traditional norms and social values, as well as to mental constructs that guide, organize, and regulate the people's way of living and making sense of their world. It is the sum of the experience and knowledge of a given social group that forms the basis of decision making in the face of challenges both familiar and unfamiliar. (p. 6)

Encompassing cultural traditions, values, belief systems, and world views, knowledge was traditionally imparted to the community by the Elders in Indigenous communities. Indigenous knowledge is relational in that it "is not learned in formal education settings [or] in isolation from the Earth or from other people" (Sefa Dei, Hall, & Goldin Rosenberg, 2000, p. 7). When referring to the communicative norms that guided and governed Indigenous people, Ross (1992) noted the importance of learning through listening, and that there was great potential for learning by listening to stories. This supposed an authentic openness to the richness of relationship and experience that was embedded deep within the stories. In the wise and insightful words of Yvonne Poitras Pratt, our colleague and Métis scholar, "Within each person lies a story that has the power to change their lives and, if shared, the potential to transform the world of others. As life reveals, some stories call out to us, some stories lay hidden in the recesses, and still others overtake all else—it is this living quality of stories that makes them such a potent tool of transformation and of domination" (2011, p. 1). Poitras Pratt went on to say, "As humans, we hunger for storytelling in all its forms. Stories link us to our humanity—they bring us joy, tears, laughter, surprise, and every other imaginable human emotion" (2011, p. 35). Our individual stories connect us to the larger narrative of relationships, communities, and societies where we live, work, and learn, and carry the potential to bring meaning to our lives.

Storytelling always has and continues to play an important role in knowledge sharing and knowledge transfer within Indigenous communities:

> The role of storytelling has been, and remains, a powerful and primary means of knowledge transfer. While vestiges of the oral tradition remain in most Aboriginal communities, especially amongst the older residents, it is important to acknowledge that these important cultural traditions, including that of storytelling, were severely disrupted as a direct result of colonizing tactics (Adams, 1975; Barkwell & Chartrand, 1989; Bourgeault, 1982; Campbell, 1973; Dickason, 1997; Frideres, 1998; LaRocque, 1975; Royal Commission on Aboriginal Peoples, 1993). This disruption has meant that many people today "hunger" for knowledge of their roots and their cultural legacies (Woodard, 1989, p. 4). (Poitras Pratt, 2011, p. 178)

Drawing further from her doctoral dissertation (2011) titled *Meaningful Media: An Ethnography of a Digital Strategy Within a Métis Community*,[1] Poitras Pratt connected self-narrative—knowing oneself—to functioning within her own Aboriginal identity. Although a direct reference from

Yvonne's good work, we have received her permission to offer the following excerpt as a voice from the field:

 As a Métis scholar who is instinctively drawn to 'give back' to my community of origin, I am reminded time and again that a "person must first know him- or herself and his or her family line, tribal nation and responsibilities to all relations if he or she is to function within an Aboriginal identity" (Graveline, 1998; McCaskill, 1987). To operate within an Aboriginal world view and to assert an Aboriginal identity means that we must also act according to a framework of values which inform how we view life, the natural world and our place within the world (Graveline, 1998, p. 57). Our interconnectedness and interrelatedness reinforces the fact that we are personally accountable for the welfare of others, where achieving our full humanity is perceived as a collective responsibility rather than an individual undertaking. This value system emerges in the narrative framework that the Fishing Lake digital stories are premised on—a personal responsibility to collective survival requires the ability to adapt—yet is balanced with an individual responsibility to adapt to changing life circumstances. Thus, my story follows the path of all my relations. (Poitras Pratt, 2011, p. 206)

Yvonne's reflections are a powerful reminder that our individual narratives are *not* so individual at all. Rather, they are intimately interconnected with the storied lives of those who have come before us and to the unwritten stories we have yet to experience, individually and collectively.

## Concluding Comments

Our goal, in this chapter, was to remind you that ways of learning involve so much more than the intellect. If we pay attention and listen, our bodies, our emotions, our spirit, the arts, and our relationships all offer incredible and multi-faceted approaches to our learning. In addition, we are reminded by the example offered through Indigenous epistemology and perspectives that how we are located within the world profoundly informs our pathways of learning.

Now, as we complete our exploration of how we learn—from traditional theories of learning, to the big four theories of adult learning, and finally other theories of adult learning—we return to the question we asked at the outset of chapter 6: "What did you learn today?" and we hope that your response reflects the complexity of possibilities we have unpacked in these three chapters. It isn't a neat and tidy event that has a beginning, middle, and end; rather, learning is woven through the tapestry of our stories that are located in a particular place and time.

## Endnote

1  Yvonne Poitras Pratt's doctoral dissertation (2011) titled *Meaningful Media: An Ethnography of a Digital Strategy Within a Métis Community* "is an ethnographic exploration of a collaborative and community-centred research project involving the researcher and the community of Fishing Lake Métis settlement situated in north-eastern Alberta. This study represents a digital strategy that sought decolonizing goals through Métis-specific research activities, community partnering and the culturally appropriate and meaningful appropriation of digital media. The project met several identified community needs, including the restoration of intergenerational connections and the revitalization of storytelling traditions, through a creative process realized through a collaboratively-led digital-storytelling workshop and related media activities. Fittingly, the work continues on in Fishing Lake." (Dissertation abstract)

# PART IV

## Contexts and Praxis: Engaging in Learning

What is a workplace? What counts as work? What and whom are valued and devalued? What is meant by professional work and learning contexts? Is there a relationship between adult learning, reflective practice, and the professional locations we are situated in?

How has technology impacted work and learning environments? What are some implications of uneven access to technology in some work, learning, and community contexts?

What are some ethical issues when considering international and global contexts of work and learning? What cultural sensitivities and competencies do we need to work and live within and across diverse cultural contexts? What is meant by *pluralized knowledge*? How do I as learner and educator (formal or informal), make a contribution to the greater good?

In part 4, our concluding theme, we revisit who we are as learners and as facilitators of learning, and how our work and learning contexts provide rich opportunities and potential in support of our learning and the learning of others.

# CHAPTER 9

# Contexts of Work and Learning

## LYNN

I have always been curious. I have always asked questions. As an undergraduate student, I have a vivid memory of being scolded by one of my professors in the third year of my Bachelor of Nursing program. The professor always spent at least part of a class reviewing the correct answers to multiple-choice questions on the exams, once they had been graded. Quite possibly I had been a bit too persistent with my rationale, lobbying the professor to see my point of view (and possibly award me another point or two) on a particular question. I cannot actually remember the topic for the exam, but I remember the exasperated tone of voice she used when she said to me, "Lynn, just answer the question!" Context was always important to me. I wanted to add details to the lives of the fictional patients in my exams who underwent a bowel resection or experienced a psychotic break. As I did this, I went beyond the black-and-white thinking that was being asked of me. It was not surprising that years later, I applied to and was accepted for a Master of Nursing program.

One month into my Master of Nursing (MN) studies, I became pregnant with my first baby. This added a layer of complexity to pursuing this degree. I would be able to complete the first year of my studies (my baby was, conveniently, due in June); but how would I manage to complete my MN with an infant? This is where I came to appreciate, as a lifelong learner, the importance of support and priorities. Our newborn son was the first priority for both my husband and me. It was decided that my husband would scale back his commitments at his place of work. We would then share the care of our son as I completed my studies.

Nearing the completion of my MN program, I felt as though my brain was a Rubik's cube. Although the same pieces of my brain were still there, the pieces were no longer in the same place and they certainly were no longer connected with anything that was familiar to me. Like a Rubik's cube, the pieces of what I thought I knew to be true had been reconfigured. I was studying the role of the public health nurse in shelters for abused women. One professor in particular, a quiet and brilliant woman, invited me to think differently as she drew her thoughts related to my topic on the page of my notebook. She made looping and squiggly connections to nursing theories and encouraged me to do the same. Context remained all-important as I considered the nurse in the shelter, not only in the context of nursing, but also within contexts of power, gender, and culture.

Years passed, another baby was born, and both of our babies grew into teenagers. I remained curious in my work life as a registered nurse. My interest in nurses at shelters expanded to a broad interest in violence against women. I had more questions and they seemed to be expanding. I wondered about nurses and exemplary screening for intimate partner violence, young adults and their understandings of healthy/unhealthy/violent intimate partner relationships, and the role of media in portraying intimate partner violence. Again, it came as no surprise when I commenced PhD studies, several years later!

Right now, it feels as though I am tap dancing in ski boots and juggling eggs. I am a mother of teenagers and a daughter of aging parents. Some refer to me as a member of the "sandwich generation;" others have called me "crazy" for being "my age" and going back to school. This is what it is like to be a lifelong learner as a mom, wife, daughter, registered nurse, and a PhD student. When I think of the order of these roles, I am certain they are accurately prioritized, in order of importance. My roles in my family come first. Without the support, understanding, and patience of my family, my lifelong learning journey may not have unfolded at all, much less in the way that I have described.

—Lynn Corcoran, Graduate Student

## Introduction

Lynn's references to context have many layers and dimensions. She speaks of *formal learning contexts*—as an undergraduate student in the Bachelor of Nursing program; of *contextual learning*—where meaning making is dependent on locating learning experiences and linkages with something that holds meaning and relevance; of *contexts of support*—counting on family members to have their hand on her back as she attempts to juggle the many priorities in her life; of *professional contexts*—as a nurse working in a shelter for abused women; and of *contexts of power, gender, and culture*—issues, factors, and other sociocultural influences that impact how we see ourselves, make sense of the world, and respond in the world. Indeed, *contexts* is a broad-brush term that spans location, dynamics, issues pertaining to learning and educative practice, sociocultural and political layers and influences, availability or lack of resources and supports, and other environmental factors and frameworks (broadly defined) in any given situation, setting, or experience.

## Situating Work and Learning

In the early 1990s, work-related learning was contextualized as work activities that occurred within formal, work-for-pay, employee/employer workplace contexts (Merriam & Clark, 1991). In the past 20-plus years, our understanding and appreciation of work and learning *and* workplace learning has shifted and expanded significantly.

Other theories of adult learning we made reference to bring our entire person, our whole self, into whatever work and learning context we are in. Where we participate and locate ourselves as "workers" and "learners" represents diverse spaces, places, purposes, and types of engagements. Griff Foley, a leading international adult educator and scholar, addressed *how* and *where* work and learning intersect in *Dimensions of Adult Learning: Adult Education and Training in a Global Era* (2004). Citing the good work of Michael Welton (1995), a Canadian historian who has written extensively on educational history and critical social theory, Foley (2004) stated, "[We] might consider differences arising from *where* something is learned, *how* it is structured, the relative *power* of participants, the identity and *life world* of learners, and the *type and degree* of incentives or coercion" (p. 172). Foley asserted that "any of these will colour the experiences of both learners and practitioners" (2004, p. 172) and that recognizing the context of *where* work and learning are situated, are located, and intersect is paramount.

Locating work and learning within contexts of agency and the social world, "Learning should enhance working people's individual and collective agency in the social world and also in the process of representing the world" (Livingstone & Sawchuk, 2004, p. 28). Fenwick (2003) took up the interplay and interconnectivity of power and knowledge and promoted the moral purpose and potential of workplace learning to "[enable] flexible, expansive, integrated persons and communities" (p. 228) by providing individuals with learning opportunities "to *participate* fully, meaningfully, fairly, and compassionately in existing systems, and to *resist* when those systems become over-controlling, harmful, or dehumanizing" (p. 228). Bruce Spencer, adult educator and scholar whose work focuses on workers' education, labour unions, and workplace union organization, adds to the discourse by addressing the lack of focus on labour education within work and learning contexts.

 Three central factors that contribute to adult educators neglecting the role of labour education are the contradictory nature of unionism; the lack of knowledge about what unions do in union education programs; and the decline of union influence in North America which masks the fact that Labour education remains the most numerous form of "non-formal adult education" available to Canadians (Spencer, 2006).

The democratic impulse, particularly at the local level, is ever present, as is the challenge to employers represented by the collective values of organized labour. Unions in Canada have retained a higher membership density generally and, in common with many unions in the USA, are building coalitions with NSMs. The dominant union philosophy in Canada since the 1980s is "social unionism," as expressed by Shirley Carr, past-president of the Canadian Labour Congress (CLC). Labour unions in Canada "have always been a very effective social movement ... we are prepared to pursue economic and social issues, and we always will" (Kumar & Ryan, 1988, p. 14). Another former CLC president, Bob White, was an advocate for the notion of linking up with other social movements—environmentalists, women's groups, aboriginal peoples, etc.—to influence the political and economic agenda (Kumar & Ryan, 1988, p. 14). Finally, labour education is much broader than mainstream union training courses might suggest.

—Dr. Bruce Spencer, Professor, Athabasca University

Conceptual lenses and theoretical underpinnings that inform our critiques and discourses around workplaces as learning environments and work-related learning processes that take shape within workplace contexts add diversity in scope, perspective, approach, and emphasis. Peter Sawchuk, from the Ontario Institute for Studies in Education (OISE) and international scholar on labour education/studies and the sociology of work, elaborated on some of the burgeoning literature generated over the past several decades:[1]

The field of workplace learning research from the final quarter of the twentieth and into the twenty-first century has demonstrated an accelerated expansion of conceptualizations, dissection, and even vivisection (by action and interventionist researchers). The multi-disciplinarity of the literature has seen a proliferation of identified skill types: from common notions of 'soft' and 'hard' skills, general education, and vocationally specific skills, literacy, communication, comprehension, multi-tasking skills, procedural and declarative knowledge, through to somewhat more theoretically robust

formulations of such things as work-related emotional skill, articu-
lation skill, relational skills, and aesthetic skill.…. Conceptualization
of work-related learning processes has expanded as well. It is now
common currency among researchers to recognize not simply individual, taught, self-directed learning, but that learning also includes
formal, non-formal, informal and tacit aspects, experiential and
incidental learning, reflective learning, legitimate peripheral participation, and learning 'activity' to name only a sampling. In turn,
debate has moved in ever-widening circles from individual cognition to include emotion, biography, identity and meaning, power
and resistance, social legitimacy and illegitimacy, and the social
constructivist roles of communities of practice, meditational processes and participatory structures at the firm, sector, national and
international levels. (2011, pp. 165–166)

These perspectives represent only a smattering of critical perspectives
and research on work and learning, workplaces, sites of learning, and
learning processes. Drawing from this rich discourse, it is abundantly
clear that work and learning are multi-faceted, multi-dimensional, and
interrelated. Spaces and places of work and learning are also relational,
political, and highly complex.

## Spaces and Places of Work and Learning

When focusing more specifically on sites of work and learning spaces
and environments, some critical questions warrant attention: *What is
a workplace? What counts as work? What and whom are valued and
validated? What do we mean by professional work and learning contexts?*
And, *what is the relationship between adult learning, reflective practice,
and the professional locations we are situated in as teachers, social workers, community workers, adult educators, human resource consultants,
business and industry personnel, vocational instructors, trainers, artists,
and so forth?* Tara Fenwick, professor of professional education at the

University of Stirling, in Scotland, cautioned against limiting workspaces and places to traditional locations:

> *Workplace* can be an organization, website, kitchen table, even a car. Work varies widely across public, private, or not-for-profit sectors, and among activities of trades workers, managers, self-employed professionals, farmers, or domestic workers. Indeed, *work* itself is a slippery category for it can be paid or unpaid, based in action or reflection, material or virtual, in or out of the home, or more often in various overlapping spaces among these categories. And just as neither workplace nor work can be referred to as generic, universal phenomena, so does learning in work take multiple forms, purposes, and qualities. (2003, p. 228)

## Unpaid Work and Learning

Colleen recalls a conversation she had with a younger sister, a few months back, that focused on providing support for their 94-year-old father who continued to live independently in the house he had built 52 years prior. Although he was in excellent health, they were concerned about his general well-being and the deepening sense of loneliness he experienced that was, in no small way, triggered by the death of their mother. Many of his friends had died several years prior and this also contributed to his loneliness. Although he tried to present a stoic posture on the outside, they both knew that he was experiencing a deepening sense of fatigue and depression in that he was no longer able to do all the things he once did with great vigour, energy, and focus. Her sister then made reference to being "the one who *did not work*" and, in light of this, would likely be the daughter to assume some of the extra care that their aging father needed. Colleen was struck by this admission as she was always in awe of the care, compassion, time, and support that her sister extended to friends, family, and many others in her local neighbourhood and community. Her sister was the local stop for stray animals that aimlessly wandered to her door. She provided after-school care for a young girl whose mother struggled financially; her sister refused to be paid for caring for this young girl. She was a constant, loving presence in the life of her mother-in-law who was dying of cancer and to other family members, whenever a need or life crisis surfaced. She regularly opened her home to host family celebrations and, in spite of her own physical limitations brought about by a serious car accident many years prior, she cleaned her father's house, continually stocked his freezer with baked goods, and spent hours helping him with his garden. Colleen reminded her sister that she did, in fact, do very important work and that all of this was no less significant because it was not validated with a paycheque or formal title. In other words, this was, in fact, real and valued work.

This story speaks to the many individuals who contribute significantly to the lives and well-being of others—to heartfelt work, motivated by love and a genuine desire to be authentically present to others. This work is neither situated in nor defined by any traditional, formal, or paid workplace context. We refer to strong, capable, engaged, and generous human beings who volunteer their time and energy, unconditionally, to individuals, to causes, and to their greater communities.

Volunteer work of individuals and non-profit organizations is multi-dimensional in that it speaks to active citizenship, contributing to and supporting the learning needs and well-being of others, engagement in communities, participatory democracy, and mobilizing for social change. Testimony to this important work is made visible in the dedication and focus of those who give their time and other resources to one-on-one programs to support relationship development with children and youth; literacy initiatives; work with new immigrants; participating in the operations of cooperatives, such as housing; environmental causes; community forums and lobby groups; and to others in the community who are left destitute after a major storm, flood, or fire. Non-profit organizations depend heavily on volunteers to offer "gifts in kind," by way of time, donations, and other resources, in support of their organization. Simply put, in light of diminishing resources, many non-profits could not survive without this.

There remains so much to be learned about volunteer cultures—from volunteers and volunteer organizations, and from the dimensions of learning associated with and in volunteer work. Duguid, Slade, and Schugurensky (2006) elaborated:

> Two factors may explain the scant attention paid in the past to this issue. First, unpaid work (such as household work and volunteer work) is seldom considered as 'real work' by policy-makers and even by large sectors of the population, and therefore the mainstream literature on labour force training tends to focus on paid labour, often within the formal sector of the economy. Second, the field of informal learning has been at the margins of educational research, partly because such learning is not formalized and hence is more difficult to research (Livingstone, 2002; Brown, 2000; Colley, Hodkinson, & Malcom, 2004; Foley, 1999; Eraut, 2000). Indeed, most studies on education and work focus on formal and non-formal education. (p. 1)

English and Mayo (2012) paid tribute to the Commission of the European Communities' publication *A Memorandum on Lifelong Learning*. This document expanded what is valued and validated as a learning context by recognizing that diverse sites of learning, education, and practice encompassed "schools, training centres, universities, museums, churches, mosques and other religious institutions, the workplace, libraries, the media, youth centres, hospitals, old people's homes and others" (p. 14). These paid and unpaid contexts of learning and teaching represent only some of the sites where we might learn or educate others.

Acknowledging that "feminist and nonprofit literatures have provided much evidence of the economic contributions of unpaid work and [that] policy-makers, researchers and the population at large are taking notice that non-market activities are important to the economy" (p. 1), Duguid, Slade, and Schugurensky (2006) noted a slow change in perspectives and attitudes expressed in the literature, by policy-makers and by society at large, as to how unpaid work is viewed, valued, and validated.

## Professional Contexts

Evans, Guile, and Harris (2011) stated that "work-based learning (WBL) is, at root, about relationships between the two fundamental human and social processes of working and learning [and that] [d]ifferent discourses about what these relationships can and should be are dominant at different times" (p. 149). For those who educate on WBL, the authors maintained that "the first challenge ... is to clarify the version and values of WBL to which they subscribe" (2011, p. 149).

Professional work and learning contexts vary in how regulatory bodies define professional development, the pre-service and in-service standards required to achieve and sustain a specific professional designation, and which types of activities are recognized as contributing to the professional learning and development of individuals within a given professional context. Learning in a professional context also "portrays the holistic nature of engagement beyond the description of a formal standard and unearths instead a transformative search by individuals for their [professional] identities" (McNally & Blake, 2010, p. xiii).

Professional development terminology varies within and across professional contexts. Knowledge, skills, abilities, competencies, performance outcomes, and capabilities are some of the terms used to describe individual professional performance. Applying a wide-angle lens, professional learning communities, communities of practice (CoPs), team learning, job learning, peer coaching, professional networks, partnership programs, work groups, and formal mentoring (to name a few) are designed to extend beyond individual professional development and focus more on group learning, group functioning, group performance, and development. Organizations and professional governing bodies refer to these initiatives as staff training, professional development, staff development, leadership development, capacity building, and building human capital.

Professional development may be shaped more formally as one-on-one engagements, online courses or course packs, workshops, seminars, conferences, symposiums, or lecture series. Delivery modes and mediums include face-to-face (f2f) delivery and virtual forums such as webinars, video chats, teleconferencing, Skype, and YouTube. An increased reliance on virtual delivery has emerged as organizations attempt to capture a broader audience, no longer defined nor determined by geographical boundaries and location. There are additional layers needing consideration when navigating the professional development landscape.

## ANNE-LIISA

 I have come to believe that, in many ways, our conversations—how we verbally record, interpret, and narrate our experiences, continue to shape and influence who we are and who we have yet to become. Each conversation, in any given day, context, and circumstance, provides a rich opportunity to revisit what we claim to know and to reflect on the underlying assumptions that inform our knowing. The key to fully engaging in life and learning is to participate thoughtfully, intentionally, and reverently in conversations and dialogue with individuals who see and experience life from other standpoints.

I have come to imagine organizations as complex networks of conversations taking place simultaneously and sequentially. As we, as workers, engage in conversations during our work, we are recording and creating our experience and reality of our work in the present tense. Essentially we are defining and redefining our organizations. We carry with us the history and culture of our organizations through the conversations we have had in the past and present. And these conversations influence our expectations of the future. The more we repeat the same conversations, the more they become embedded into our understanding of who we are and what the organization is in the context of our work. Each conversation, and the conversational pattern to which it contributes, holds the potential through which learning and creativity may emerge.

However, the environment in which our organizations are operating is rapidly changing. We, as employees and knowledge workers, are charged with the responsibility to keep up. Learning in the workplace has become a necessity for organizational survival. In our attempt to keep up, we, as employees, race from one agenda item to another. We pursue our personal and corporate goals with a vengeance. Resources, due to macro-environmental factors, have become more and more scarce. Thus, in the pursuit of our goals and much-needed resources, we become combative and competitive—consequently, many of our conversations are reflective of this fact. Conversations in this scenario are rarely exploratory; mostly they become about winning, or about protecting one's "turf" or ego. These conversations inhibit learning and creativity.

In North America we are acculturated to speak up and share what is on our minds. Consequently, in our desire to share our point of view—or defend it, we cut others off. With the multitude of tasks at work and our challenges in balancing our home and work lives, we are often unable to hear ourselves think. Many of us have a continuous loop of conversation constantly playing in our heads. The silos we have created, through our competitive environments, have impeded our ability to reach out or connect with each other. As a result, in our disconnected state, we feel empty, alone, and unfulfilled.

There is such pressure to conform and toe the party line that at times our conversations become stagnant and predictable. We become indoctrinated into a corporate culture so much so that we adopt the existing language and the conversation. Ultimately, the conversational pattern repeats itself over and over again. Listening to these conversations, it becomes apparent that those participating are engaging without truly committing, let alone truly connecting and hearing themselves or one another. One might assume we are merely going through the motions. Subsequently, our conversations have become superficial, without depth or authenticity. The networks of conversation, through their repetitive nature, become weak and worn. Very little deep learning is taking place under these circumstances.

That being said, there are those of us who, feeling overwhelmed with the "noise" of our lives—the endless loop of conversations that play over and over again in our heads—and feeling frustrated with the competition, inauthenticity, and predictability of organizational conversation, want things to be different. We look for ways to quiet the internal chatter so we can reconnect with, and hear, our authentic deepest selves. We inject pauses during our conversations with others so we can meet and connect with the other in an open, loving, and respectful way—breaking down the barriers that separate us. We explore ways in which we can still the organizational din so we can allow spirit back into our work. We understand that we are interconnected and it is our hope that cultivating the environment through which we may reconnect with our deepest selves, with each other, and with spirit, we may shift the existing conversational patterns inhibiting our learning. I have come to learn that injecting a pause into our work—in other words, our conversations—significantly influences our individual and workplace learning. Silence, I believe, connects us to ourselves, to each other, and to the universe. Silence enables our conversations to shift and expand and to be real. Silence connects us to learning.

—Anne-Liisa Longmore, Graduate Student

Anne-Liisa's reflection emphasizes the importance of relationships with others in the workplace and on how authentic engagement, through conversation and dialogue, has shaped her lifelong learning journey. Terms like *just-in-time* and *fast, flexible, and focused* learning are applied to individuals and organizations, emphasizing the need to remain competitive and cutting-edge in a knowledge- and labour market–oriented, globalized world. How do we balance this current focus with the need to create space for engagement and thoughtful dialogue?

The aforementioned terminology clearly illustrates the values, vision, and expectations of an organization. The common ground across organizations is that professional development is often linked with and designed to contribute to the overall functioning, success, enhancement, and competitiveness of an organization, profession, or field more than it is to the life and learning needs of individuals within these contexts. We further argue that a development of practice that primarily focuses on crafting specific techniques and skills "may lead away from an evolving reflection on [our] practice" (Whitelaw, Sears, & Campbell, 2004, p. 12); reflective work that extends beyond specific competencies articulated by the organization or profession we are located in. Pondering the busyness and frenetic activity that continues to drive our work lives and personal agendas, a current reality where organizations and individuals attempt to do more and more with less and less time and resources, Anne-Liisa invites more focused attention on creating spaces for conversation and dialogue in our day-to-day. One of her greatest insights during her graduate studies and in her work as an educator and business strategy consultant was to recognize the importance of creating space for conversations and the potential for learning through conversations when this space was supported and encouraged by leaders and others within organizations.

Organizational cultures and norms carry great weight and this puts tremendous pressure on individuals to align with and conform to spoken and unspoken expectations and agendas of an organization. It is under this great weight that the individual and collective voice are often minimized, devalued, and disregarded. Power relations and politics within organizations and professions contribute significantly to this marginalization of voice and compete with a "pedagogy of hope, one where the possibility of democratic transformation of education and society is still alive" (Brookfield, 2005a, p. 6). A "pedagogy of hope" is informed by the questioning of hegemonic ideologies, discourses, assumptions, and practices. Brookfield's response is to argue for a more critical approach "to help adults realize the ways dominant ideology limits and circumscribes what people feel is possible in life, then raising awareness of how this happens" (p. 6).

One of the highly esteemed voices from the field, Leona English, speaks to those working in the health care profession.

Adult health learning (AHL) is an integral part of community living. When we consider that our health is determined by social factors such as geography, education, employment, income, gender, and biology, it is clear that learning about and acting to promote health is essential. While there is still an important place for health care professionals in preventing and treating diseases, there is also a need to broaden the understanding of health learning to include the contributions of adult educators and community developers who bring their expertise to bear on this work. They have an analysis of power structures, experience in participatory processes, and an understanding of informal learning to inform their engagement with communities. Whether adult educators are utilizing a health impact assessment tool with community groups, working to improve local transportation, or setting up community gardens and kitchens, they are working to honour community knowledge and skill, or improving the health of citizens. Adult educators have a diversity of skills and abilities needed to support community-based activism, research teams, and policy groups that are inclusive, and which contribute to stronger citizenship.

—Dr. Leona English, Professor, St. Francis Xavier University

Leona encourages health care professionals to advocate for adult health learning by seeing individuals as citizens—as co-learners, individuals capable of knowing their own needs and working to make their communities healthier. In this way, adult health learning professionals, and those they support, engage with, and provide care for, are actively engaged and give voice to the co-creation of collaborative and empowering learning relationships.

## Jay

Jay Tuason, a PhD graduate in workplace and adult learning and a voice from the field gives testimony as someone who experienced transformation as a graduate student and, subsequently, transitioned from a high-ranking executive position in the corporate world to the role of adult educator in a post-secondary institution. Jay speaks to the courage and commitment it takes to listen to our inner voice and passion, and to follow our heart.

 I had a very successful career in the financial services industry. I was a branch manager of a head office branch, an area
manager in one of the most affluent areas in Vancouver, a
sales manager, a division manager, the chair of several councils, on the
board of charity groups, had travelled extensively for work and had also
received special perks and bonuses throughout my career. Although I
had advanced quickly in the corporate world, the career and workplace
I thought I'd wanted was somehow lacking. I realized that there was
more to life than the climb up the corporate ladder. I began to reflect
on what it was I really wanted to do with my life and career; I wanted
to find the passion again. Prompted by a longing to do, be, and feel
more, I returned to the classroom.

This longing overrode some of my self-doubt about going back
to school. I began very slowly to explore learning opportunities and
challenges and to reflect on what and how I wanted to "be." The first
major step into the world of adult education was the MBA program. I
could relate to comments by Brookfield (1990) on the imposter syndrome, in that I felt I did not belong in a graduate-level course with
people who, to my mind, seemed much smarter than me. Solomon and
Flores (2001) described these feelings as normal emotions; trust, by
necessity, involves uncertainty. With each step, however, my fear and
self-doubt lessened and my passion and self-trust grew.

With the support of family, friends, and my MBA cohort, I thrived. I was
learning to trust myself and, in turn, had surrounded myself with those
whom I could trust and rely on. I had what Brookfield (1990) called a supportive learning community, one that was founded on trust. Filled with this
newfound self-trust and confidence in my abilities, I went on to complete
a Master of Education in Adult Community, and Higher Education and
then a PhD in Workplace and Adult Learning at the University of Calgary.

Shortly after starting my PhD program, I realized that the time had come to leave the financial services industry. To stay any longer would mean compromising my values and beliefs. In fact, I believe I stayed too long. Although I tried to fool myself into believing I was making a difference in people's lives, my heart was telling me otherwise. The façade I was trying to maintain was cracking. I looked in the mirror and knew that I could not accomplish my hopes, dreams, and goals if I remained. I left my six-figure salary and began teaching full-time. The decision to leave the corporate world to become an adult educator has been one of the best decisions of my life.

I teach at a local polytechnic university where I feel valued as an individual and find deep meaning in my work and in the relationships I've developed with colleagues and students. I work in an environment where I can make a difference, develop trusting connections, and make meaningful contributions. Equally as important, I have learned to trust myself.

—Dr. Jay Tuason, Adult Educator,
Kwantlen Polytechnic University

Jay transitioned from one professional context to another that was completely unrelated—from the corporate banking industry to teaching adult learners at a university in British Columbia. She traded in a six-figure salary for currency of another kind, one that brought her a deeper sense of life balance and satisfaction. How is it, she pondered, that I can leave something that feels so familiar and where I have experienced so much success, yet, at the same time, feel like I am finally going home!

In the years that followed, Jay spoke of a sense of oneness experienced when she stepped from underneath the "shoulds" and "oughts" that guided her earlier career decision-making when moving up the corporate ladder. Although Jay had acquired a wealth of knowledge, skills, and abilities in the corporate banking sector, she began to feel deeply disconnected in that, regardless of how lucrative, the work she was doing was no longer the work she felt drawn to do.

## *Shifts and Transitions*

Colleen experienced a similar shift when she transitioned from her work as a social worker in crisis intervention to adult educator in a vocational, post-secondary institution.

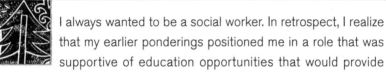

I always wanted to be a social worker. In retrospect, I realize that my earlier ponderings positioned me in a role that was supportive of education opportunities that would provide more options for individuals reliant on social services. I have always believed that we have so much more potential than we realize and that this potential is often impeded by barriers like being short of finances, family issues, health concerns, and sociocultural influences. My work as a social worker was always with those considered to be on the fringes—in the margins of society.

I struggled with trying to provide these supports when my clients were experiencing extreme crisis. So, most of my time as a social worker with the provincial government focused on crisis intervention. It was at this time that I volunteered to co-lead a continuing education course in support of young, unmarried single mothers on the topic of parenting. I loved the opportunity to work with some amazing young moms who were looking forward to being the best moms that they could be. They were not necessarily in crisis, although they were experiencing many stresses and challenges. It was after this that I realized I needed to make a career change; I transitioned from social worker to adult educator. I could have continued to work with these individuals as their social worker but I experienced a greater sense of satisfaction and empowerment when I engaged with them in an educative environment. That was 33 years ago!

Within our work contexts, as teachers, social workers, community developers, human resource training and development specialists, health care professionals, instructors in post-secondary or continuing education environments, artists, business and industry workers, formal leaders in corporate settings or in adult education institutions, community developers, or as individuals working in community-based non-profit organizations (an inexhaustive list), we encourage critical reflection. By integrating reflection into our day-to-day practice, we remain actively engaged in an intentional and thoughtful meaning-making process to inform the work that we do, why we continue to do what we do, and what we need in support of our ongoing growth and development.

In *Enhancing Teaching Practice for Student Learning: A Framework for Professional Development in Alberta,* published by the Alberta Teacher's Association (n.d.), professional development (PD) is described as "... a complex process. It requires collaboration, informed decision-making and an understanding of adult learning" (p. 4). This document refers to the importance of collaborative dialogue that is ongoing and to "being responsive to changing, contextual variables [that] requires ongoing monitoring and refinement" (p. 6). More specifically, when addressing the roles and responsibilities of teachers, Alberta Education referred to "Alberta's teachers [as] lifelong learners [and to how] professional development and other learning opportunities equip them with the tools and knowledge they need to help students reach their full potential" (n.d., para. 1). Within the health care context, the Canadian Nurses Association takes up lifelong learning and calls upon Canadian registered nurses to continue to enhance their knowledge, skills, and abilities in order to remain current and accountable for providing competent nursing care, citing this as a professional responsibility. The Alberta College of Social Workers refers to "continuing competence" and to social workers developing a professional development portfolio in support of her/his learning and development goals. These are only three examples of the work of professional bodies to support and inform ongoing professional development of its members.

Organizations and professional bodies expect that we remain current, relevant, and effective in our work. Participation in formal professional development initiatives is identified as the best pathway to achieve performance goals. The thrust that drives ongoing in-service professional

development and the goals and learning outcomes that inform professional development activities, responds to an organization or to a professional association's commitment to the greater community that their
"human" resources will have ongoing, enhanced, and sustained currency
and capacity. Indeed, we cannot argue with this conception as we live in
an ever-changing world, a world that demands keeping abreast of new
developments informed by sound and solid research; by the changing
and emerging needs of individuals, communities, and societies; and by
best practices. Consider, as you reflect on what fascinates you, what drew
you to the choices you have made regarding the work you are preparing
to do or the work you are doing now, and on what one needs to do to
remain current in the field. What are the expectations of your profession,
your chosen vocation, your life work? What language (terminology, jar-
gon) is used when referring to ongoing development and learning? What
is unique about these expectations and the learning required for your
field and scope of practice? What supports and resources are available?
What barriers or challenges do you need to navigate to access what it is
you need to know, and how you will learn what it is you want and need
to learn? We also assert that professional development extends beyond
the dictates of organizations and professional bodies. If we believe that
we bring our "whole selves" into our work contexts, the potential for
learning at a personal and a professional level cannot and should not be
conceived as separate.

## Concluding Comments

Locating ourselves as lifelong adult learners, be this in formal, informal,
paid, unpaid, professional, business and industry, non-profit, or other
community contexts, requires that we rethink what motivates us, how
we identify what we value, what we need, what we want to learn, how we
want to learn, and what we hope to contribute. Newman (2000) spoke to
the difficulty of balancing our own interpretations of meaning, purpose,
and contributions with the culture, values, beliefs, expectations, and

performance measures embedded in the organizational cultures and contexts we are in.

In this chapter, we explored diversity of work and learning contexts and different understandings of learning and professional development within these contexts. Student narratives and voices from the field provided rich fodder that invite our own reflections on work and learning and the diverse contexts that we work and learn in. We were also reminded that work presents in many different ways and contexts and that what counts as work or not—what is valued and validated—should not be determined by formal organizational structures or a paycheque. Indeed, significantly more attention that focuses on unpaid workspaces, informal learning, and volunteer cultures is needed. Duguid, Slade, and Schugurensky (2006) argued that

> Although many studies on voluntary work in Canada have been undertaken (Hall, Barr, Easwaramoorthy, Sokolowsky, & Salaman, 2005; Hall, McKeown, & Roberts, 2001), little is known yet about the learning dimension of volunteer work. The research literature on the extent, modes and effectiveness of volunteers' acquisition of new skills, knowledge, attitudes and values, and on the relationship between formal, non-formal and informal learning in this process is scarce." (p. 1)

Unpaid work, still perceived by many as "not real work," contributes significantly to communities, to larger society, and to the economy. Duguid, Slade, and Schugurensky (2006) contended that "the recognition of the economic and social contribution of volunteer work, compounded with the new awareness of the impressive nature and scope of this contribution, are helping to recognize that volunteer [unpaid work] is indeed 'real work'" (p. 2).

## Endnote

1  See *The SAGE Handbook of Workplace Learning* (2011): Chapter 12.

# CHAPTER 10

# Moving Forward:
# Learning and Leading

## JACQUELINE

 Without a doubt, the Internet has significantly changed, and continues to change, the face of teaching and learning. Today, an increasing number of adult learners takes advantage of online learning opportunities, and more universities, colleges, workplaces, and other educational institutions offer e-learning courses and training programs (Canadian Council on Learning, 2009). My formal online learning journey began in September, 2006. I wanted to make a career change and decided to return to university to pursue a Master of Education degree. The MEd program was course-based and could be fully completed online. When I started my MEd degree, I was working full-time, and like many other adult learners, the online program allowed me the flexibility to continue working, while studying in the evenings and on weekends.

Today, adult learners enrolled in formal education programs often juggle their studies with many other obligations, such as caring for children and elderly parents, work responsibilities, and community commitments. They are more likely to be employed full-time and to enroll in a program or take courses on a part-time basis (Polson, 2003). I was one of many adult learners for whom the Internet and the expansion of e-learning opportunities made pursuing further education more accessible, affordable, and flexible.

Perhaps even more significant than the expansion of formal e-learning courses and programs is the opportunity for adults to engage in informal and self-directed learning on the Internet. The development of Web 2.0 tools has significantly contributed to the creation of online learning spaces. "Web 2.0 applications enable users with little technical knowledge to construct and share their own media and information products ... [and] make it possible to pool the collaborative efforts of potentially millions of users" (Harrison & Barthel, 2009, p. 157).

—Jaqueline Warrell, Graduate Student

## Introduction

In this final chapter, we highlight some of the trends in adult education that have shifted and shaped the learning experiences of adult learners. Technology is certainly a trend that continues to impact the adult education landscape and learners' experiences. Jacqueline's narrative captures some of her journey as a graduate student and is testimony to this. In consideration of future directions, we also highlight other trends and challenges as we move forward, experienced in whichever roles we assume in supporting our own learning and the learning of others, today or in the years to come.

Some of us may assume more formal roles as educators and facilitators of adult learning in any number of diverse work and learning contexts. You may have come to this text as a student enrolled in a nursing, teacher education, business, or social work program. You may be taking a continuing education course or certificate. Perhaps you are an artist who is interested in supporting the learning needs of other adult learners who aspire to be artists one day. Or are you a coach or mentor, working with adults who are disabled; a community worker engaged with street youth or the homeless? Do you work in a training and development capacity in business and industry? Are you an instructor in a community or vocational college? Wherever we are located, personally or professionally, we do share some common ground as lifelong adult learners in that we all contribute, formally or informally, to the learning needs and experiences of other adults we encounter and engage with along the way. It is likely that we may not even realize the impact we have on the learning journeys of others. Each one of us has a story to tell, a story shaped over a number of years, a narrative of our lived experiences. Our narratives are also connected to one another in ways that we may never have considered previously.

In consideration of future trends in adult education and adult learning, we have chosen to briefly highlight four key themes in this final chapter: technology and learning, learning from one another, who we are as adult learners, and the critical importance of taking up leadership (formally or informally) in support of the learning needs of others.

## Technology and Learning: Supports for Success

Jacqueline's experience provides testimony to how technology has enhanced and supported her learning journey as a graduate student. After reading Jacqueline's reflection, Colleen smiles. Computers were certainly not a part of her early experience.

### Turning Back the Pages

It was the mid-1970s. Colleen was a young, single parent of a one-year-old. She recalls purchasing a complete set of hardcover Encyclopedia Britannica books that included a very large atlas. She was building a reference library to guide her little boy's school projects in the years to come. *"In retrospect, it was so important to me that my son have access to information and knowledge to support his learning in school. Encyclopedia Britannica represented a pathway to knowledge—to topics, geography, facts, and figures that would provide him a window to a world that extended far beyond what he could possibly access in his day-to-day experiences."* In the mid-1980s, a Commodore 64, 8-bit home computer was purchased. A dot matrix printer replaced the home typewriter and floppy disks were used to store data that spanned household recipes and budgets, personal letters, and work-related documents. In the early 1990s, Colleen enrolled in a "distance delivery" course through Athabasca University. Distance delivery translated to receiving a large box of paper-based course materials in the mail—textbooks, floppy disks, and a reading package. The box also housed a complete set of cassette tapes on course-related topics and a notation that indicated the day and time, every week, when she could telephone her tutor with questions about the course, clarify assignment expectations, and draw support. This progressive mode of delivery built on an earlier "correspondence course" model.

Computer pricing dropped rapidly in the 1980s and early 1990s. Purchasing technology became much more affordable and this provided households, workplaces, and educational institutions easier access to technologies and supports. This timing aligned with the introduction of a worldwide interconnectivity of networks—referred to as the Internet—in 1982. In 1991, when the World Wide Web was launched, the Internet was still relatively unknown to the common folk. By 1995, and with the launch of Windows 95, excitement for technology to support and enhance education, work and learning, and personal use had escalated. The possibilities and potential were endless. The World Wide Web and the Internet were becoming household names and the world, as we knew it, had been transformed.

## Back to the Present

It is hard to imagine a world without computers, especially for anyone born post–Internet and the World Wide Web. For those of us who do recall life before this type of technology, learning within formal education contexts brings back memories of homework sheets reproduced by Gestetner copiers and classroom activities designed around workbooks, chalkboards, and textbooks. In the present day, in industrialized countries, learners are equipped with any number or combination of handheld learning devices, laptop computers, apps, and other mobile technologies to support their learning. Assistive technologies to support individuals located across a continuum of abilities and learning challenges are also widely available to those who have the resources, supports, and ability to access these technologies. What warrants our ongoing attention, focus, and commitment, however, are learners and communities who reside beyond these aforementioned parameters of privilege. We refer here to many of our First Nations, Métis, and Inuit populations in Canada where socioeconomic and cultural barriers add additional layers of challenge to technology access and support. As we move forward in our thinking and adult education praxis, addressing disparities to access is paramount if the democratization of education is to be achieved. Failure to do so will only serve to maintain the status quo where, "social disparity ... use of the Internet and other information technologies continue to be dominated by persons with higher education and income, because equipment is often unavailable to the others and because there is still wide-spread technological illiteracy" (UNESCO Institute for Education, 1997, p. 5).

Democratizing adult education extends far beyond access, however; it involves deep and thoughtful integration of content, processes, and supports that are authentically respectful of different cultures and alternative ways of learning and knowing. Within any learning culture and context, be this informal, formal, or non-formal, technology is *not* a replacement for the human factor. In a 2010 qualitative study that Colleen conducted with researchers from Bow Valley College and in partnership with other provincial colleges, eCampusAlberta, the Alberta Rural Development Network (ARDN), and the Ministry of Advanced Education and Technology, "the learning needs of Aboriginal adult learners residing in selected First Nations communities in rural Alberta" (Kawalilak, Little Mustache-Wells, Connell, & Beamer, 2012, para. 1) were explored. The study sought to gain a deeper understanding of interest, readiness, needs, and supports related to e-learning access, opportunities, and challenges for Aboriginal adult learners located in rural communities. Researchers engaged in open dialogue with Aboriginal adult learners, Aboriginal and non-Aboriginal instructors, Elders from the community, and other un-enrolled community members who often

212 Contexts and Praxis: Engaging in Learning

frequented the rural learning centres to connect with one another and for social engagement. The importance of the "human factor" in learning emerged as a dominant theme in this study. More specifically,

> how relationships significantly impact learners and learning pro-
> cesses received the most attention. *I need to be with others when*
> *learning.* With an emphasis on one-on-one teacher/student contact
> within a larger group context, teachers were referred to as *my men-*
> *tor* and *someone who walks with me in learning.* Feeling connected
> to peers meant a *family atmosphere here at school … the good part of*
> *family. That's why I come … It's all about relationships. It all comes*
> *back to this.* (para. 55)

Most post-secondary institutions across Canada have adopted blended learning as a way to capture and balance the best of both worlds—the human factor and the benefits of technology-supported teaching and learning. Blended learning is defined as "the organic integration of thoughtfully selected and complementary face-to-face and online approaches and technologies" (Garrison & Vaughan, 2008, p. 148). At the University of Calgary, the Faculty of Social Work offers a blended learning Learning Circles program:

> The Learning Circles program is an accredited Bachelor of Social
> Work, which is designed for students in rural, remote, and/or
> Aboriginal communities across Canada. The program is delivered
> through a blended learning format, allowing students to complete
> their social work degree in their own community, while maintain-
> ing full-time employment. To complete their degree in 24 months,
> students are required to participate in synchronous or real-time
> (e.g. online chats, audio conferences) and asynchronous (e.g.
> posting to discussion board, exercises) learning activities and to
> travel to Calgary once each year for a period of one week. (Human
> Resources and Skills Development Canada, 2011, p. 9)

Randy Garrison, a voice from the field and international scholar who has advanced our thinking and practice on blended learning, shares his perspective.

 I have described blended learning as the thoughtful integration of face-to-face and online learning. This succinct definition of blended learning rationally integrates the best of face-to-face and online learning. The strength and challenge of blended learning is combining the immediate exchanges of synchronous verbal communication with reflective asynchronous written communication. Blended learning is a way of thinking about learning that avoids either/or choices. It allows learners to be separate and connected: to be reflective yet critically engaged in discourse. Blended approaches provide opportunities for the responsibility to construct personal meaning as well as sustained opportunities to share and challenge ideas for purposes of mutual understanding.

The great strength of blended learning is to sustain learning communities where thinking can be challenged and the experiences of learners shared over time. A pioneer of adult education, Eduard Lindeman, made it clear that adult education is cooperative and with emphasis placed on discussion. Active engagement and reflection embedded in critical discourse is a hallmark of adulthood. This speaks to the strength of blended approaches to learning. Considering the vicissitudes of adulthood, the accessibility to and possibilities for engagement offered by blended learning makes this a natural and powerful fit to meet the needs of adult learners.

—Dr. Randy Garrison, Professor, University of Calgary

We return to Jacqueline's reflection and her focus on social media as providing another dimension to adult education and learning in the twenty-first century.

The Internet is no longer a place for adult learners to simply find, read, and passively accept information. Instead, learners are challenged to become active participants in their learning, and to engage in the ongoing creation and dissemination of knowledge. Social media platforms such as YouTube, blogs, wikis, file/photo sharing applications, and social networking sites are only some examples of online spaces that have become a part of people's personal learning network. A personal learning network (PLN) refers to the people, resources, and content one chooses to connect with and to engage in learning and information sharing (Richardson & Mancabelli, 2011).

As a PhD student and avid user of social media, online social networking sites (SNS) became an important part of my PLN. Currently, three of the most popular SNS in Canada are Facebook, Twitter, and LinkedIn, and like other many other Canadians these SNS have increasingly become a part of my daily life (Ipsos Reid Corporation, 2012). Although I initially viewed social networking as primarily a social activity, I also discovered it could be a powerful learning tool. On SNS, people are encouraged to share ideas, engage in dialogue, and negotiate new understandings (Chatti, Klamma, Jarke, & Naeve, 2007). For me, online social networking was a way to connect with other graduate students, professors, subject matter experts, and business professionals, both locally and globally. I experienced SNS as conversational spaces for creating knowledge and reflecting on learning, and for participating in online learning communities. In online learning communities, people learn through telling stories, sharing jokes, giving ideas and examples, asking questions, providing feedback, posting resources, discussing challenges, and reflecting on topics of interest (Aceto, Dondi, & Marzotto, 2010; Chatti et al., 2007)

My PLN is unique. The multitude and variety of social media and Web 2.0 applications has afforded me with increased ability to shape, tailor, and personalize my learning experience. Further, they have given me the opportunity to learn and express myself in diverse ways and to choose which tools I want to use and which people and content I want to interact with. I see the Internet and social media as continuing to push twenty-first century adult learning and education beyond the walls of the classroom and into the everyday interactions and activities of adult learners.

—Jaqueline Warrell, Graduate Student

Social networking and social networking devices were also noted for their potential in motivating learners to develop technology literacies, with teachers and community leaders citing "social networking devices as untapped potential in rural adult learning environments" (Kawalilak, Little Mustache-Wells, Connell, & Beamer, 2012, para. 58). Jacqueline's call to explore the potential of social media to support learning beyond formal classroom learning positions social media as an emerging technology. Social media is also being used within formal education environments to address the needs of adult learners located in different geographical regions, and within work, learning, and cultural contexts, for more social engagement, interaction, and collaboration. The literature supports the notion that social media and digital technology may also assist in leveraging gaps in adult literacy education, language learning, basic skills education, and environmental education. Clearly, we have only begun to scratch the surface!

As we ponder the future in an attempt to discern what distance learning might entail for adult learners over these next several years, the only thing we can predict with any certainty is that change will be ongoing, rapidly moving us into horizons of learning that we have not even begun to anticipate. Indeed, we recognize that the landscape in distance learning is shifting so rapidly, that by the time you, the reader, have this book in your hands, some of our commentary about this topic will be out-of-date! For example, unheard of by the mainstream even a few years ago, MOOCs—Massive Open Online Courses—are free, non-credit online university-level courses that allow unlimited numbers of learners to enroll in and have open access to course content. In 2012, both the *New York Times* (Pappano, 2012) and *Inside Higher Education* (Watters, 2012) heralded MOOCs as the most important and talked about trend in distance learning. However, even though more universities are climbing onboard this platform of learning, dialogue is emerging regarding dissatisfaction with the teaching and learning dynamics within a MOOC:

> Much of what's being lauded as "revolutionary" and as "disrupting" traditional teaching practices here simply involves videotaping lectures and putting them online. While MOOCs might be changing education by scaling this online delivery, we need to ask, "Are they really changing how people teach?".... MOOCs are, however, changing how people learn, if for no other reason than they are offering lectures, quizzes, educational resources, and possibly even credentialing to anyone with Internet access. (Watters, 2012)

What is particularly interesting regarding the discourse on the emergence of MOOCs in higher education is that, while it is acknowledged that MOOCs are having an impact on course delivery, it is too soon to tell if they will fundamentally affect how distance learning is offered, both within the post-secondary and the private sectors. The phrase "it is too soon to tell" is important for us to remember because MOOCs are symptomatic of the speed of change within distance learning; something new is constantly being introduced and we need to continually engage with and reflect on whether and how each new initiative will have an impact in this important context of adult learning.

## Welcoming Differences: Learning from One Another

Learning from one another, a theme that emerges throughout this text, speaks to our courage to step beyond our comfortable and familiar to engage *with* and to learn together, *through* and *from* differences. Learning from one another prompts us to lean into questions like *What do we mean by internationalizing education? How do we indigenize education? What is involved in democratizing education?* And *what are the politics, power structures, and power differentials embedded within?*

## Some Critical Questions

Our colleague and voice from the field, Shibao Guo, shares his perspective on creating a more inclusive society that welcomes and responds to the needs of immigrant populations in formal education, in work and learning environments, and in society at large.

Canada is an immigrant society. Immigration has played an important role in transforming Canada into an ethno-culturally diverse and prosperous nation. The 2011 Census of Canada shows that, between 2006 and 2011, about 1.2 million newcomers arrived in Canada, which means that Canada has the highest proportion of foreign-born population among G8 countries at 20.6 percent. Among them, a large number are adult learners. Despite the fact new immigrants bring significant human capital resources to Canada, research shows that many immigrants experience devaluation and denigration of their international credentials and prior work experience after arriving in Canada. As a consequence, they suffer unemployment and underemployment, poor economic performance, and downward social mobility. It is important to ask why such inequities occur in a democratic society like Canada, where democratic principles are upheld and where immigrants are "welcome." My research shows non-recognition of international credentials and prior work experience can be attributed to a deficit model of difference, which leads us to believe that differences are a deficiency, and that the knowledge of immigrant professionals, particularly those from developing countries, is incompatible and inferior, and hence invalid. The soberness of the issue requires us to consider a paradigm shift in adopting recognitive justice so we recognize and accept differences as valid and valuable expressions of the human experience.

—Dr. Shibao Guo, Associate Professor, University of Calgary

Shibao advocates for more focused attention to advance the democratization of adult education and for a deeper commitment to the co-creation of respectful and inclusive work and learning environments, formal and informal. Within contexts of formal learning, what is needed to *re*vision curriculum to represent and capture pedagogical perspectives and approaches that reside beyond what we typically read and study? Internationalizing learning and education demands attention and action to design curriculum that presents a broader knowledge base and perspective—we refer here to scholarship and practice that is inclusive of non-Western, conceptual, and theoretical lenses and praxis. What are some of the ethical issues involved when we consider international, global contexts? What cultural sensitivities and competencies are needed to live and to work within diverse cultural contexts? What do we mean by pluralized knowledge? How do we create space to explore and value other ways of knowing? As we consider future directions of adult education and how adult education intersects with global education, sustainability, and internationalization, how do we *step beyond* our comfortable and familiar to be open and to deeply and authentically engage *with* and *in* a more diverse and complex world? And how do we, as learners and educators, move toward a deeper understanding of the complexities and diverse relationships between the world that feels familiar to us and a "self-other" world? What do we need to let go of if we are to purposefully, intentionally, and thoughtfully lean into what some will refer to and experience as "the unfamiliar" and "the uncomfortable"? Vanbalkom, Paul, and Kawalilak (2010),[1] in a concept paper intended to support a deepened understanding and appreciation as to the importance of internationalization from a Faculty of Education perspective, spoke to the consequences when we fail to attend to these questions: "Without properly acknowledging internationalism's effect-affect on who we are and what we do, will not our ethnocentrism seek to convince us that our traditional paradigms are the only place-holders of Truths? Is internationalization then not that academic, ethical, social, and cultural interruption that invites complexity, diversity, and otherness into our heads, hearts, and hands?" (p. 7).

These same questions are at the forefront when reflecting on what indigenizing education means and entails. Over the past many years, there has been significant focus on how adult education contributes to the learning needs of Indigenous communities. We reposition this question and ask, How do non-Indigenous adult learners and educators benefit and grow from gaining a deeper understanding of other ways of knowing and being? Does our curriculum provide thoughtful spaces to ask and to ponder these critical questions? How do we loosen our grip on tightly held beliefs, values, notions, assumptions, and agendas in support of co-creating these thoughtful spaces? These questions extend beyond superficial, mechanical changes. They challenge us to find the courage to situate ourselves beyond the routines and practices of local ways and to advocate for deep curricula change and transformation—transformation that can only be achieved by moving *beyond* appreciation, to actually support deep engagement *with* differences if we ever hope to achieve a rich and deep understanding of diversity. Maureen Coady, a voice from the field, and associate professor from St. Francis Xavier University, speaks to engaging with community in support of creating spaces for knowledge sharing and informed, collective action.

 Community development (CD) is the planned evolution of all aspects of community well-being (economic, social, environmental, and cultural). It is a process whereby community members come together to take collective action and generate solutions to common problems, as defined by them. Communities may be geographic, may be issue- or interest-based, or may exist within organizations and social systems. Community development processes may emerge spontaneously from inside the community, or be stimulated by an outside catalyst. As an educational concept, community development is a process of learning that is supportive of advancement, betterment, capacity building, empowerment, and enhancement. The adult educator's concern is with helping community members to connect with each other and their existing resources, and to become more self-directed in driving their own development. Adult education's purpose in this context is to foster learning that enhances sustainable community capacity and self-reliance.

—Dr. Maureen Coady, Associate Professor,

St. Francis Xavier University

Community engagement and community development processes co-create space for reciprocity of learning, knowledge sharing, and informed collective action. We refer here to empowerment, individually and collectively, and to agency of voice and action, in support of *all* community members. Engaging with differences provides a pathway to overcome the gaps and the legacy that has been created, a legacy that has contributed to fragmentation and separation from rich and vibrant cultures and traditions different from our own, a legacy that needs to be broken and healed. There is no easy way to heal the broken legacy of separation and fragmentation, brought about by differences, that exists within and between cultures. It is *not* about gathering facts and evidence in order for us to believe in the possibilities and potential of coming together in oneness. It *is* about believing in the possibilities in order to see and experience the healing. In the words of First Nations National Chief Shawn A-in-chut Atleo who spoke at the opening of the Iniikokaan (Buffalo Lodge) Aboriginal Centre at Bow Valley College,

it requires not that we will believe it when we see it … when we know in our hearts, just like the Elders in our ceremonies … that [we] believe, fully, with every fibre in our being, that we will see it when we believe it … This is the moment where we break these patterns that we've been involved in … This is a moment where we reach out to say "walk with us".… Let us work together to overcome. (Bow Valley College, 2013, November 15)

For reciprocity to emerge, to be experienced, and to be transformational, letting go of tightly held agendas is paramount. The paradox is that *stepping in* demands a willingness to *step back*, in order to move forward—a willingness to consider that what we thought we knew might only be a very small piece of a much bigger story. And if we have the courage to breathe in deeply and to *really* take a step back, we may discover that many of our assumptions have been faulty all along.

## Back to Ourselves as Learners and Educators

We have travelled over a great deal of terrain in this book, including a look at technology and learning from one another in this chapter. At this point, as we prepare to bring this text to a close, we bring the focus back to ourselves as learners and educators. Looking back at ideas offered in this volume—who we are as learners, philosophies of learning, historical trends within our field, educational theories, and a look into future trends—we invite you to consider how they have impacted you as learner/educator and as educator/learner. We deliberately intertwine the terms *learner* and *educator* because the educator role—be that coach, facilitator, or formal classroom teacher—should be undergirded by a learning stance. Conversely, if you see yourself as a learner foremost, we encourage you to also regard yourself as an educator. As we have already pointed out, much of our learning happens informally in multiple contexts: through dialogue at a community meeting, with significant contributions from each member in a community of practice, or when you pull together an important report with a colleague at work. We all have the opportunity to lead, to teach, to facilitate, and to educate while we are learning. In the following discussion we offer some thoughts on how to move forward as learner and educator based on several of the key concepts and themes explored in this text. While we consider each role separately, we suggest that there are potential benefits if we blur the distinctions.

## *Our Pathway as Learners*

Even though the first suggestion we offer may seem deceptively simple and easy to take up, its absence would make any other ideas we have to offer irrelevant. Here it is: *See yourself as a learner—a learner capable of success, especially on your terms.* We turn to the story of Teresa to illuminate what we mean. Teresa was a research participant in a study that Janet and her colleague Tara Hyland-Russell (Groen & Hyland-Russell, 2009) conducted, which focused on stories of transformative learning for adult learners enrolled in one of the Radical Humanities 101 programs across Canada. Teresa, a 53-year-old grandmother living in Thunder Bay, Ontario, had been attending a program at Lakehead University for one term when she sat down to talk to Janet and Tara. Even though she had lived in Thunder Bay all of her life, she did not see the university as part of her life. She had never entered the grounds of Lakehead University, feeling that this space was for other people: people who were smarter than she, people who were successful in high school and went on to university and great careers. That wasn't her story. She had a tumultuous and unstable upbringing and she did not see herself as a learner. Then her counsellor told her about the Radical Humanities program at Lakehead University. Gradually, as she participated in the program, she saw herself differently: she could learn. She engaged in discussions. She had great ideas and she realized that she loved the whole process! She was a learner! She is now passing her love of learning and the idea that the university is a shared space—open to everyone—on to her granddaughter. She wants her granddaughter to love learning, to be curious, and to see that spaces of learning, such as the university, are also there for her. Here are some of Teresa's thoughts about how she has changed her view of the university and, more importantly, herself:

[The university is] for anyone. I was actually glad to be able to get a library card, because my daughter's oldest—she didn't want to learn. I said, "Well, what kind of homework do you have?" and she replied, "I have to do an autobiography of this musician." I said,

"Have you thought of a musician?" and she said, "No". "Well come with me," I said, picking her up. "Let's go to university. [The university], it's okay; it's not scary or nothing. It's inviting to go there". (Groen & Hyland-Russell, 2009, p. 56)

As we think a little more deeply about Teresa's story, we realize the ongoing narratives we hold about ourselves and our sociocultural context and shifting life roles inform how we see ourselves. As a result, we may hold multiple stories about ourselves as learners, some more positive than others. We might see ourselves as "successful" in mathematics, but not in writing. We may tell ourselves that we cannot create a piece of art, but that we can create an amazing meal. We ask you to challenge your perceptions about yourself as a learner in general, and as a learner in specific contexts. Where do these perceptions come from? What experiences are causing you to put boundaries around yourself? What messages might you be receiving from society that are inhibiting? What societal structures are impeding you? How might these perceptions and structures be limiting for you and, in turn—when we consider Teresa's grandchild—have an impact on the learning opportunities of those whom you influence?

As we deepen our consideration of how we think about ourselves as learners, we realize many of the dynamics shaping our perceptions of self as learner and the actual process of learning itself are highly relational. For example, returning to Teresa's story, aspects of her personal story and the larger societal structures placed boundaries on beliefs she held about herself as learner. Conversely, it was through the encouragement and support of a counsellor at a social service agency that she enrolled in the program. Then, within the actual learning space itself, with the provision of a safe and encouraging learning space and the practical supports of a warm meal and free bus tickets, the boundaries placed around the possibility of learning began to dissolve for Teresa.

Continuing the notion of boundaries, we encourage you to challenge boundaries you might be placing around *how you learn*. While the dominant discourse within formal education places a premium on cognitive approaches to learning, we urge you to challenge these boundaries and to consider that there are multiple pathways for learning. Learning through your body, the arts, your emotions, and relationships are some of the ways we learn, and they all offer the opportunity to deepen our experience of learning.

Finally, we encourage you to be aware that the possibilities for learning are not bounded by a specific place, time, class, workshop, or lecture. We have come to realize the contexts for learning are boundless and that most learning happens informally, beyond the bricks and mortar of face-to-face classroom environments. What is key, however, is a heightened awareness of and openness to the possibility of learning, not only through multiple approaches, but in multiple contexts: within your workplace, within your home, through your volunteer work, and yes, within the classroom. As you engage in learning within these contexts, we hope that you will be emboldened to question and to challenge boundaries: *What am I learning and why? What dominant messages are being communicated? Who has power? What knowledge is valued? Who is validated? What voice do I have and who will listen?*

## Our Pathway as Educators

In a similar vein as our recommendations to you as learner, we are reaching beyond techniques in our offering of suggestions to you as educator. We ask you to go deeper to consider your beliefs about who you are as an educator and, in turn, how this manifested within your practice, formally in an instructor role and/or informally in daily interactions with others. While instructional approaches are important, we align ourselves with the following statement by Palmer (1998), *"good teaching cannot be reduced to technique; good teaching comes from the identity and integrity of the teacher"* (p. 10). Therefore, we turn to the notion of authenticity and teaching to inform our reflection on our pathway as educators.

At its most basic, an authentic approach to teaching makes a connection between an educator's identity and integrity and his or her ability to create safe and potentially transformative spaces of learning. A three-year grounded theory research study conducted by Cranton and Carusetta (2004a, 2004b), in which they explored how faculty members speak about authenticity, helps us illuminate some of its qualities:

> Authenticity is not just genuineness and openness, though that forms a central part of being authentic, but it is socially situated. It involves helping others, relating to others, and caring for the authenticity of others around us. And moving outward further, it involves knowing who we are within our social world, how we are shaped by the world, and how we position ourselves in that world. Being authentic is being conscious of self, other, relationships, and context through critical reflection. (Cranton & Carusetta, 2004b, p. 289)

When we reflect on these qualities, they mirror many of the considerations we just offered to you as a learner—understand who you are as an educator, recognize that you are located within a particular sociocultural context, and continually engage in critical reflection about your practice. We ask you to consider many of the same questions posed to you as a learner, replacing the word *learner* with *educator*: Who am I as educator and how to do I bring myself into this space? What role do I play in creating a safe learning space? What messages are being communicated and what might be suppressed? Who is being valued here and who might feel devalued in my approach? Am I open to learning while instructing, facilitating, coaching, teaching, or engaging in dialogue?

We refer to Ernie, an 82-year-old philosophy professor who taught a philosophy course in one of the Radical Humanities programs, to illuminate how authenticity informs his practice (Groen & Hyland-Russell, 2009). As Ernie related his experience, most of his story focused on how much he learned from the program's students. He placed a high value on understanding how the students' experiences informed their connection to the content, and he appreciated the gifts of insight they brought to their interpretation of Plato. In turn, as he was still teaching a few under-graduate philosophy courses a year as a sessional instructor, he spoke about the changes in his "regular" teaching practice as a result of his experiences within the Radical Humanities program. He now connects a little more deeply with his students, wanting to know their stories, and he has adjusted course assignments to allow for more personal, yet critical, reflection on philosophical perspectives presented in his courses.

At the end of the course, the students in the Radical Humanities pro-gram offered Ernie a gift: a walking staff and a handmade royal blue velvet cape embellished with their names, all hand embroidered in gold thread. As he leaves his home to teach at the university, he passes by the cape and staff, hooked onto the coat stand by the front door, serving as a daily reminder about the importance of being open to the wisdom offered to him by his students. We remind you, while Ernie is a formal instructor in an academic setting, the gems offered in his story are appli-cable to all of us, whether or not we hold a formal position as instructor, teacher, professor, coach, or facilitator. Notions of openness, genuine listening, deep engagement, creating safe spaces, and critical reflection on our practice are available to all of us regardless of role.

As we close this section on our pathway as educators, we turn to one final aspect of authenticity. Charles Taylor (1991) reminded us that authenticity is about so much more than self-realization, self-awareness, and congruence between values and actions. Authentic engagement as a learner and educator should occur against the backdrop of societal issues that are crucial, or the "horizons of significance" in which we understand ourselves in our various roles: "The understanding that independent of my will there is something noble, courageous, and hence significant in giving shape to my own life" (Taylor, 1991, p. 39). Underlying the notion of a pathway of learning and educating is the bigger question: where is the pathway heading? How do I, as learner and educator, make a contri-bution to the greater good? Widening the lens to the field of adult educa-tion and learning, Nesbit (2006) reminded us we are "part of a broader and vital mission for 'really useful knowledge' that helps create a more equitable world at individual, family, community and society levels" (p. 16). We turn now to an exploration of some horizons of significance for all of us as adult learners and educators.

## Around the Next Bend: Adult Education, Learning, and Leading

In 2009, Gordon Selman and his son Mark Selman (Selman & Selman, 2009) penned an article entitled "The Life and Death of the Canadian Adult Education Movement." When Gordon Selman started his academic career in the 1950s, just as scholarship in the area of adult education was emerging, he believed he was part of something important, highlighting many of the contributions we noted in chapter 5 to provide evidence that the earlier "leaders in the field continued to share the conviction that adult education had a vital role to play in both the personal and professional lives of adults" (Selman & Selman, 2009, p. 19). However, over the duration of his career, Selman argued that adult education and learning shifted its focus and efforts to become more professionalized and institutionalized. We lost our horizon of significance as we set up graduate programs in adult education and launched research agendas, instead of engaging in social movements. In addition, the term *lifelong learning* was being pulled away from its inclusive community roots, only to be appropriated by governments and their policies. Mark Selman (Selman & Selman, 2009) concurred, noting as we gained stature within post-secondary institutions, corporate settings, and government agendas, we retreated from collective action—no longer were we a movement involved in social change. He stated, "The actual practice of adult education as a means to address the interests of people facing disadvantages, or aimed at the public good is not well supported and is sometimes actively discouraged" (p. 23). These words challenge the very heart of adult education's vision to contribute really useful knowledge that has an impact on the lives of individuals and communities.

Tom Nesbit (2011) directly refuted the arguments proffered by Gordon and Mark Selman, offering compelling evidence that the field of adult education and learning is not only alive and well, but that we are increasingly relevant as we continue to make substantial contributions that reflect our aspirations to make a difference in the lives of those around us. We are not retreating into our institutions, rather "there is evidence to suggest that the opposite is true: levels of social action and interest are increasing.... Canadian adult education remains as involved in such collective action as it has been throughout its history" (Nesbit, 2011, p. 4). In addition, Nesbit argued that the tight connection between the scholarship of adult education and community-based learning is irrefutable, in particular in the growing research emphasis on challenging inequities. For example, in Donovan Plumb's (2009) overview of Canadian adult education research agendas, he noted the following trends: research on heteronormative biases in Canadian adult education theory and practice; an exploration of ways that adult education can contribute to deepening capacities for spirituality; an examination of how globalization is destroying Indigenous cultures and the environment that sustains all of us; a focus on unions as a key space for adult learning; and finally, pulling the curtain back on dramatic inequities of human rights, poverty, and violence triggered by contemporary capitalism. In an article we wrote examining research trends in Canadian adult education (Groen & Kawalilak, 2013), we noted a similar research foci contributing to "the 'liberatory' tradition of adult education: citizenship, gender, health, adult literacy, immigration, transmigration, transformative learning, diversity, race, consumerism, and adult learning communities in varied contexts" (p. 36).

While Nesbit asserted that we, as adult educators and practitioners, continue to be deeply involved in education that contributes to the co-creation of just, equitable, and vital communities at the local, national, and international level, we are also reminded that we should not be complacent. In all of our pathways of learning and educating, we *all* have a role to play, in our own unique ways, in supporting the well-being of those lives we touch.

## Concluding Comments

There is so much more to explore and we are cognizant of not attending to many other questions, topics, and themes that contribute to the rich, ongoing discourse on adult education and adult learning. For this we apologize.

In many ways, we liken this to inviting you to dinner and only providing you with an array of appetizers. Now, it feels like we are sending you off without having offered you a main course. This is always the quandary for authors who are humbled in their attempt to highlight, capture, and explore key themes in a text that is bound by a certain number of pages.

We do, however, hope that what we have provided here is a morsel of different voices, perspectives, and promptings that will encourage you to explore more broadly and deeply. We are *all* adult learners. We *all* have stories to tell and knowledge to be gained from our experiences and from the stories and experiences of others. It is important to know that a field of scholarship and practice exists in Canada and beyond—a field that pays great tribute to and places great value on the experiences we hold as adult learners, regardless of our work, learning, cultural, or socioeconomic contexts. In this way, we all remain connected to a narrative of work and learning that extends beyond our own individual experiences.

Some of us assume or will assume more formal roles in the education and facilitation of learning of others. Some of us will not take on these formal roles. What is most important to remember, however, is that, regardless of our discipline or context, we are all navigating a pathway of lifelong learning and our learning journeys are interconnected with those we work, learn, and live with along the way. If we have the courage to be open to the unknown and unexpected, we will recognize that we have so much to learn from one another and that our greatest potential for learning is gained from authentically engaging with others who experience and view the world through a lens that is different from our own.

We extend our deepest gratitude to you for journeying with us through this text. We remain fascinated and excited about the potential and possibilities for learning and knowledge sharing that we have yet to experience. Our hope is that you embrace this same excitement and fascination for learning as your own learning journey continues to unfold. Our narratives as lifelong adult learners are, indeed, a work in progress!

## Endnote

1  Vanbalkom, Paul, & Kawalilak (2010). *The faculty and internationalisation: Otherwise necessarily and responsibly engaged.* Unpublished Concept Paper prepared for the Faculty of Education, University of Calgary, (p. 7).

# References

Aceto, S., Dondi, C., & Marzotto, P. (2010). *Pedagogical innovations in new learning communities*. Retrieved from ftp.jrc.es/EURdoc/JRC59474.pdf

Alberta Education. (n.d.). *Role of teachers: Professional development*. Retrieved from www.education.alberta.ca

Alberta Human Rights Commission (2014). Retrieved from http://www.albertahumanrights.ab.ca/

Alberta Teacher's Association. (n.d.). *Enhancing teaching practice for student learning: A framework for professional development in Alberta*. Retrieved from www.teachers.ab.ca/SiteCollectionDocuments/ATA/Professional%20 Development/PD_Framework.pdf

Alexander, A. (1997). *The Antigonish movement: Moses Coady and adult education today*. Toronto, ON: Thompson Educational.

Althusser, L. (1971). *Lenin and philosophy*. New York, NY: Monthly Review Press.

Atleo, M. (2013). The zone of Canadian Aboriginal adult education. In T. Nesbit, S. Bringham, N. Taber, & T. Gibb (Eds.), *Building on critical traditions: Adult education and learning in Canada* (pp. 39–50). Toronto, ON: Thompson Press.

Attwood, B., & Magowan, F. (2001). *Telling stories: Indigenous history and memory in Australia and New Zealand*. Crows Nest, Australia: Allen & Unwin.

Beard, C., & Wilson, J. (2002). *The power of experiential learning*. London, England: Kogan Page.

Beder, H. (1990). Purposes and philosophies of adult education. In S. B. Merriam & P. Cunningham (Eds.), *Handbook of adult education and continuing education* (pp. 37–50). San Francisco, CA: Jossey-Bass.

Belenky, M. F., Clinchy, B. M., Goldberger, N. R., & Tarule, J. M. (1986). *Women's ways of knowing: The development of self, voice, and mind*. New York, NY: Basic Books.

Bell, B., Gaventa, J., & Peters, J. (1990). *We make the road by walking: Conversations on education and social change, Myles Horton and Paulo Freire*. Philadelphia, PA: Temple University Press.

Berman, M. (1981). *The Reenchantment of the world*. Ithaca, NY: Cornell University Press.

Bibby, R. (2004). *Restless gods: The renaissance of religion in Canada*. Toronto, ON: Novalis.

Bohm, D. (1996). *On dialogue*. London, England: Routledge.

Bohm, D. (1998). What is dialogue? In L. Ellinor & G. Gerard, *Dialogue: Rediscover the transforming power of conversation* (pp. 19–27). New York, NY: John Wiley & Sons.

Bohm, D., Factor, D., & Garrett, P. (1998). *Dialogue: A proposal.* Retrieved from www.david-bohm.net/dialogue/dialogue_proposal.html

Boucouvalas, M. (2005). Cognition. In L. English (Ed.), *The international encyclopedia of adult education* (pp. 111–113). London, England: Palgrave MacMillan.

Boud, D. (2005). Experiential learning. In L. English (Ed.), *The international encyclopedia of adult education* (pp. 243–245). London, England: Palgrave MacMillan.

Boud, D., & Miller, N. (Eds.). (1996). *Working with experience: Animating learning.* London, England: Routledge.

Bourdieu, P. (2005). Habitus. In J. Hillier & E. Rooksby (Eds.), *Habitus: A sense of place* (pp. 43–52). Aldershot, England: Ashgate Publishing.

Bow Valley College. (2013, November 15). Keynote address [Video file]. *Bow Valley College unveils the Iniikokaan (Buffalo Lodge) Aboriginal Centre.* Retrieved from bowvalleycollege.ca/news/news-archive/bvc-unveils-the-iniikokaan-(buffalo-lodge)-aboriginal-centre.html

Bratton, J., Mills, J. H., Pyrch, T., & Sawchuk, P. (2004). *Workplace learning: A critical introduction.* Aurora, ON: Garamond Press.

Brookfield, S. D. (1990). *The skilful teacher.* New York, NY: Jossey-Bass.

Brookfield, S. D. (2005a). *The power of critical theory: Liberating adult learning and teaching.* San Francisco, CA: Jossey-Bass.

Brookfield, S. D. (2005b). Philosophy. In L. English (Ed.), *The international encyclopedia of adult education* (pp. 475–480). London, England: Palgrave MacMillan.

Buber, M. (1970). *I and thou.* New York, NY: Scriber Classics.

Butler-Kisber, L. (2010). *Qualitative inquiry: Thematic, narrative and arts-informed perspectives.* London, England: SAGE Publications.

Canadian Council on Learning. (2009). *State of e-learning in Canada.* Retrieved from www.ccl-cca.ca/pdfs/E-learning/E-Learning_Report_FINAL-E.PDF

Canadian Literacy and Learning Network. (2013). *Literacy Statistics.* Retrieved from www.literacy.ca/literacy/literacy-sub/

Candy, P. (1991). *Self-direction for lifelong learning.* San Francisco, CA: Jossey-Bass.

Capra, F. (1996). *The web of life: A new scientific understanding of living systems.* New York, NY: Random House.

Castellano, M. B. (2000). Updating Aboriginal traditions of knowledge. In G. J. Sefa Dei, B. L. Hall & D. Goldin Rosenburg (Eds.), *Indigenous knowledges in global contexts.* Toronto, ON: University of Toronto Press.

Chatti, M. A., Klamma, R., Jarke, M., & Naeve, A. (2007). The Web 2.0 driven SECI model based learning process. In J. M. Spector, D. G. Sampson, T. Okamoto, Kinshuk, S. A. Cerri, M. Ueno, & A. Kashihara (Eds.), *Proceedings of the 7th IEEE International Conference on Advanced Learning Technologies, ICALT 2007, July 18–20 2007* (pp. 780–782). Niigata, Japan: IEEE Computer Society.

Clark, J., & Dirkx, J. (2000). Models of the self: A reflective dialogue. In B. Hayes and A. Wilson (Eds.), *Handbook 2000—Adult and Continuing Education* (pp. 101–116). San Francisco, CA: Jossey-Bass.

Clark, M. C. (2005). Embodied learning. In L. English (Ed.), *The international encyclopedia of adult education* (pp. 210–213). London, England: Palgrave MacMillan.

Clover, D., & Butterwick, S. (2013). Fear of glue, fear of thread: Reflections on teaching arts-based practice. In D. Clover & K. Sanford (Eds.), *Arts-based Education, Research and Community Cultural Development in the Contemporary University: International Perspectives* (pp. 66–80). Manchester, England: Manchester University Press.

Coady, M. (2000, March). Moses Coady's message: Standing the test of time. *Coady International Institute Newsletter, 20*(1). Retrieved from collections. stfx.ca/cdm/compoundobject/collection/stfx_coady/id/2906/rec/1

Cole, A., & Knowles, G. (2001). *Lives in context: The art of life history research.* Walnut Creek, CA: AltaMira Press.

Collins, D. (1998). *Organizational change: Sociological perspectives.* New York, NY: Routledge.

Council of Ministers of Education, Canada. (2008, July). *Education in Canada.* Retrieved from www.cicic.ca/docs/cmec/EducationCanada2008.en.pdf

Cranton, P. (2005). Transformative learning. In L. English (Ed.), *The international encyclopedia of adult education* (pp. 630–637). London, England: Palgrave MacMillan.

Cranton, P. (2013). Adult learning theory. In T. Nesbit, S. Bringham, N. Taber, & T. Gibb (Eds.), *Building on critical traditions* (pp. 95–106). Toronto, ON: Thompson Educational.

Cranton, P., & Carusetta, E. (2004a). Perspectives on authenticity in teaching. *Adult Education Quarterly, 55,* 5–22.

Cranton, P., & Carusetta, E. (2004b). Developing authenticity as a transforming process. *Journal of Transformative Education, 2,* 276–293.

Cross-Durant, A. (1984). Basil Yeaxlee and lifelong education: Caught in time. *International Journal of Lifelong Education, 3*(4), 279–291.

Darkenwald, G., & Merriam, S. B. (1982). *Adult education: Foundations of practice.* New York, NY: Harper & Row.

Davis, B., & Sumara, D. (2006). *Complexity and education: inquiries into learning, teaching, and research.* Mahway, NJ: Lawrence Erlbaum Associates.

Davis, B., Sumara, D., & Luce-Kapler, R. (2008). *Engaging minds: Changing teaching in complex times* (2nd ed.). New York, NY: Routledge.

Davis, J. (n.d.). *Myles Horton: The radical hillbilly.* Retrieved from www.uawregion8.net/Activist-HOF/M-Horton.htm

Delors, J., et. al (1996). *Learning: The treasure within: Report to UNESCO of the international commission on education for the twenty-first century.* Retrieved from plato.acadiau.ca/courses/pols/conley/QUEBEC98/DELORS~1/delors_e.pdf

Dewey, J. (1938). *Experience and education.* New York, NY: Collier Books.

Dirkx, J. (1997). Nurturing soul in adult learning. *New Directions for Adult and Continuing Education, 74,* 79–88.

Dirkx, J. (2001). The power of feeling: Emotion, imagination and the construction of meaning in adulthood. *New Directions for Adult and Continuing Education, 89,* 63–72.

Dirkx, J. (2007). Nurturing soul in adult learning. In P. Cranton (Ed.), *Transformative learning in action: Insights from practice* (pp. 79–88). San Francisco, CA: Jossey-Bass.

Dirkx, J. (2008). Adult learning and the emotional self. *New Directions for Adult and Continuing Education, 120*, 7–18.

Doll, W. C., Fleener, M. J., Trueit, D., & St. Julien, J. (2005). *Chaos, complexity, curriculum, and culture.* New York, NY: Peter Lang.

Dominicé, P. (2000). *Learning from our lives: Using educational biographies with adults.* San Francisco, CA: Jossey-Bass.

Duerk, J. (1993). *I sit listening to the wind: Woman's encounter within herself.* San Diego, CA: LuraMedia.

Duguid, F., Slade, B., & Schugurensky, D. (2006, July 4–6). *Unpaid work, informal learning and volunteer cultures.* Paper presented at the 36th Annual SCUTREA Conference, Trinity and All Saints College, Leeds. Retrieved from www.wallnetwork.ca/resources/Duguid_etalSCUTREA2006.pdf

Eco, U. (1989). *The open work.* Cambridge, MA: Harvard University Press.

Elfert, M., & Rubenson, K. (2013). Adult education policies in Canada: Skills without humanity. In T. Nesbit, S. M. Brigham, N. Taber, & T. Gibb (Eds.), *Building on critical traditions: Adult education and learning in Canada* (pp. 238–247). Toronto, ON: Thompson Educational.

Elias, J., & Merriam, S. (1980). *Philosophical foundations of adult education.* Malabar, FL: Krieger.

Elias, J., & Merriam, S. (2005). *Philosophical foundations of adult education* (3rd ed.). Malabar, FL: Krieger.

English, E., & Mayo, P. (2012). *Learning with adults: A critical pedagogical introduction.* Rotterdam, Netherlands: Sense Publishers.

English, L. (2006). Postfoundationalism in adult education. In T. Fenwick, T. Nesbit & B.Spencer (Eds.), *Contexts of adult education: Canadian perspectives* (pp. 105–117). Toronto, ON: Thompson.

English, L., & Gillen, M. (2000). Editors' notes. *New Directions for Adult and Continuing Education, 85*, 1–5.

The European Older People's Platform. (2007). *Lifelong learning—A tool for all ages.* Retrieved from www.age-platform.eu/images/stories/EN/AGE_leaflet_lifelong_learning.pdf

Evans, K., Guile, D., & Harris, J. (2011). Rethinking work-based learning: For education professionals and professionals who educate. In M. Malloch, L. Cairns, K. Evans, & B. N. O'Connor (Eds.), *The SAGE Handbook of Workplace Learning* (pp. 149–162). Thousand Oaks, CA: SAGE Publications.

Fenwick, T. (2003). *Learning through experience: Troubling orthodoxies and intersecting questions.* Malabar, FL: Krieger.

Field, J. (2006). *Lifelong learning and the new educational order.* Staffordshire, England: Trentham Books.

Foley, G. (Ed.). (2004). *Dimensions of adult learning: Adult education and training in a global era.* Berkshire, England: Open University Press.

Fowler, J. (1981). *Stages of faith.* New York, NY: HarperCollins.

Freiler, T. (2008). Learning through the body. *New Directions for Adult and Continuing Education, 119,* 37–48.

Freire, P. (1970). *Pedagogy of the oppressed.* New York, NY: Continuum International Publishing Group.

Freire, P. (2006). *Pedagogy of the oppressed* (30th Anniversary Edition). New York, NY: Continuum International Publishing Group.

Gadotti, M. (1994). *Reading Paulo Freire: His life and work* (J. Milton, Trans.). Albany, NY: State University of New York Press.

Garrison, D. R. (1997). Self-directed learning: Toward a comprehensive model. *Adult Education Quarterly, 48*(1), 18–33.

Garrison, D. R., & Vaughan, N. (2008). *Blended learning in higher education.* San Francisco, CA: Jossey-Bass.

Gilligan, C. (1982). *In a different voice.* Cambridge, MA: Harvard University Press.

Goldberger, N., Tarule, J., Clinchy, B., & Belenky, M. (Eds.). (1996). *Knowledge, difference, and power: Essays inspired by women's ways of knowing.* New York, NY: Basic Books.

Gould, R. (1990). The therapeutic learning program. In J. Mezirow et al. (Eds.), *Fostering critical reflection in adulthood: Guide to transformative and emancipatory learning* (pp. 134–156). San Francisco, CA: Jossey-Bass.

Gouthro, P. (2005). A critical feminist analysis of the homeplace as learning site: Expanding the discourse of lifelong learning to include adult women learners. *International Journal of Lifelong Education, 24*(1), 5–19.

Grace, A. P. (1996). Striking a critical pose: Andragogy—missing links, missing values. *International Journal of Lifelong Education, 15*(5), 382–392.

Grace. A. P., & Kelland. M. (Eds.). (2006). *Canadian association for the study of adult education (CASAE): 25th anniversary memory book (1981–2006).* Retrieved from www.casae-aceea.ca/?q=history

Gramsci, A. (1971). *Selections from the prison notebooks* (Q. Hoare & G. M. Smith, Trans.). London, England: Lawrence & Wishart.

Griffin, V. (2001). Holistic learning. In T. Barer-Stein & M. Kompf (Eds.), *The craft of teaching adults* (3rd ed.) (pp. 107–139). Toronto, ON: Culture Concepts.

Groen, J. (2012). Kindred spirits? Challenges and opportunities for the faculties of education and social work in the emerging teaching focus on spirituality. In J. Groen, D. Coholic, & J. Graham (Eds.), *Spirituality in education and social work: Theory, practice and pedagogies* (pp. 77–94). Waterloo, ON: Wilfrid Laurier Press.

Groen, J., & Hyland-Russell, T. (2009). *Radical humanities: A pathway toward transformational learning for marginalized non-traditional adult learners.* Ottawa, ON: The Canadian Council on Learning.

Groen, J., & Kawalilak, C. (2013). The tapestry of adult education research in Canada. In T. Nesbit, S. Brigham, T. Gibb, & N. Taber (Eds.), *Building on critical traditions: Adult education and learning in Canada* (pp. 29–38). Toronto, ON: Thompson Press.

Gutek, G. (2014). *Philosophical, ideological, and theoretical perspectives on education* (2nd ed.). New York, NY: Pearson.

Habermas, J. (1971). *Knowledge and human interests.* Boston, MA: Beacon Press.

Hall, B. L., Clover, D. E., Crowther, J., and Scandrett, E. (2012). *Learning and education for a better world: The role of social movements.* Rotterdam, Netherlands: Sense Publishing.

Hansman, C. A., & Mott, V. W. (2010). Adult learners. In C. E. Kasworm, A. D. Rose, & J. M. Ross-Gordon (Eds.), *Handbook of adult and continuing education* (pp. 13–23). Thousand Oaks, CA: SAGE Publications, Inc.

Harrison, T. M., & Barthel, B. (2009). Wielding new media in Web 2.0: Exploring the history of engagement with the collaborative construction of media products. *New Media & Society, 11*(1–2), 155–178.

Hart, M. A. (2010). Indigenous worldviews, knowledge, and research: The development of an indigenous research paradigm. *Journal of Indigenous Voices in Social Work, 1*(1), 1–16.

Hartree, A. (1984). Malcolm Knowles' theory of andragogy: A critique. *International Journal of Lifelong Education, 3*(3), 203–210.

Havecker, C. (1991). *Understanding aboriginal culture* (Y. Malykke, Ed.). Sydney, Australia: Cosmos Periodicals.

Hayes, E., & Flannery, D. (2000). *Women as learners: The significance of gender in adult learning.* San Francisco, CA: Jossey-Bass.

Hillier, J., & Rooksby, E. (Eds.). (2005). *Habitus: A sense of place.* Aldershot, England: Ashgate Publishing.

Hochschild, A. (1989). *The second shift.* New York, NY: Viking Penguin Press.

Human Resources and Skills Development Canada. (2011). *Innovative practices research project: COHERE report on blended learning.* Retrieved from cohere.ca/wp-content/uploads/2011/11/REPORT-ON-BLENDED-LEARNING-FINAL1.pdf

Inglis, T. (1997). Empowerment and emancipation. *Adult Education Quarterly, 48*(1), 3–17.

Ipsos Reid Corporation. (2012). *The Ipsos Canadian inter@ctive Reid report: 2012 fact guide.* Retrieved from theexchangenetwork.ca/upload/docs/IpsosReid-Canadian%20Internet%20FactGuide.pdf

James, C. (2010). *Seeing ourselves: Exploring race, ethnicity and culture* (4th ed.). Toronto, ON: Thompson Educational.

Jarvis, P. (2006). *Towards a comprehensive theory of human learning: Vol. 1.* London, England: Routledge.

Kawalilak, C. (2004). *Illumination: An adult educator's journey—Dialogues with adult educators and adult learners in Indigenous Western Australia* (Unpublished doctoral dissertation). University of Calgary, Canada.

Kawalilak, C., Little Mustache-Wells, N., Connell, L., & Beamer, K. (2012). E-learning access, opportunities, and challenges for Aboriginal adult learners located in rural communities. *College Quarterly, 15*(2). Retrieved from www.collegequarterly.ca/2012-vol15-num02-spring/kawalilak-wells.html

Kechnie, M. C. (2003). *Organizing rural women: The Federated Women's Institutes of Ontario, 1897–1919.* Montreal, QC: McGill-Queen's University Press.

Kegan, R. (1994). *In over our heads: The mental demands of modern life.* Cambridge, MA: Harvard University Press.

Knowles, M. (1980). *The modern practice of adult education: From pedagogy to andragogy* (2nd ed.). New York, NY: Cambridge Books.

Knowles, M. (1990). *The adult learner: A neglected species.* New York, NY: Gulf Publishing.

Kolb, D. (1984). *Experiential learning: Experience as the source of learning and development.* Englewood Cliffs, NJ: Prentice Hall.

Kumar, P., & Ryan, D. (1988). *Canadian union movement in the 1980s: Perspectives from union leaders.* Kingston, ON: McGill-Queen's University Press.

Laidlaw, A. F. (1961). *The campus and the community: The global impact of the Antigonish movement.* Montreal, QC: Harvest House.

Lange, E. (2006). Challenging social philosophobia. In T. Fenwick, T. Nesbit, & B. Spencer (Eds.), *Contexts of adult education: Canadian perspectives* (pp. 92–104). Toronto, ON: Thompson.

Lange, E. A. (2013). Interrogating transformative learning theory. In T. Nesbit, S. Brigham, T. Gibb, & N. Taber (Eds.). *Contexts of adult education* (pp. 107–118). Toronto: Thompson Educational Publishing.

Lawrence, L. (2005). Artistic ways of knowing: Expanded opportunities for teaching and learning. *New Directions for Adult and Continuing Education, 2005*(107), 3–11.

Leach, L. (2005). Self-directed learning. In L. English (Ed.), *The international encyclopedia of adult education* (pp. 565–569). London, England: Palgrave MacMillan.

LeDoux, J. (2002). *The synaptic self: How our brains become who we are.* New York, NY: Viking Penguin.

Lefrancois, G. (1996). *The lifespan* (6th ed.). Belmont, CA: Wadsworth.

Levinson, D. (1978). *The seasons of a man's life.* New York, NY: Knopf.

Levinson, D. & Levinson, J. (1996). *The seasons of a woman's life.* New York, NY: Knopf.

Lindeman, E. C. (1945). The sociology of adult education. *Journal of Educational Sociology, 19*(1), 4–13.

Lindeman, E. C. (1961). *The meaning of adult education.* New York, NY: Harvest House. (Original work published in 1926.)

Livingstone, D. W., & Raykov, M. (2013). *Adult learning trends in Canada: Basic findings of the WALL 1998, 2004 and 2010 surveys.* Toronto, ON: Centre for the Study of Education and Work, Ontario Institute for Studies in Education, University of Toronto.

Livingstone, D. W., & Sawchuk, P. H. (2004). *Hidden knowledge: Organized labour in the information age.* Aurora, ON: Garamond Press.

Loevinger, J. (1976). *Ego development: Conceptions and theories.* San Francisco, CA: Jossey-Bass.

Lotz, J., & Welton, M. (1997). *Father Jimmy: The life and times of Jimmy Tompkins.* Cape Breton Island, NS: Breton Books.

MacKeracher, D. (2004). *Making sense of adult learning* (2nd ed.), Toronto, ON: University of Toronto Press.

MacKeracher, D. (2009). Social change in historical perspective. P. Cranton, & L. English (Eds.), *New Directions for Adult and Continuing Education, 124,* 25–35.

Macy, J., & Johnstone, C. (2012). *Active hope: How to face this mess we're in without going crazy.* Novato, CA: New World Library.

Maslow, A. (1970). *Motivation and personality* (2nd ed.). New York, NY: McGraw-Hill.

McNally, J., & Blake, A. (Eds.). (2010). *Improving learning in a professional context: A research perspective on the new teacher in school.* New York, NY: Routledge.

Merriam, S. (2005). How adult life transitions foster learning and development. *New Directions for Adult and Continuing Education, 108,* 3–14.

Merriam, S., & Brockett, R. (1997). *The profession and practice of adult education.* San Francisco, CA: Jossey-Bass.

Merriam, S., Caffarella, R., & Baumgartner, L. (2007). *Learning in adulthood: A comprehensive guide* (3rd ed.). San Francisco, CA: Jossey-Bass.

Merriam, S., & Clark, M. C. (1991). *Lifelines: Patterns of work, love, and learning in adulthood.* San Francisco, CA: Jossey-Bass.

Merriam, S., & Clark, M. C. (2006). Learning and development: The connection to adulthood. In C. Hoare (Ed.), *Handbook of adult development and learning* (pp. 27–52). Oxford, England: Oxford University Press.

Mezirow, J. (1978). Perspective transformation. *Adult Education Quarterly, 28*(2), 100–110.

Mezirow, J. (1996). Contemporary paradigms of learning. *Adult Education Quarterly, 46*(3), 158–172.

Mezirow, J. (2012). Learning to thinking like an adult. In E. Taylor, P. Cranton, & Associates (Eds.), *The handbook of transformative learning* (pp. 73–95). San Francisco, CA: Jossey-Bass.

Mezirow, J., & Associates. (2000). *Learning as transformation.* San Francisco, CA: Jossey-Bass.

Michelson, E. (1998). Re-membering: The return of the body to experiential learning. *Studies in Continuing Education, 20*(2), 217–232.

Miller, J. (2012). Contemplative practices in teacher education: What I have learned. In J. Groen, D. Coholic, & J. Graham (Eds.), *Spirituality in education and social work: Theory, practice and pedagogies* (pp. 77–94). Waterloo, ON: Wilfrid Laurier Press.

National Research and Development Centre. (2010, July). *Study on European terminology in adult learning for a common language and common understanding and monitoring of the sector.* Retrieved from www.anc.edu.ro/uploads/images/Legislatie/adultreport_en.pdf

Nesbit, T. (2006). Introduction. In T. Fenwick, T. Nesbit, & B. Spencer (Eds.), *Contexts of adult education: Canadian perspectives.* Toronto, ON: Thompson Educational.

Nesbit, T. (2011). Canadian adult education: Still a movement. *Canadian Journal of University Continuing Education, 37*(1), 1–13.

Newman, M., (2000). Program development in adult education and training. In G. Foley (Ed), *Understanding adult education and training* (2nd Ed.) (pp. 59–80). New South Wales, Australia: Allen & Unwin.

Nishitani, K. (1991). *Nishida Kitaro.* Berkeley, CA: University of California Press.

Olsen, M. E., Lodwick, D. G., & Dunlap, R. E. (1992). *Viewing the world ecologically.* San Francisco, CA: Westview Press.

Organization for Economic Co-operation and Development (OECD). (2002). *Thematic review on adult learning.* Retrieved from www.oecd.org/education/innovation-education/thematicreviewonadultlearning-mainpage.htm

Palmer, P. (1998). *The courage to teach: Exploring the inner landscape of a teacher's life.* San Francisco, CA: Jossey-Bass.

Palmer, P. (2002). *Stories of the courage to teach: Honoring the teacher's heart.* San Francisco, CA: Jossey-Bass.

Pappano, L. (2012, November 11). The year of the MOOC. *New York Times.* Retrieved from www.nytimes.com/2012/11/04/education/edlife/massive-open-online-courses-are-multiplying-at-a-rapid-pace.html?pagewanted=all

Piaget, J. (1973). *The child's conception of the world.* London, England: Paladin.

Plumb, D. (2009). Critical adult education in Canada in the time of CASAE. *New Directions for Adult and Continuing Education, 124,* 5–15.

Poitras Pratt, Y. (2011). *Meaningful media: An ethnography of a digital strategy within a Métis community* (Unpublished doctoral dissertation). University of Calgary, Canada.

Polanyi, M. (1966). *The tacit dimension.* Chicago, IL: University of Chicago Press.

Polanyi, M. (1969). *Knowing and being: Essays by Michael Polyani.* Chicago, IL: University of Chicago Press.

Polson, C. J. (2003). Adult graduate students challenge institutions to change. *New Directions for Student Services, 102,* 59–68.

Pratt, D. (1993). Andragogy after twenty-five years. In S. Merriam (Ed.), *An update on adult learning theory: New directions for adult and continuing education, no. 57* (pp. 15–24). San Francisco, CA: Jossey-Bass.

Price, D. W. (1999). Philosophy and the adult educator. *Adult Learning, 11*(2), 3–5.

Reuter-Lorenz, P., & Lustig, C. (2005). Brain aging: Reorganizing discoveries about the aging mind. *Current Opinions in Neurobiology, 15,* 245–251.

Rice, B. (2005). *Seeing the world with Aboriginal eyes: A four directional perspective on human and non-human values, cultures and relationships on Turtle Island.* Winnipeg, MB: Aboriginal Issues Press.

Richardson, W., & Mancabelli, R. (2011). *Personal learning networks: Using the power of connections to transform education.* Bloomington, IN: Solution Tree Press.

Roberts, S. M., & Pruitt, E. Z. (2003). *Schools as professional learning communities: Collaborative activities and strategies for professional development.* Thousand Oaks, CA: Corwin Press.

Rogers, C. (1961). *On becoming a person.* Boston, MA: Houghton Mifflin.

Ross, R. (1992). *Dancing with a ghost: Exploring Indian reality.* Toronto, ON: McClelland & Stewart.

Rossiter, M. (2005). Relational learning. In L. English (Ed.), *The international encyclopedia of adult education* (pp. 548–552). London, England: Palgrave MacMillan.

Sandlin, J. (2005). Andragogy and its discontents: An analysis of andragogy from three critical perspectives. *PAACE Journal of Lifelong Learning, 1*(14), 25–42.

Sarbin, T. (Ed.). (1993). Narrative as the root metaphor for contextualism. In S. Jayes, L. Hayes, J. Reese, & T. Sarbin (Eds.), *Varieties of scientific contextualism* (pp. 51–65). Reno, NV: Context Press.

Sawchuk, P. H. (2011). Researching workplace learning: An overview and critique. In M. Malloch, L. Cairns, K. Evans, & B. N. O'Connor (Eds.), *The SAGE handbook of workplace learning* (pp. 165–180). Thousand Oaks, CA: SAGE Publications.

Schlossberg, N. (1989). *Overwhelmed: Coping with life's ups and downs.* Lanham, MD: Lezington Books.

Schlossberg, N., Waters, E., & Goodman, J. (1995). *Counseling adults in transition: Linking practice with theory* (2nd ed.). New York, NY: Springer.

Sefa Dei, G., Hall, B., & Goldin Rosenberg, D. (Eds.). (2000). *Indigenous knowledges in global contexts: Multiple readings of our world.* Toronto, ON: University of Toronto Press.

Selman, G., Cooke, M., Selman, M., & Dampier, P. (1998). *The foundations of adult education in Canada* (2nd ed.). Toronto, ON: Thompson Educational.

Selman, G., & Selman, M. (2009). The life and death of the Canadian adult education movement. *Canadian Journal of University Continuing Education, 35*(2), 13–28.

Shugg, O. J. W. (n.d.). *Farm radio forum.* Retrieved from www.thecanadianencyclopedia.com/articles/farm-radio-forum

Sinnott, J. (1994). The relationship of postformal thought, adult learning, and lifespan development. In J. D. Sinnott (Ed.), *Interdisciplinary handbook of adult lifespan learning* (pp. 105–119). Westpost, CT: Greenwood Press.

Smith, B., & Sparkes, A. C. (2008). Contrasting Perspectives on Narrating Selves and Identities: An Invitation to Dialogue. *Qualitative Research, 8*(1): 5–35.

Smith, D. (2005). *Institutional ethnography: A sociology for people.* Lanham, MD: AltaMira Press.

Solomon, R. C. (2007). *True to our feelings: What emotions are really telling us.* New York, NY: Oxford University Press.

Solomon, R. C., & Flores, F. (2001). *Building trust in business, politics, relationships, and life.* New York, NY: Oxford University Press.

Spencer, B. (2006). *The purposes of adult education: A short introduction.* Toronto, ON: Thompson Educational.

Spencer, B., & Kelly, J. (2013). *Work and learning: An introduction.* Toronto, ON: Thompson Educational.

Statistics Canada. (2012). *Life expectancy at birth, by sex, by province.* Retrieved from www.statcan.gc.ca/tables-tableaux/sum-som/l01/cst01/health26-eng.htm

Swartz, J. (2008). Uncovering science in adult education: Welcome complexity theory. In D. Flowers & S. Bracken (Eds.), *Proceedings of the Adult Education Research Conference.* St. Louis, MO: University of Missouri.

Taber, N., & Gouthro, P. (2006). Women and adult education in Canadian society. In T. Fenwick, T. Nesbit, & B. Spencer (Eds.), *Contexts of adult education: Canadian perspectives* (pp. 58–67). Toronto, ON: Thompson Educational.

Talbert, J. E., & McLaughlin, M. W. (1994). Teacher professionalism in local school context. *American Journal of Education, 102,* 123–153.

Taylor, C. (1991). *The malaise of modernity: CBC Massey lecture series.* Toronto, ON: Anansi.

Taylor, E. (2008). Transformative learning theory. In S. Merriam (Ed.), *Third update on adult learning theory: New directions for adult and continuing education, no. 119* (pp. 5–15). San Francisco, CA: Jossey-Bass.

Taylor, P. (1993) *The texts of Paulo Freire.* Buckingham, England: Open University Press.

Tennant, M. (2006). *Psychology and adult learning* (3rd ed.). London, England: Routledge.

Tisdell, E. J. (1995). *Creating inclusive learning environments for adults: Insights from multicultural education and feminist pedagogy.* Columbus, OH. Retrieved from ERIC database. (ED384827)

Tisdell, E. J. (2003). *Exploring spirituality and culture in adult and higher education.* San Francisco, CA: Jossey-Bass.

Tough, A. (1967). *Learning without a teacher: A study of tasks and assistance during adult self-teaching projects.* Toronto, ON: The Ontario Institute for Studies in Adult Education.

Tough, A. (1971). *The adult's learning projects: A fresh approach to theory and practice in adult learning.* Toronto, ON: Ontario Institute for Studies in Education.

UNESCO. (1980). *Recommendation on the Development of Adult Education.* Ottawa, ON: Canadian Commission for UNESCO.

UNESCO Institute for Education. (1997). *New information technologies: A key for adult learning.* Retrieved from www.unesco.org/education/uie/confintea/pdf/7a.pdf

Usher, R. (1993). Experiential learning or learning from experience: Does it make a difference? In D. Boud, R. Cohen, & D. Walker (Eds.), *Using experience for learning* (pp. 169–180). Buckingham, England: Society for Research into Higher Education and Open University Press.

Usher, R., Bryant, I., & Johnston, R. (1997). *Adult education and the postmodern challenge: Learning beyond the limits.* London, England: Routledge.

Vella, J. (2002). *Learning to listen—Learning to teach: The power of dialogue in educating adults* (2nd ed.). San Francisco, CA: John Wiley & Sons.

Vogel, L. J. (2000). Reckoning with the spiritual lives of adult educators. In L. M. English & M. A. Gillen (Eds.), *New directions for adult and continuing education: Addressing the spiritual dimensions of adult learning. What can educators do, no. 85* (pp. 17–27). San Francisco, CA: Jossey-Bass.

Vygotsky, L. (1978). Interaction between learning and development. In *Mind and Society* (pp. 79–91). Cambridge, MA: Harvard University Press.

Walter, P. (2009). Philosophies of adult environmental education. *Adult Education Quarterly, 60*(1), 3–25.

Watters, A. (2012, December 18). *Top ed-tech trends of 2012: MOOCs.* Retrieved from www.insidehighered.com/blogs/hack-higher-education/top-ed-tech-trends-2012-moocs

Weil, S., & McGill, I. (1989). *Making sense of experiential learning.* London, England: Open University Press.

Welton, M. (Ed.). (1995). *In defense of the lifeworld: Critical perspectives on adult learning.* Albany, NY: State University of New York Press.

Wenger, E. (1998). *Communities of practice: Learning, meaning, and identity.* Cambridge, England: Cambridge University Press.

Wenger, E. (n.d.). *Communities of practice: A brief introduction.* Retrieved from wenger-trayner.com/wp-content/uploads/2012/01/06-Brief-introduction-to-communities-of-practice.pdf

Werquin, P. (2010). *Recognising non-formal and informal learning: Outcomes, policies and practices.* Paris, France: OECD Publishing.

Wheatley, M. J. (2009). *Turning to one another: Simple conversations to restore hope to the future.* San Francisco, CA: Berrett-Koehler Publishers, Inc.

Whitelaw, C., Sears, M., & Campbell, K. (2004). Transformative learning in a faculty professional development context. *Journal of Transformative Education, 2*(9), 9–27.

Winchester, I. (2013). On seeing our deepest intellectual, educational and practical traditions from a non-western perspective. *Interchange, 43*, 67–69.

# Index

198, 218. *See also* andragogy; Freire, Paulo
Peters, J., 102, 105
philosophical orientations in adult education,
73–97
   behaviourist. *See under* correspondence
    theories
   feminist, 92–94. *See also* feminism
   humanist. *See under* coherence theories
   liberal, 78. *See also* Plato
   post-modernist, 89–90
   post-structuralist, 90–92
   progressive, 79–80
   radical/critical. *See* coherence theories,
    critical theory
Piaget, Jean, 41–42, 129, 150
Plato, 77–78, 94, 125
Plumb, D., 228
pluralized knowledge, 183, 218. *See also*
  difference; diversity
Poitras Pratt, Yvonne, 179–81, 182
Polanyi, M., 18, 165
positionality, 6, 57, 69, 171–72. *See also*
  difference; diversity; identities
post-formal thought. *See* adult development,
  cognitive
post-secondary education. *See under* education
power
   Foucault and disciplinary power, 90–92
   and relational learning, 172–74
   relations of, 14, 46, 56–57, 63–69, 80–82,
    85, 148, 176–77, 186–90, 198–99,
    216, 224
   and social change, 103–104, 130–31
   *See also* empowerment
Pratt, D., 144
pre-service teacher education, 3–4, 194
Price, D. W., 79–80
prior learning assessment and recognition
  (PLAR), 24–25, 93, 152
professional development, 3, 15, 17, 74, 123,
  194–98, 203–205
professional learning community. *See*
  communities of practice
Pruitt, E. Z., 21
psychoanalysis, 43, 157–58
psychology, 125, 128, 130, 135, 139, 144, 158
Pyrch, T., 178

queer. *See* sexual and gender minorities

race, 23, 38, 47
   and learning, 51, 57, 64–65, 82, 89, 94,
    158, 228

and power, 14, 104, 130, 133
   *See also* culture; difference; diversity
Radical Humanities program, 222, 225–26
Raykov, M., 113–14
Reading Camp Association, 106
reflective thinking, 33, 39–41, 45–46, 60, 75–76,
  88, 150–52, 150, 165, 175, 183, 190, 198, 213
relational learning, 15, 28, 37, 46–47, 55, 62,
  149, 170–74, 179, 190, 223
religion, 4, 12, 33–34, 51, 54, 57–60, 82, 89,
  105, 193. *See also* faith; spirituality
Reuter-Lorenz, P., 39
Rice, B., 179
Roberts, S. M., 21
Rogers, C., 46, 81, 128–29
Rooksby, E., 57
Ross, R., 179
Rossiter, M., 171
Roy, Carol, 84–85, 110
Rubenson, K., 111

Sandlin, J., 143–44
Sarbin, T., 48
Sawchuk, Peter H., 178, 188–89
Schlossberg, N., 44, 45
Schugurensky, D., 193–94, 205
Sears, M., 198
Sefa Dei, G., 95, 179
the self, 14, 63, 69, 81–82, 89, 122, 135, 140,
  143, 157, 187, 223–26
   and connectedness, 171–72, 178
   non-unitary, 47–48
   self-actualization, 36, 46, 81–82, 101,
    128–29, 226
   unitary, 45–46, 149
   *See also* identities
self-directed learning, 81, 89, 91, 128–29,
  139–49, 151, 153, 175, 190, 208, 220
Selman, Gordon, 101, 227–28
Selman, Mark, 101, 227–28
sexual and gender minorities, 68–69
sexual orientation, 4, 23, 57, 64–65, 82, 89,
  130, 171
Sinnott, J. D., 42
situated cognition, 130
Slade, B., 193–94, 205
Smith, B., 57
Smith, D., 57
Smith, Laurel, 160–62
Smith, Monty, 168
social action, 67–68, 86, 107–110, 228
socioeconomic status, 4, 6–7, 14, 17, 32, 38,
  51–52, 64–65, 82, 93–94, 117, 171, 211, 229